INTEREST GROUPS
AND
CONGRESS

LONGMAN CLASSICS in POLITICAL SCIENCE

INTEREST GROUPS AND CONGRESS

LOBBYING, CONTRIBUTIONS, AND INFLUENCE

JOHN R. WRIGHT
The George Washington University

With new foreword by
Bruce I. Oppenheimer
Vanderbilt University

New York   San Francisco   Boston
London   Toronto   Sydney   Tokyo   Singapore   Madrid
Mexico City   Munich   Paris   Cape Town   Hong Kong   Montreal

Vice President and Publisher: Priscilla McGeehon
Executive Editor: Eric Stano
Senior Marketing Manager: Megan Galvin-Fak
Production Coordinator: Shafiena Ghani
Cover Designer/Manager: Wendy Fredericks
Cover Photo: ©Dale Atkins/AP/Wide World Photos
Technical Desktop Manager: Heather A. Peres
Publishing Services Manager: Alfred Dorsey
Printer and Binder: RR Donnelley & Sons, Inc.–Harrisonburg
Cover Printer: Coral Graphics Services, Inc.

Library of Congress Cataloging-in-Publication Data

Wright, John R.
    Interest groups and Congress : lobbying, contributions, and
influence / John R. Wright.
        p. cm.
    Includes bibliographical references
    ISBN 0-02-430301-1
    1. Pressure groups—United States. I. Title
JK1118.W75   1995
324'.4'0973—dc20

                                                                95-24147

                                                                CIP

Please visit our website at http://www.ablongman.com

ISBN 0-321-12187-2

2345678910—DOH—050403

With the exception of David Truman's masterful *The Governmental Process: Political Interests and Public Opinion*, the classic books (and by classic books I mean here those that scholars read and cite more than two decades after their initial publication) on interest groups in modern political science share two notable features. They are short books, often less than 200 pages, and they contribute primarily to the theoretical understanding of interest groups rather than reporting on empirical research. This group includes, but is not limited to, Olson's *The Logic of Collective Action*, Schattschneider's *The Semisovereign People*, and Freeman's *The Political Process: Bureau–Legislative Committee Relations*. This may be a testament to the value of the concise statement of ideas and to the durability of important theoretical contributions.

Given that it was published only six years ago, John R. Wright's *Interest Groups and Congress: Lobbying, Contributions, and Influence* cannot yet be labeled an interest groups classic. Certainly its brevity and its focus on a theoretical approach to the study of interest groups are aspects that it shares with these other works. And as I will illustrate in this foreword, Wright's book has other virtues, especially in its integration of other research, its presentation of data on PACs and campaign contributions, and its conceptual richness that contribute to an expectation that it will have enduring influence. In the end, however, the importance of Wright's contribution will rest on the degree to which he is able to persuade other scholars of the efficacy of his central argument that he states on page 2 and then weaves throughout the book: ". . . interest groups achieve influence through the acquisition and strategic transmission of information that legislators need to make good public policy and to get reelected."

Whether this book becomes a classic or not, together with his other publications, it has helped to establish Jack Wright as a cutting-edge scholar in American politics and the study of interest groups. He is one of those individuals who is both well-grounded in formal theory approaches to the study of political institutions and yet recognizes the importance of empirical testing of the propositions derived from formal arguments. Included in his empirical work is research on campaign contributions and representation, the use of counteractive lobbying, interest group influence in judicial nominations, and strategic behavior in the filing of amicus curiae briefs. Thus, Wright's theory of information supply as the source of interest group influence that he presents in *Interest Groups and Congress* rests in part on his findings in a range of research projects as well as his synthesis of the work of others.

It should not surprise anyone that Wright's approach to the study of interest groups appears to be strongly influenced by his graduate school training. Having earned his Ph.D. at the University of Rochester, Wright had the advantage of being exposed to many of the leading advocates of formal approaches to the study of politics as well as to others who were strongly planted in an empirical soaking and poking for "truths." It is surely no accident that Wright's strategic behavior theory of interest groups shares a common underpinning with Keith Krehbiel's theory of legislative organization. Both have the information needs of members of Congress at their centers. But it should be noted that Wright and Krehbiel are both 1983 Rochester Ph.D.s as well. And I have always believed that one learns from and is influenced intellectually as much, if not more, by one's student cohorts in graduate school as by the faculty. (Krehbiel's book *Information and Legislative Organization* pre-dates Wright's by five years. It has influenced a number of scholars who study congressional committees and has provoked a good deal of debate in the legislative studies community.) So it is not merely the common features that Wright's book shares with classic interest group studies that suggest its potential for this status, but it is also, and more important, that it is the book of a leading and productive scholar in the field who combines excellent formal theory training and an understanding of the empirical realities of interest group behavior.

Perhaps the most critical ingredients that make *Interest Groups and Congress* essential reading for those with academic or applied concerns about the behavior of interest groups are its range of coverage, the number of important questions that Wright is able to address in this concise volume, and the care Wright has given to the organization and presentation in the book. First, after briefly setting forth his information theory of interest groups, Wright uses the existing literature to entice the reader into what he calls "The Puzzle of Interest Group Influence." Not only does this grab one's attention, but it also provides a vehicle for understanding the tensions that exist in the contradictory claims of various scholars and gives his theory toeholds that Wright uses to extend his theory throughout the book. In essence he is able to say: "If the available theories do not offer consistent answers to the key questions about interest group research, can my information theory offer more reasonable and compelling explanations?"

Second, Wright's book is historically and contextually sensitive. He understands that the environment of American politics has affected interest group development and at times has been more or less favorable to interest groups being influential in Congress. He does not see interest groups in isolation but rather understands that they are in competition with other forms of political organization for influence. Moreover, they have adapted organizationally and tactically to the contexts in which they operate. And Wright persuasively demonstrates that different forms of interest groups participate and are better suited to exerting their influence in different venues within the congressional process and in the making of public policy both inside and outside of Congress. Thus, although his model for interest group influence may be a fixed one, Wright acknowledges that the exercise and the effectiveness of his information strategy and of interest group influence will vary. He is sensitive to the changes in the political context that occur both across time and over differing institutional settings. Although the book's title and focus are on interest groups in Congress, Wright extends the coverage to examine facets of interest group activity in courts and executive agency settings. The reader accordingly learns about the constant of the theory but understands that one also needs to grasp contextual variation.

Third, Wright uses the book to address many of the most meaningful questions about interest groups in the current context. What is the purpose of lobbying? What is it that PACs are trying to achieve with campaign contributions? Are the proliferation and activity of interest groups responsible for policy gridlock and governmental inefficiency? And what are the effects of interest groups on the inequality of representation in American government? It is important to note that Wright does not simply accept pat answers or conventional wisdom. Rather he challenges them and offers instead explanations that are linked to the importance of obtaining access as a means of supplying information to members of Congress about such things as their constituents' policy preferences, the electoral consequences of pursuing their own preferences, and the substantive effects of differing policies.

In the end whether the reader finds Wright's theory of information supply as the primary source of interest group influence persuasive or not strikes me as less important than the fact that it opens up new ways of thinking about and evaluating interest group behavior. Beyond that it also provides a vehicle for questioning the accuracy of existing explanations.

Fourth, Wright's concerns are normative as well as empirical. His chapter on the consequences of interest group politics asks the "so what" questions. Inevitably, when I am teaching my classes and observe my students assiduously taking notes but otherwise appearing glassy-eyed, I realize that I've neglected to make connections between the empirical findings of political science and things that resonate in their lives. It's then that I raise the "so what" questions: "Aside from the fact that this material might be covered on the final exam, why should we care about this?" Wright poses a series of these questions and uses his theory to offer meaningful answers. What are the repercussions of interest group activity for American democracy? Does the struggle of interest groups for policy influence enhance or damage the working of Congress in trying to resolve policy conflicts? How can American government cope with the dysfunctional aspects of interest group activity without infringing on basic constitutional rights? Will proposed reforms of the campaign financing system and of lobbying regulation effectively control the excesses of interest groups and provide a greater degree of representational equality? Unlike others who prescribe cures for the interest group abuses, Wright does not offer "knee-jerk" ideological responses. Instead he relies on reasoning that is consistent with the theory he offers.

Finally, it would be a mistake to view Wright's book as just a theoretical tome. It is rich in case study material on lobbying and data on

PACs. The case studies he provides are on point and well documented and based on important policy decisions. Issues such as the Bork nomination, gays in the military, and family and medical leave are ones that continue to have relevance for ongoing policy struggles. They not only can serve as the basis for student discussion, but a faculty member can easily update the underlying debates and changes that have occurred in interest group strategies. And the PAC data offer important refinements to commonly accepted ideas about the growth of PACs and the number of them that make sizeable campaign contributions. For Wright, however, the case studies are a way to illustrate and, to a modest degree, test his proposition about the use of proactive and counteractive lobbying strategies. The former he contends is applied to change the positions of those who disagree with the interest group's policy preference, and the latter is reserved for legislators who already favor the policy position of the group but are being proactively lobbied by interest groups on the other side.

Beyond the theory and coverage that Wright provides, there is another aspect that I find particularly attractive. I suspect I am biased because Wright's view fits one that I have articulated throughout my professional career and perhaps more strongly in recent years. In our popular culture and in the weight of the interest group literature in political science of the past twenty-five years or so, it has been commonplace to equate the influence of interest groups with campaign contributions. Although Wright does not challenge the view that campaign contributions provide a source for access to members of Congress, he notes early in his book that lobbying is undoubtedly the more important means of influence. On page 8, after noting that the use of campaign contributions as a source of influence "merits a most careful and thorough examination," he argues with a good deal of vehemence:

> However, before settling on campaign money as the predominant explanation of interest group influence, other explanations for the influence of contemporary interest groups must be explored. This book offers one alternative explanation: interest groups achieve influence in the legislative process not by applying electoral or financial pressure, but by developing expertise about politics and policy and by strategically sharing this expertise with legislators through normal lobbying activities.

In Chapter 4, Wright makes his case for the importance of lobbying activities as the primary source of interest group influence in Congress. But if he is correct, and I believe he is, in his contention that "interest groups can and do exert substantial influence even without making campaign contributions and that campaign contributions and other material gifts and favors are not the primary sources of interest group influence in the legislative process," then why is it that so much of the political science empirical literature on interest groups in recent years (as well the journalistic coverage) focuses on campaign contributions rather than on lobbying? The answer to this question lies in the availability of and access to data on the former and the lack of and inaccessibility of data on the latter. The reporting requirements under the Federal Election Campaign Act of 1971 and its subsequent amendments and the collection and ease of access to this information from the Federal Election Commission have provided a wealth of data for various tests of hypotheses about the influence of PAC and other contributions on roll call and other behaviors of members of Congress. And political scientists, not unlike Willie Sutton and robbing banks, know where the money (and in this case the data about it) is.

By contrast there is not a repository of data or information on lobbying Congress. And the interest groups engaged in lobbying are not anxious to share a detailed accounting of their activities. Aside from certain very public activities, such as testifying before congressional committees, or some information on lobbying now available under the registration and reporting requirements of the Lobbying Disclosure Act of 1995, much of the information about money and the activity of lobbying is not accessible. It is no wonder that much of the early work on interest groups (pressure groups) merely inferred their influence from their presence on the scene in Congress when decisions were made. When an interest group's position held sway, it was assumed that the interest group had exerted pressure to get its way. While working on my dissertation, which was later revised and published in the book *Oil and the Congressional Process: The Limits of Symbolic Politics*, I became all too aware of the difficulties of studying the strategic behaviors of the oil industry in influencing decisions in two policy areas using the more rigorous methods of social science with which I had been trained.

It is ironic that some of the best analysis of interest group lobbying has been done in studying efforts to lobby the Supreme Court, not Congress. Because the Supreme Court is so immune from many of the standard methods of lobbying employed in Congress, interest groups are largely limited to using amicus curiae briefs. And because those briefs are public record, scholars, including Wright, have had easy access to them. But contacts between interest groups and members of Congress are so frequent and varied and often private that it is far more difficult to develop data about them.

So while there has been a mushrooming of studies about campaign contributions and PAC activity and their role in influencing congressional behavior, there has been relatively little scholarly work of an empirical nature on lobbying activities. This becomes ironically clear in *Interest Groups and Congress*. For although Wright correctly contends that lobbying is a more critical part of influencing Congress than are PAC contributions, Chapter 5 on Political Action Committees is 25 percent longer than Chapter 4 on Legislative Lobbying. In large part this is because of the disproportionate amount of scholarly research that has been devoted to the first, a condition attested to in the footnote citations in the two chapters.

I do not mean this observation to be a criticism of Wright. Any scholar writing these chapters would face a similar dilemma. Thus, for me, at least, one way to evaluate the significance of this book will be the degree to which Wright persuades a new generation of interest group scholars to study the influence of lobbying activity rather than campaign contributions. But that is perhaps an unfair test. After all, when I think of the major empirical studies of lobbying activity in Congress, the list is a short one. Schattschneider's study of the Smoot–Hawley tariff, Bauer, Poole, and Dexter's *American Business and Public Policy*, and John Mark Hansen's book on the farm lobby come to mind. That's three major works in a period of more than 60 years. Hopefully, Wright's book will sufficiently stimulate a new generation of scholars (or even some established ones) to take up the challenge of studying lobbying in a more systematic way.

Aside from motivating scholarly research, Wright's book provides an excellent vehicle for organizing classroom discussion on interest groups. Let me suggest some of the areas that students might explore:

1. It is clear from reading Wright that parties and interest groups are in competition when it comes to influencing the behaviors of House members and senators. Over the past decade or more there is ample evidence that parties and party leaders in Congress have become stronger. One result is that policy formulation has become more a

party function and less a congressional committee function. How might interest groups be affected by this change? Might they change their choices of venue in their lobbying activities? Have they become less important in influencing the behavior of members?

2. Wright is critical of the service bureau view of interest groups. Yet at the time that view was articulated might it have been a correct one? What has changed in the political context that has made the service bureau role insufficient if interest groups were to maintain an influential role in congressional decision making?

3. Will the passage of a major piece of campaign finance legislation in 2002 (McCain–Feingold) affect the influence of interest groups? Why did it leave PACs untouched although in the early 1990s PACs were the focus of campaign finance reform proposals? What will be the effect of the ban on soft money on interest group and PAC influence? How will the increase doubling of the limits on individual contributions to congressional campaigns affect the way interest groups use money to influence elections?

4. Why is it that journalists and reformers see campaign contributions from PACs and individuals associated with interest groups as so central to the influence of interest groups in Congress? What makes them reach conclusions that are quite different from the ones Wright puts forward?

5. Should efforts be made to assist unorganized interests in getting access and influence? Is it a desirable goal if we want a more level playing field in efforts to influence congressional decision making? Are there feasible ways to achieve this goal?

Given the major role that interest groups play in all facets of contemporary American government, the limited amount of research on them is certainly regretable as well. I suspect that gets reflected in the undergraduate and graduate curriculums of political science departments at major universities and that interest group courses are offered on a less regular basis than is warranted. And even at large Ph.D. granting institutions, one may not find a single faculty member who lists interest groups as his or her primary focus of research specialization. Hopefully, Wright's book and other research that it stimulates will help rectify that situation as well.

BRUCE I. OPPENHEIMER
Vanderbilt University

CONTENTS

CHAPTER 4

LEGISLATIVE LOBBYING 75

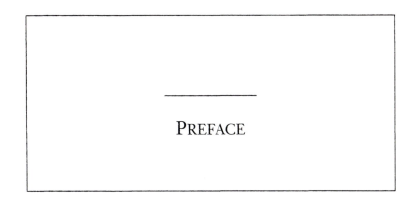

PREFACE

The academic research on American interest groups has experienced a surge in both volume and technical complexity over the past decade. Thanks to the Federal Election Campaign Act of 1971 and subsequent amendments in 1974, data on campaign contributions from organized interests to congressional candidates are now easily and widely available. These data have opened new research questions and possibilities, to which scholars have applied a variety of statistical techniques. Interest group research has also benefited from an increased theoretical interest in organizations and their activities. Recent developments in game theoretic approaches to information problems have been particularly important for placing the long-recognized relationship between information and lobbying on firm theoretical footing. Scholars are now able to address abstract questions about the relationship between groups and legislators that have traditionally been quite difficult to analyze with empirical approaches alone.

These are welcome developments to those interested in understanding and explaining interest group politics in the United States. Unfortunately, these developments come at some cost. The research results in the professional literature are often difficult to work through, especially for undergraduates and even beginning graduate students. Technical obstacles make it more difficult to understand how various research findings relate to one another, or what they imply for our understanding of the political process in general.

My purpose in writing this book is to make research on interest groups more accessible, especially to advanced undergraduate and beginning graduate students. My intent is to bridge the abstract and

technical research on interest groups in the professional journals—
especially the "informational" approach—and the more intuitive and
practical demands of the student and layperson. As such, I have tried
to present the major arguments and theoretical concepts in nontech-
nical terms and to illustrate them with actual examples of lobbying
campaigns. This approach necessarily involves simplification and
some loss of precision. Thus any errors or ambiguities that have
occurred in translating and reformulating arguments or results are
wholly mine, not those of the original research.

A number of people contributed to the writing of this book.
Bruce Nichols first planted the idea in my mind and encouraged me
to get started. My good friends James Brask and Dennis Winters
both encouraged and inspired me along the way. Richard Fenno
provided invaluable support throughout the project as teacher,
friend, and critic. David Austen-Smith not only read the manuscript,
but also helped me develop and interpret some of the theoretical
ideas presented in the book. Greg Caldiera and Lee Sigelman read
and commented on major portions of the manuscript. Craig Volden
provided a number of useful comments, as did students in my graduate seminars at George Washington University. I have also benefited
from careful reviews by Bruce I. Oppenheimer, Vanderbilt University; John F. Bibby, University of Wisconsin, Milwaukee; Burdett
Loomis, University of Kansas; Elizabeth Paddock, Drury College;
Marjorie Hershey, Indiana University; Frank J. Sorauf, University of
Minnesota; Richard Fenno, University of Rochester; Eric Uslaner,
University of Maryland; John Mark Hansen, University of Chicago.
Last but not least, I am grateful to my wife Jane, without whom this
book would not have been written.

INTEREST GROUPS
AND
CONGRESS

CHAPTER 1

INTRODUCTION

A Gallup Poll conducted in 1988 revealed that 92 percent of the American public supported a waiting period and background check of anyone wishing to purchase a handgun, and that 90 percent of gun *owners* also supported a waiting period.[1] The U.S. House of Representatives was evidently unimpressed by these polling figures. On September 15, 1988, the U.S. House voted 228–182 to delete the Brady amendment from the Omnibus Drug Act, thereby rejecting a proposed seven-day waiting period and background check for anyone seeking to purchase a handgun. Efforts to pass the Brady amendment failed again in the House in 1989 and 1990 and, even though successful in 1991, failed in the Senate in 1992. Not until 1993, five years after its initial introduction, was the Brady provision finally passed by Congress and signed into law by the president.

Leading the lobbying effort against the Brady amendment over this period was the National Rifle Association of America (NRA), an organization of 2.6 million members, 400 full-time employees, an annual operating budget of $88 million, and $128 million in assets.[2] In 1988 the NRA spent between $1.5 and $3 million on its lobbying effort against the Brady amendment alone. This sum could not be matched by a much smaller coalition of police officers and handgun opponents, described by one of its leaders as only a "shoestring

---

[1]George Gallup, Jr., *The Gallup Poll: Public Opinion 1988* (Wilmington, DE: Scholarly Resources, 1989), p. 213.
[2]The NRA, as Josh Sugarmann notes, "is more than an organization—it is an American institution." See Josh Sugarmann, *National Rifle Association: Money, Firepower, Fear* (Washington, DC: National Press Books, 1992), p. 13.

operation."[3] Only when public fear about crime emerged as a potentially volatile political issue in 1993 was Congress persuaded to pass the Brady amendment.

The participation and success of the NRA and its allies in this case illustrate a basic reality of the American political process: organization and action are often far more influential than public opinion for determining policy outcomes. Passionate and well-organized minorities can and frequently do thwart lukewarm majorities in American politics, and although public opinion may ultimately triumph in the end, special interests can prevail for significant periods of time. This feature of the process has provoked a good deal of discussion, debate, and dismay over the years. Some have decried the power of minority interests as a violation of the one-person-one-vote principle; others, a subversion of the public interest.[4] In 1946 Senator Robert La Follette protested that far too often "the true attitude of public opinion is distorted and obscured by the pressures of special interest groups." Noting the "swarms of lobbyists" seeking to protect and advance their own narrow interests, La Follette complained that "legislators find it difficult to discover the real majority will and to legislate in the public interest."[5] Concern about the ability of special interest groups to manipulate legislative policy is certainly no less, and perhaps even greater, today than it was in 1946.

The purpose of this book is to explain how, why, and to what extent special interests achieve influence over the legislative branch of American national government. The central argument is that interest groups achieve influence through the acquisition and strategic transmission of information that legislators need to make good public policy and to get reelected. Indeed, most of what interest groups and lobbyists do involves acquiring expert information about policy and politics and reporting this information to legislators.

---

[3]NRA expenditures and quotation are from Nadine Cohodas, "NRA Shows It Still Has What It Takes to Overcome Gun-Control Advocates," *Congressional Quarterly Weekly Report* (September 17, 1988): 2564.

[4]For example, Philip M. Stern, *The Best Congress Money Can Buy* (New York: Pantheon Books, 1988).

[5]*Legislative Reorganization Act of 1946.* Seventy-ninth Congress, second session. Senate Report No. 1400, pp. 4–5.

Interest groups employ policy experts—economists and scientists—as well as legislative experts—often former congressional committee staffers. They frequently conduct studies of their own or else commission university faculty or other established experts to conduct studies. They testify before congressional committees. They retain expensive and well-known Washington law firms to represent them in adjudicatory proceedings before the courts and federal agencies. They make campaign contributions and engage in voter mobilization and registration drives to demonstrate their understanding of electoral politics and to make clear who they consider to be their legislative friends. They meet one-on-one with legislators and their staffs in Washington, and they undertake grassroots lobbying campaigns as a way of demonstrating to members of Congress the political costs and benefits of various policy alternatives.

Interest group scholars have recognized the importance of information in the lobbying process for many years.[6] Until recently, however, scholars have not explicitly considered how interest groups might manipulate legislators' beliefs or behavior strategically through the content of the information they present.[7] The lobbyist has traditionally been portrayed as a "service bureau" when providing information to legislators, not as a strategic purveyor of information or possible manipulator of legislators' per-

[6]See, for example, David B. Truman, *The Governmental Process: Political Interests and Public Opinion* (New York: Knopf, 1951); Lester W. Milbrath, *The Washington Lobbyists* (Chicago: Rand McNally, 1963); Kay Lehman Schlozman and John T. Tierney, *Organized Interests and American Democracy* (New York: Harper and Row, 1986), pp. 297–300; Jeffrey M. Berry, *The Interest Group Society*, Second Edition (Boston: Scott Foresman/Little, Brown, 1989), pp. 143–146; John Mark Hansen, *Gaining Access: Congress and the Farm Lobby, 1919–1981* (Chicago: University of Chicago Press, 1991); Richard Smith, "Advocacy, Interpretation, and Influence in the U.S. Congress," *American Political Science Review* 78 (1984): 44–63; and William P. Browne and Won K. Paik, "Beyond the Domain: Recasting Network Politics in the Postreform Congress," *American Journal of Political Science*, 37 (1993): 1054–1078.
[7]The theoretical properties of information problems as they relate to lobbying and legislatures have been developed formally only in the last few years, but work in this area is developing rapidly. See David Austen-Smith and John R. Wright, "Competitive Lobbying for Legislators' Votes," *Social Choice and Welfare* 9 (1991): 229–257; Eric Rasmusen, "Costly Lobbying as a Signal of Conviction." Working paper, Yale Law School, 1991; Jan Potters, *Lobbying and Pressure: Theory and Experiments* (Tinbergen Institute Research Series, No. 36, Thesis Publishers:

ceptions.[8] Even today, the prevailing assumption among interest group scholars is that lobbyists may shade the truth from time to time, but they do not deliberately distort it for their own advantage.[9]

My working assumption in this book is quite different. I assume that interest groups have both the opportunity and incentive to present information that misleads legislators into thinking that policies are working, or will work, better than they actually are or that there is greater or less political support for policies than exists in fact and that groups do sometimes deliberately distort information for their own advantage. However, to suggest that groups have both the opportunity and incentive to mislead legislators is not to assert that they always do so, or even that they do so frequently. The point is merely that whenever groups have information that legislators do not, the *possibility* of manipulation exists, and it then becomes a theoretical and empirical issue as to whether and to what extent it occurs. Concerns about interest groups and manipulation of the legislative process are far too important to resolve simply by assuming that groups never exaggerate, distort, or mislead.

The possibility of manipulation raises important questions about the role of interest groups in the political process. What kinds of information do groups specialize in, and how do they acquire it? Why, and to what extent, do legislators depend on this information?

(continued)
Amsterdam, The Netherlands, 1992); Scott Ainsworth, "Regulating Lobbyists and Interest Group Influence," *Journal of Politics* 55 (1993): 41–56; Richard Ball, "Political Lobbying as Welfare Improving Signalling," Working paper, Department of Agricultural and Resource Economics, University of California at Berkeley, 1991; Abraham H. Wu, "A Theory of Campaign Contributions and Lobbying," manuscript, Stanford University, 1992; David Austen-Smith, "Information and Influence: Lobbying for Agendas and Votes," *American Journal of Political Science* 37 (1993): 799–833; and Scott Ainsworth and Itai Sened, "The Role of Lobbyists: Entrepreneurs with Two Audiences," *American Journal of Political Science* 37 (1993): 834–866.

[8]Raymond A. Bauer, Ithiel de Sola Pool, and Lewis Anthony Dexter, *American Business and Public Policy* (New York: Atherton, 1963), p. 353.

[9]Schlozman and Tierney, in *Organized Interests and American Democracy*, acknowledge that groups sometimes "attempt to place the facts in a favorable light," but they assert that "organizations avoid outright misrepresentation." See p. 298. For a similar conclusion, see Berry, *The Interest Group Society*, pp. 144–145.

Strategically, how do lobbyists use the information they have, and how do legislators respond? To what extent, and under what situations, can legislators trust lobbyists and rely on their expertise? What, if anything, constrains interest groups from manipulating the process? These are some of the questions to which this book is addressed.

The Puzzle of Interest Group Influence

The proposition that interest groups are often influential in congressional politics may come as little surprise to inside observers of the process, but it challenges a long accepted tenet in the political science literature. Several independent research efforts during the early 1960s concluded that legislators' policy choices are constrained hardly at all by interest group lobbying. This conclusion provided a significant counterpoint to research of earlier decades when groups were thought to be highly influential because of their ability to pressure legislators. Characteristic of the pressure group school is the work of Earl Latham, who in the early 1950s argued that the legislative vote on any issue tends to represent the "balance of power among the contending groups at the moment of voting," and that a representative's "ideas, principles, prejudices, programs, precepts, slogans, and preachments" all represent "adjustment to the dominant group combination among his constituents."[10]

Challenging this pressure perspective in the early 1960s was Lester Milbrath's analysis of lobbying as a "communications" process. Milbrath concluded that organized interests hold little influence over legislative outcomes because most lobbying simply reinforces representatives' positions but does not alter them.[11] Central to Milbrath's perspective is the notion that elected officials attend selectively to messages that they wish to hear. By determining which messages will be received, representatives determine which

[10]Earl Latham, "The Group Basis of Politics: Notes for a Theory." *American Political Science Review* 46 (1952): 376–397. Quotations are from pages 390 and 391, respectively.

[11]See Lester W. Milbrath, "Lobbying as a Communication Process," *Public Opinion Quarterly* 24 (1960): 33–53; and Lester W. Milbrath, *The Washington Lobbyists* (Chicago: Rand McNally, 1963).

communication channels will be open or closed, and thus they determine which messages will be sent. Interest groups, according to Milbrath, "create messages and choose means of transmission which are most likely to ensure clear and favorable reception of the message by the intended receiver."[12] It follows, then, that "lobbyists do not bother to communicate with those they know are opposed; this is both painful and thought to be a waste of time."[13]

Following in the tradition of Milbrath, Raymond Bauer and his associates traced the flow of demands on tariff legislation from the business community to representatives in Washington, arguing that legislators seldom received clear signals from business interests in their constituencies.[14] Interfering with the communication process were a variety of factors: trade policy was not an issue of high salience to the business community as a whole, many corporate leaders were unable to assess accurately which policies were in their best interests, and individual businesspeople often did not communicate with their elected representatives. Bauer, Pool, and Dexter found that interest groups were anything but omnipotent, as they struggled to overcome shortages of money, personnel, information, and time. Faced with a shortage of resources, most groups concentrated their interactions with people on the same side of the issue as their own. They concluded that "lobbyists tended to establish liaison only with the congressmen and senators on their own side," and that "direct persuasion of uncommitted or opposed congressmen and senators was a minor activity of the lobbies."[15] They viewed the lobbyist as merely a "service bureau" for "congressmen already agreeing with him."[16]

Providing additional impetus for the revision of the pressure perspective in the 1960s were studies of individual political behavior.

---

[12]Milbrath, *The Washington Lobbyists*, p. 189.

[13]Ibid., p. 217.

[14]Raymond A. Bauer, Ithiel de Sola Pool, and Lewis Anthony Dexter, *American Business and Public Policy* (New York: Atherton, 1963).

[15]Bauer, et al., *American Business and Public Policy*, p. 442.

[16]Ibid., p. 353. The notion that legislators make up their minds prior to hearing from interest groups was advanced in a number of other important academic works during the 1960s. Matthews, in his classic study of the U.S. Senate, argued that most lobbying of U.S. senators was directed at those "already convinced;" and Harmon

Voting studies, which revealed how little citizens knew about their representatives' policy stands and demonstrated the relatively small role that policy considerations played in voting decisions, helped dispel the notion that groups could pressure legislators by mobilizing electoral support for or against them on the basis of their policy choices. When combined with the research findings of Milbrath, Bauer, and others, factors such as party, constituency, and ideology soon supplanted groups as the most important determinants of congressional behavior.

The research findings on interest groups and Congress during the 1960s represent an important milestone in our understanding about how interest groups operate in Washington. Clearly, groups do not get their way by simply applying pressure to elected representatives. The rejection of the pressure perspective, while inevitable and largely justified, nevertheless has left a void in our intellectual understanding of interest groups and their relationship to Congress. Now, with the growing organizational presence of groups in Washington and with the increased visibility of their campaign contributions through political action committees (PACs), the image of interest groups as mere "service bureaus" is no longer adequate. Yet, there is no common understanding among scholars and journalists about exactly how groups achieve influence. Far too often, those who demand quick answers propose the most simple and cynical of all explanations: groups buy influence through their campaign contributions.

The belief that interest groups are able to purchase legislative influence with campaign contributions has sufficient currency, and

---

(continued)
Zeigler observed that the success of the lobbyist "depends more upon the degree to which legislators agree with the professed ideals of the group...than upon the ability of the lobbyist to manipulate or persuade." (pp. 267–68). See Donald R. Matthews, *U.S. Senators and Their World* (New York: Random House, 1960), p. 182; and Harmon Zeigler, *Interest Groups in American Society* (Englewood Cliffs: Prentice-Hall, 1964), pp. 267–268. Also see Lewis Anthony Dexter, *How Organizations Are Represented in Washington* (Indianapolis: Bobbs-Merrill, 1969); Andrew M. Scott and Margaret A. Hunt, *Congress and Lobbies* (Chapel Hill: University of North Carolina Press, 1966); and John C. Wahlke, Heinz Eulau, William Buchanan, and Leroy Ferguson, *The Legislative System* (New York: Wiley, 1962).

the implications for the political system are so significant, that it merits a most careful and thorough examination. However, before settling on campaign money as the predominant explanation of interest group influence, other explanations for the influence of contemporary interest groups must be explored. This book offers one alternative explanation: interest groups achieve influence in the legislative process not by applying electoral or financial pressure, but by developing expertise about politics and policy and by strategically sharing this expertise with legislators through normal lobbying activities. I argue that groups can and do exert substantial influence even without making campaign contributions and that campaign contributions and other material gifts or favors are not the primary sources of interest group influence in the legislative process.

The remainder of the book is organized as follows: Chapter 2 provides some background information on the evolution, organization, and regulation of interest groups in the American political system. Chapter 3 then places the legislative activities of interest groups in the broader context of the policy making system and the legislative process. The decision of whether to pursue a legislative strategy is considered, and the basic legislative strategies available to interest groups are reviewed. Chapter 3 also integrates interest groups into traditional models of legislative decision making, explaining where and how lobbying information figures into legislators' decisions to follow the preferences of party leaders, constituents, or their own convictions. Chapter 4 examines the role of information in legislative lobbying. The discussion focuses on the kinds of information groups acquire, how they acquire it, and how they use it strategically to achieve their objectives of access and influence. In Chapter 5, I return to political action committees. I discuss the place of campaign contributions in the legislative process, and I consider some of the consequences of PACs for the nature of representation in American politics. Contributions, I argue, are an important adjunct to lobbying—they help establish access, and they indicate which groups have useful lobbying information to offer—but I conclude that they are neither necessary nor sufficient for gaining influence. Finally, I discuss some of the consequences of interest group politics, both positive and negative, in Chapter 6; and in Chapter 7, I conclude the book by reviewing the campaign finance and lobbying reforms of the 103rd Congress.

C H A P T E R 2

THE HISTORY, ORGANIZATION, AND REGULATION OF INTEREST GROUPS

The range of organized political interests in the United States is fully as broad and diverse as the economic and social concerns of the nation itself. Jeffrey Birnbaum has aptly noted that organized groups represent interests from soup to nuts and from head to toe—from the Campbell Soup Company to the Peanut Butter and Nut Processors Association and from the Headwear Institute of America to the American Podiatric Medical Association.[1] The range of political groups also spans a broad organizational spectrum from large and wealthy to small and modest. The American Association of Retired Persons claims 28 million members and an annual operating budget of $239 million, whereas the Animal Reform Movement has only 5000 members and an annual operating budget of $100,000. There are also "peak" organizations such as the Business Roundtable, an elite group of chief executive officers from 200 corporations, and grassroots organizations such as the National Organization for the Reform of Marijuana Laws (NORML).

Just how many political organizations and lobbyists exist in the United States is unclear. The most comprehensive guide to organized interests in Washington, D.C., is *Washington Representatives*, a compilation of "persons working to influence government policies

---

[1]From Jeffrey Birnbaum, *The Lobbyists: How Influence Peddlers Get Their Way in Washington* (New York: Times Books, 1992) p. 36.

and actions to advance their own and their client's interest."[2] It lists more than 12,500 individuals affiliated with more than 11,600 groups, companies, and law and public relations firms represented in the nation's capital. Other sources routinely place the number of Washington lobbyists at 80,000, although the definition of *lobbyist* used for this estimate and the actual method of estimation are unclear.[3] If one defines a lobbyist as anyone working in a professional capacity for a Washington-based interest group or law firm, then the 80,000 figure may be realistic. There obviously are not 80,000 lobbyists trekking up to Capitol Hill everyday, though.

One indirect measure of lobbying in the nation's capital is the number of lawyers belonging to the Washington, D.C., bar. The membership in the D.C. bar in 1993 totalled 61,110—one lawyer for every 10 residents of the District of Columbia. By comparison, there is only one lawyer for every 181 residents in the state of Illinois.[4] If the District of Columbia had the same ratio of lawyers to citizens as Illinois, there would be only 3366 lawyers in Washington, not 61,100, which means there are roughly 58,000 "extra" lawyers in the nation's capital. Some of these 58,000 are employed by the federal government, but many thousands are employed in the private sector, and their job is to try to influence the form and substance of federal policies.

---

[2]*Washington Representatives* (Washington, DC: Columbia Books, 1990) compiles information from lobby and foreign agent registrations, federal election commission files, annual company reports to regulatory agencies, and other agency documents and public records.

[3]See Helen Dewar, "Major Overhaul of Lobbying Laws Clears Senate, 95–2," *The Washington Post*, May 7, 1993, A, 1:5; and Birnbaum, *The Lobbyists*, p. 38. Robert Salisbury also uses the figure of 80,000 and claims the actual number is at least in the 50,000 range. See Robert H. Salisbury, "Washington Lobbyists: A Collective Portrait," in Allan J. Cigler and Burdette A. Loomis (eds.), *Interest Group Politics*, Second Edition (Washington, DC: Congressional Quarterly Press, 1986), p. 149. For additional estimates of the number of lobbyists in Washington, see the figures and citations in John P. Heinz, Edward O. Laumann, Robert L. Nelson, and Robert H. Salisbury, *The Hollow Core: Private Interests in National Policy Making* (Cambridge, MA: Harvard University Press, 1993), p. 10.

[4]The Chicago office of the Illinois Bar Association reported 63,385 lawyers registered as of July 13, 1993.

The cost of all of this political activity is also unknown. *Public Interest Profiles* reported the proposed budgets of 208 organizations for 1988, and these totalled $1.6 billion.[5] These organizations are probably not representative of all political organizations, however. The average budget of these organizations was $7.7 million, which is almost surely higher than the average of all organizations, since *Public Interest Profiles* compiles data on only the most visible public interest groups. Still, even if one adopts a conservative estimate of an average budget of roughly one million dollars each among the 11,600 organizations reportedly based in Washington, DC, the total operating cost of the lobbying industry is in the neighborhood of $12 billion annually.

By any standard, the money and human resources of the lobbying industry is substantial.[6] The interest group system as we observe it today, however, is far different from what existed in earlier times. The diversity, number, and strength of interest groups in the contemporary United States reflects many years of adaptation to changes in the nation's economic, political, social, and legal environments.

The Evolution of Interest Groups

The rapid economic and social development in the United States immediately following the Civil War created a new and uncertain political environment for members of Congress. Congress emerged as the dominant force in national policy making, and members' electoral constituencies became far more heterogeneous and complex than ever before. In this new and uncertain political environment, the informational needs of members of Congress were greater than

[5]Foundation for Public Affairs, *Public Interest Profiles*, 1988–1989 (Washington, DC: Congressional Quarterly, Inc., 1988).

[6]The overall size of the lobbying industry, as formidable as it may be, is dwarfed by the financial giants of American enterprise. General Motors (GM), for example, has nearly ten times as many employees worldwide and nearly ten times the annual operating budget of all lobbying groups combined. Based on its *First Quarter Report, 1991*, GM's annual costs and expenses exceeded $120 billion with more than 735,000 employees worldwide.

at any previous time, and it was in this environment that the American interest group system evolved.

Although the evolution of interest groups in the United States did not begin in earnest until after the Civil War, the groundwork for their development was laid much earlier in several key provisions of the U.S. Constitution. These constitutional provisions have had a profound effect on the American political party system, which in turn has had a major impact on the interest group system.

Constitutional Underpinnings

The place of special interests in American politics today is largely a consequence of two competing political values expressed in the U.S. Constitution: a concern for liberty and freedom of political expression on the one hand, and the desire to prevent tyranny on the other. James Madison's *Federalist* No. 10 is the classic justification for the various constitutional checks and balances, which disperse power and make it difficult for any single group of citizens to control the entire government.[7] Madison, whose thinking was strongly influenced by the English philosopher David Hume, believed that it is natural for people to differ, and in differing, to form into factions, or parties. The problem with factions, according to Madison and his contemporaries Jefferson and Hamilton, is their potential for subverting government and the public good. Factions, in Madison's words, are mischievous.

Madison's primary concern in *Federalist* No. 10 was with *majority* factions—typically, but not exclusively, political parties as we know them today—not minority factions such as contemporary interest groups.[8] Although he recognized that minority factions could lead to disorder and conflict, Madison believed that it is the possibility of tyranny by the majority that poses the greatest threat to individual liberties. Madison did not recommend that factions be forbidden or repressed, a practice that would conflict with the fun-

---

[7]James Madison, "Federalist No. 10," in Alexander Hamilton, James Madison, and John Jay, *The Federalist Papers* (Cutchogue, NY: Buccaneer Books, 1992), pp. 42–49.
[8]See Richard Hofstadter, *The Idea of a Party System* (Berkeley: University of California Press, 1969), p. 66.

damental values of liberty and freedom of expression, but instead that their negative tendencies be held in check and controlled through explicit constitutional safeguards.[9]

Formal mechanisms in the U.S. Constitution for controlling majority factions include the requirements that the president be elected separately from members of Congress and that members of Congress reside in the states from which they are elected. These provisions disperse power horizontally—across national institutions of government—and vertically—from national to local political jurisdictions. Separation of the executive and legislative branches eased fears among the smaller states in 1787 that large states, which presumably would control the Congress, would also control the presidency; and geographic representation ensured that control over elected representatives would rest with local rather than national interests, thereby lessening the influence of the national government over state decisions.

These basic constitutional provisions have had a profound effect on the abilities of modern political parties to control and manage American government. Historically, control of the government has frequently been divided between the two major political parties, neither of which has been capable of exerting much discipline over its members. A single party has controlled the presidency and a majority in the U.S. House and Senate in just 43 of the 70 Congresses—61 percent—that have convened from 1855 to 1993. Even in times of single-party control of the government, voting defections within both major parties have been common. Since World War II, a majority of Democrats has voted against a majority of Republicans only 44 percent of the time on average in the U.S. House of Representatives and only 45 percent of the time on average in the U.S. Senate.[10] American legislators have little incentive to toe the party line for the simple reason that a cohesive majority is not required to

[9]Despite their avowed aversion to parties, Jefferson, Hamilton, and Madison were the leading figures in the development of the first American party system. See Joseph Charles, *The Origins of the American Party System* (New York: Harper and Row, 1956); and John H. Aldrich and Ruth W. Grant, "The Antifederalists, the First Congress, and the First Parties," *Journal of Politics* 55 (1993): 295–326.

[10]See Samuel C. Patterson and Gregory A. Caldeira, "Party Voting in the United States Congress," *British Journal of Political Science* 18 (1988): 111–131.

maintain control of the government or to preclude calling new elections, as is the case in parliamentary regimes.[11] In the absence of party discipline, American legislators look to their geographic constituencies rather than to their parties for voting cues.[12]

Madison and his contemporaries succeeded brilliantly in designing a constitutional system to attenuate the power of majority factions, but in doing so, they also created unanticipated opportunities for minority factions to be influential. When political parties are unable to take clear responsibility for governing, and when they cannot maintain cohesion and discipline among those elected under their labels, special interests have opportunities to gain access to the key points of decision within the government. David Truman explains that when a single party succeeds regularly in electing both an executive and a majority in the legislature, channels of access "will be predominantly those within the party leadership, and the pattern will be relatively stable and orderly."[13] He notes, however, that when "the party is merely an abstract term referring to an aggregation of relatively independent factions," as in the case of the United States, then the channels of access "will be numerous, and the patterns of influence within the legislature will be diverse, constantly shifting, and more openly in conflict."[14]

[11]For elaboration on this point, see Leon D. Epstein, *Political Parties in Western Democracies* (New Brunswick, NJ: Transaction Books, 1982), pp. 318–332; and Austin Ranney, "Candidate Selection and Party Cohesion in Britain and the United States," in William J. Crotty, Donald M. Freeman, and Douglas S. Gatlin (eds.), *Political Parties and Political Behavior* (Boston: Allyn and Bacon, 1971), pp. 248–264.

[12]For a classic explanation of how geographic representation prevents national leaders from controlling their partisans, see William H. Riker, *Federalism: Origin, Operation, Significance* (Boston: Little, Brown, 1964), pp. 91–101. Other political scientists attribute somewhat greater importance to the role of parties in structuring the behavior of legislators. See, for example, David W. Rohde, *Parties and Leaders in the Postreform House* (Chicago: University of Chicago Press, 1991); and Gary W. Cox and Mathew D. McCubbins, *Legislative Leviathan: Party Government in the House* (Berkeley: University of California Press, 1993). For counterarguments, see Keith Krehbiel, "Where's the Party"? *British Journal of Political Science* 23 (1993): 235–266.

[13]David B. Truman, *The Governmental Process: Political Interests and Public Opinion* (New York: Knopf, 1951), p. 325.

[14]Ibid., p. 325.

One important consequence of this "diffusion of access" is that legislators will be much more accessible to interests within their local constituencies, especially *organized* interests. Simply put, interest groups will thrive in an environment in which legislators take their behavioral cues from heterogeneous constituencies rather than from cohesive political parties. E. E. Schattschneider has summed up the situation succinctly:

> If the parties exercised the power to govern effectively, *they would shut out the pressure groups.* The fact that American parties govern only spasmodically and fitfully amid a multitude of lapses of control provides the opportunity for the cheap and easy use of pressure tactics.[15]

Although the constitution makes no specific mention of interest groups, or even political parties for that matter, it has influenced the evolution of both. The weakness of the political parties in their ability to control and manage the government is an intended consequence of the efforts by the founding fathers to inhibit majority factions; the prevalence of special interests, however, is an unintended consequence of weak parties. The U.S. Constitution indirectly laid the groundwork for a strong interest group system, but that system, unlike the political party system, did not evolve right away. It took nearly 70 years from the development of the first party system in 1800 until groups began to form and proliferate at a significant rate.

The Formation and Maintenance of Interest Groups

Although trade unions and associations have historical roots dating to the beginning of the republic, interest groups of regional or national scope as we know them today did not develop significantly until after the Civil War, and even then, pronounced growth did not really begin to take place until the late 1800s. Table 2.1 lists a few of the early organizations and their founding dates.

In what is known as the "disturbance theory" of interest group formation, David Truman argued that organizations will form when

[15]E. E. Schattschneider, *Party Government* (New York: Holt, Rinehart and Winston, 1941), p. 192.

Table 2.1 Selected Organizations and Their Founding Dates

American Medical Association	1847
National Grange	1867
National Rifle Association	1871
American Bankers Association	1875
American Federation of Labor	1886
Sierra Club	1892
National Association of Manufacturers	1895
National Audubon Society	1905
National Association for the Advancement of Colored People	1909
U.S. Chamber of Commerce	1912
American Jewish Congress	1918
American Farm Bureau Federation	1919
National League of Cities	1924

the interests common to unorganized groups of individuals are disturbed by economic, social, political, or technological change.[16] As society becomes increasingly complex and interconnected, Truman argued that individuals have greater difficulty resolving their differences and grievances on their own and instead must seek intervention from the government. It is at this time that political organizations will begin to take shape. Once interest groups begin to form, they will then tend to form in "wavelike" fashion, according to Truman, because policies designed to address one group's needs typically disturb the interests of other unorganized citizens, who then form groups to seek governmental intervention to protect and advance their particular interests.

The period from 1870 to 1900 was rife with disturbances favorable to the formation of interest groups in the United States. The economic, social, and political upheaval following the Civil War destabilized relationships within and between numerous groups of individuals. The completion of the railroads and the introduction of the telegraph dramatically altered communication and transporta-

---

[16]David B. Truman, *The Governmental Process*, Chapters 3 and 4.

tion patterns; immigration and population growth gave rise to new economic and social relationships; and commercial and territorial expansion in the West, combined with the task of maintaining order and rebuilding the infrastructure in the South, increased demands for routine services such as post offices, law enforcement, internal improvements, customs agents, and so forth. The process of industrialization created further economic and political tensions and uncertainties. The period 1870 to 1900 witnessed three economic depressions: a major one from 1873 to 1879, a minor one in the mid-1880s, and the collapse of 1893. Overall, the period from 1870 to 1900 was one when conditions were finally right for the widespread growth of organized interests in the United States.[17]

Margaret Susan Thompson points out that in addition to the unprecedented economic and social upheaval at the end of the Civil War, political conditions in the 1870s were also favorable to the formation of groups and, in particular, the lobbying of Congress.[18] Two factors—the ascendancy of congressional power associated with the impeachment proceedings against Andrew Johnson and the growing heterogeneity of congressional constituencies—were instrumental in the growth of congressional lobbying and interest group activity. Congress, by enacting a comprehensive program on reconstruction in 1865 over the determined opposition of the president, established political preeminence over federal policy making and, as a consequence, became the focal institution for receiving and processing the conflicting demands of many newly recognized interests. Then, as congressional constituencies diversified economically and socially, the presence of multiple and competing interests began to force legislators to develop "representational priorities."[19] Thompson notes that legislators at this time had to determine which were their "meaningful" constituencies, and organization was the critical means

---

[17]Although a major wave of interest group formation occurred after the Civil War, James Q. Wilson points out that a number of national organizations were first organized in the 30 years prior to the Civil War. See James Q. Wilson, *Political Organizations* (New York: Basic Books, 1970): pp. 195–211.

[18]Margaret Susan Thompson, *The Spider Web: Congress and Lobbying in the Age of Grant* (Ithaca, NY: Cornell University Press, 1985).

[19]Thompson, *The Spider Web*, pp. 130–131.

by which interests achieved such designation. Thompson refers to the nascent organization of interests during the 1870s as "clienteles" rather than interest groups, for even though numerous subgroups of the population began making significant demands on the government during the 1870s, there was not a great deal of formal organization then as we know it today.[20] Still, even these nascent groups began to provide important information to members of Congress about the interests and priorities of their constituents.

One example of how interest groups formed in response to economic and political disturbances during the post-Civil War period is provided by the organization of postal workers. Even before the Civil War, the volume of mail had grown tremendously in response to the development of railroads and the resulting decrease in the costs of postage. But in 1863, another significant increase in the volume of mail occurred when Congress lowered the long-distance postage rates.[21] This created additional strains for letter carriers and postal clerks who already were greatly overworked. Then, in 1868, the Post Office Department refused to apply the "eight-hour" law—a law enacted that same year by Congress stipulating that eight hours constituted a day's work for laborers, workmen, and mechanics—to letter carriers on the grounds that they were government employees, not laborers, workmen, or mechanics. Finally, implementation of civil service following passage of the Pendleton Act in 1883 eliminated what little political clout the letter carriers had enjoyed. Once the patronage system was eliminated, politicians lost interest in the letter carriers and no longer intervened on their behalf.

In response to these deteriorating circumstances, the letter carriers organized into the National Association of Letter Carriers in 1889. Once organized, the letter carriers had a significant advantage over the unorganized postal clerks in the competition for wages. At the time, wages for all postal workers, letter carriers and clerks alike, were provided through a single congressional appropriation to the

---

[20]Thompson, *The Spider Web*, pp. 136–137.

[21]For this and other historical facts leading to organization of postal workers, see John Walsh and Garth Mangum, *Labor Struggle in the Post Office: From Selective Lobbying to Collective Bargaining* (Armonk, NY: M. E. Sharpe, 1992), p. 47.

Post Office Department, and the letter carriers used their organizational clout to claim a disproportionate share of the annual appropriation. Thus, the postal clerks came under pressure to organize as well, and so in predictable "wavelike" fashion, the National Association of Post Office Clerks was established in 1894.

Changing economic, social, and political conditions are necessary but not sufficient circumstances for the formation and development of organized interests. Even when environmental conditions are favorable to the formation of groups, there is still a natural proclivity for individuals *not* to join political interest groups. The reason is that individuals do not always have to belong to political groups in order to enjoy the benefits they provide. Wheat farmers, for example, benefit from the price supports that Congress establishes for wheat even though they do not belong to the National Association of Wheat Growers (NAWG), which lobbies for price supports. Similarly, individuals do not have to belong to environmental groups in order to reap the benefits of a cleaner environment brought about by the lobbying efforts of groups such as the Sierra Club and the National Wildlife Federation. More generally, the lobbying benefits provided by groups such as the wheat growers and the environmentalists are consumed *jointly* by all citizens affected; that is, Congress does not guarantee a higher price for wheat only to farmers who have paid dues to the National Association of Wheat Growers, and it does not and cannot restrict the benefits of a clean environment only to individuals who have paid their dues to environmental groups.

Unlike lobbying benefits, which are available even to those who do not contribute to lobbying efforts, the costs of lobbying are borne only by those who actually pay their dues to political groups or otherwise participate in lobbying activities. This creates a major organizational problem, for when it is possible to get something for nothing, many individuals will rationally choose to free ride on the efforts of others. When there are thousands of wheat farmers, for example, and the annual dues to the National Association of Wheat Growers are $100 or less, individual wheat farmers might very well conclude that their single contributions are not very important, that the NAWG will manage quite nicely without their money because there are many other wheat farmers paying dues, and that there are much better uses for the $100 in light of the fact that the government will still provide price supports for their crop.[22] The problem for the NAWG is that if every wheat farmer reasoned this way there would be no national association, and thus probably no price supports for wheat.[23]

Given the natural proclivity for individuals to be free riders, all organizations must provide incentives of one sort or another to induce individuals to pay dues and otherwise contribute to the collective efforts of the organization. Generally speaking, individuals do not join interest groups because of benefits that can be consumed jointly; they join because of benefits that can be enjoyed *selectively* only by those individuals who pay dues to political groups. There are three main types of selective benefits. A selective *material* benefit includes such things as insurance and travel discounts and subscriptions to professional journals and other specialized information.[24] A second type of selective benefit is what Peter Clark and James Q. Wilson have labelled *solidary* incentives. These, too, derive only from group membership and involve benefits such as "socializing, congeniality, the sense of group membership and identification, the status resulting from membership, fun and conviviality, the maintenance of social distinctions, and so on."[25] The third basic type of selective benefit is an *expressive* incentive.[26] Expressive incentives are those that individuals attach to the act of expressing ideological or

---

[22]Individuals sometimes have an exaggerated sense of efficacy, in which case they believe that their small individual contribution is more important than it really is. In such cases, individuals may rationally calculate that the benefits of participation outweigh the costs. See Terry M. Moe, "A Calculus of Group Membership," *American Journal of Political Science* 24 (1980): 593–632.

[23]The seminal work on the problem of free riding as applied to interest groups is Mancur Olson's *The Logic of Collective Action* (Cambridge, MA: Harvard University Press, 1965 and 1971).

[24]Olson, *The Logic of Collective Action*, p. 133–134.

[25]Peter B. Clark and James Q. Wilson, "Incentive Systems: A Theory of Organizations," *Administrative Science Quarterly* 6 (1961): pp. 134–135.

[26]For further discussion of expressive benefits, particularly the role of political entrepreneurs in providing them, see Robert H. Salisbury, "An Exchange Theory of Interest Groups," *Midwest Journal of Political Science* 13 (1969): 1–32. Salisbury introduced the term *expressive benefit* in lieu of the term *purposive benefit* that was originally introduced by Clark and Wilson in "Incentive Systems: A Theory of Organization," pp. 135–136.

moral values such as free speech, civil rights, economic justice, or political equality. Individuals obtain these benefits when they pay dues or contribute money or time to an organization that espouses these values. What is important in receiving these benefits is the feeling of satisfaction that results from expressing political values, not necessarily the actual achievement of the values themselves.

Most organizations provide a mix of these various benefits, although different kinds of organizations typically rely more heavily on one type of benefit than another.[27] Professional and trade associations, for example, are more likely to offer selective material benefits than purposive benefits, whereas environmental groups and other organizations claiming to lobby for the public interest rely more heavily on expressive benefits. Expressive benefits are also common in organizations relying heavily on mass mailings to attract and maintain members. Many direct mail approaches use negatively worded messages to instill feelings of guilt and fear in individuals, with the hope that people will contribute money to a cause as a means of expressing their support for certain values or else assuaging their guilt and fear.[28]

That individuals are not drawn naturally to interest groups and must instead be enticed to join makes it very difficult for groups to get started. Organizations often need outside support in the form of a patron—perhaps a wealthy individual, a nonprofit foundation, or a government agency—to get over the initial hurdle of organizing collective action. In one of the leading studies on the origins and maintenance of interest groups, Jack Walker discovered that 89 percent of all citizen groups and 60 percent of all nonprofit occupational groups (e.g., the National Association of State Alcohol and Drug Abuse Directors) received financial assistance from an outside source at the time of their founding.[29] Many of these organizations continued to draw heavily from outside sources of support to main-

---

[27]For analysis of the importance of various types of benefits for group membership, see Lawrence S. Rothenberg, "Putting the Puzzle Together: Why People Join Public Interest Groups," *Public Choice* 60 (1988): 241–257.

[28]R. Kenneth Godwin, *One Billion Dollars of Influence: The Direct Marketing of Politics* (Chatham, NY: Chatham House Publishers, 1988), p. 21.

[29]Jack L. Walker, "The Origins and Maintenance of Interest Groups in America," *American Political Science Review* 77 (1983): 390–406.

tain themselves once they were launched. Walker concluded that "the number of interest groups in operation, the mixture of group types, and the level and direction of political mobilization in the United States at any point in the country's history will be determined by the composition and accessibility of the system's major patrons of political action."[30]

In summary, the proficiency that contemporary interest groups have achieved in attracting and maintaining members has evolved from a combination of factors. Most fundamental to their evolution has been a constitutional arrangement that has not only encouraged their participation but also created unanticipated opportunities for them to exert influence. Changing economic, social, and political circumstances have also played critical roles at various times throughout American history. However, even under conditions favorable to their development, the formation and maintenance of interest groups requires leadership and creative approaches for dealing with the natural inertia that individuals exhibit toward collective activities. The number of groups continues to grow each year, however, as does the diversity of the issues and viewpoints they represent.

The Organization of Interests

The size and diversity of the universe of groups in American politics often leads to confusion about what kinds of organizations qualify as political interest groups. Are corporations interest groups? How about charitable organizations such as the Salvation Army? Obviously, one cannot draw meaningful conclusions about the activities and influence of interest groups without first being explicit about what an interest group is. Here, then, is a rough and ready definition: A *political interest group, or organized interest,* is "a collection of individuals or a group of individuals linked together by professional circumstance, or by common political, economic, or social interests, that meets the following requirements: (1) its name does not appear on an election ballot; (2) it uses some portion of its collective

---

[30] Ibid., p. 406. I return to the issue of outside subsidies for interest groups in Chapter 6.

resources to try and influence decisions made by the legislative, executive, or judicial branches of national, state, or local governments; and (3) it is organized externally to the institution of government that it seeks to influence."

The first requirement distinguishes interest groups from political parties. Interest groups do not run slates of candidates under their labels; political parties do. The second requirement excludes organizations such as hobby groups, or even corporations, that do not allocate any of their resources to efforts to influence government. The third requirement eliminates coalitions of governmental officials who attempt to influence policy within the institutions in which they are employed. Within Congress, for example, the Congressional Black Caucus, a coalition of African-American members of Congress, does not qualify as an interest group; within the White House, distinct factions of presidential advisors do not qualify as interest groups.[31] The Congressional Black Caucus would be considered an interest group, however, when it attempted to influence decisions in the executive or judicial branches. By similar reasoning, the Department of Defense qualifies as an organized interest when it attempts to secure larger operating budgets from the Congress or when it lobbies against the cancellation of a weapons program. Table 2.2 displays several common types of political interest groups, all of which participate frequently before Congress.

Trade and Professional Associations

The most longstanding and perhaps most familiar type of political organization is the trade or professional association. Groups such as the American Bankers Association, the National Restaurant Association, and the Association of Trial Lawyers of America are just a few of the 2200 trade and professional associations with a permanent presence in Washington that lobby on behalf of the economic interests of their members. For example, the National Restaurant Association lobbied in 1993 against reducing the tax deduction for business

---

[31]If the Congressional Black Caucus were to be designated an interest group, then the Democratic and Republican Party Caucuses would also have to be considered interest groups, as would any regular coalition of legislators.

Table 2.2   Basic Types of Political Interest Groups

Trade and professional associations
Corporations
Labor unions
Citizen groups
State and local governmental organizations
Religious, charitable, and community groups

meals, the American Bankers Association lobbied in 1992 to allow banks to open branches across state lines, and the Association of Trial Lawyers of America lobbied in 1992 against revamping product liability laws.

The membership of these associations usually consists of individuals, but sometimes it is composed of organizations or a mix of individuals and organizations. The American Public Welfare Association, for example, is made up of federal, state, and county welfare organizations in addition to welfare administrators and other individuals interested in public welfare issues. Many national associations are also federations, having as members or affiliates regional, state, or local organizations. The American Trucking Associations has as members the 50 states plus the District of Columbia trucking associations. Affiliated with the American Medical Association are more than 400 state, county, and local medical societies. Also, belonging to the U.S. Chamber of Commerce are 180,000 businesses, 2850 state and local chambers of commerce, and 1400 trade and professional associations.

Corporations

Many corporations also take political positions and engage in political activities. For example, companies such as Dow Chemical and Shell Oil monitor the proceedings of federal regulatory agencies, Congress, and the courts. They prepare legal briefs and comments, and they lobby on their own and through their professional associations—the Chemical Manufacturers Association and the American Petroleum Institute in the cases of Dow and Shell, respectively. In its

1990 edition, *Washington Representatives* listed 1700 representatives of individual corporations.

Although corporate representation in Washington is commonplace today, Graham Wilson comments that until the late 1960s American business was remarkable for the "degree to which it failed to use the standard techniques of interest group politics."[32] Prior to the late 1960s, economic, social, and political conditions were favorable enough to business interests that organized political action was not necessary, but these circumstances changed dramatically in the early 1970s. According to Wilson, four major disturbances have contributed to the growth of corporate political activity since the early 1970s: a decline in public confidence in business, a shift in the balance of power in Washington away from probusiness elected officials, increased industrial competition abroad, and an increase in federal regulations affecting business by agencies such as the Occupational Safety and Health Administration and the Environmental Protection Agency.[33]

Labor Unions

Historically much better organized than corporations are labor unions. Over the years, unions have organized in virtually all aspects of the labor force, ranging from the United Mine Workers to the Airline Pilots Association International and the National Football League Players Association. Total union membership, however, as measured by the percentage of the nonagricultural workforce, has declined since the mid-1950s. Contrary to what many people think, the decline in unionism cannot be explained by the transition of the U.S. economy away from blue-collar jobs and toward white-collar service jobs.[34] Union membership has declined even in the blue-

[32]Graham Wilson, "American Business and Politics," in Allan J. Cigler and Burdette A. Loomis (eds.), *Interest Group Politics*, Second Edition (Washington, DC: Congressional Quarterly Press, 1986), p. 224.

[33]Wilson, ibid., pp. 227–228.

[34]For a discussion of the decline in union membership, see Paul Edward Johnson, "Organized Labor in an Era of Blue-Collar Decline," in Allan J. Cigler and Burdette A. Loomis (eds.), *Interest Group Politics*, Third Edition (Washington, DC: Congressional Quarterly Press, 1991), pp. 33–61.

collar industries, and thus a better explanation is that business has adapted to increasing wage costs associated with unions by opening nonunion plants and by providing incentives to employees not to organize. In addition, as union membership has declined generally, many unions have responded by increasing dues, which has had the effect of further reducing membership by driving out existing members. As Paul Johnson has pointed out, increasing dues leads to an "unraveling process," as wealthier members constitute larger and larger majorities in unions when poorer members leave, leading to additional increases in dues and further exiting of less wealthy members.[35]

Citizen Groups

Citizen groups constitute a large and important category of groups that has undergone tremendous growth in recent years. The defining characteristic of a citizen group is that its membership is not drawn exclusively from a particular professional, occupational, or industrial class of individuals or organizations. Groups such as the American Association of Retired Persons (AARP), the National Organization for Women (NOW), the National Rifle Association (NRA), and the Sierra Club are examples of citizen groups. Their memberships span a variety of occupations and economic concerns.

Included within this general category of citizen groups are organizations that are typically called *"public interest groups."* A public interest group, according to Jeffrey Berry, is one that lobbies for benefits that do "not selectively and materially benefit the membership and activists of the organization."[36] Clear examples of such organizations are Mothers Against Drunk Driving (MADD) and Handgun Control, Inc. Examples of organizations strictly fitting Berry's definition are difficult to find, however. Unions, trade associations, and corporations sometimes lobby for environmental benefits or on behalf of civil rights, but they are not recognized as public

---

[35]See Paul Edward Johnson, "Unraveling in Democratically Governed Groups," *Rationality and Society* 2 (1990): 4–34.

[36]Jeffrey M. Berry, *Lobbying for the People* (Princeton, NJ: Princeton University Press, 1977), p. 7.

interest groups when they do; and organizations such as AARP, NOW, and the NRA, often classified as interest groups, lobby for benefits that materially benefit their members. AARP, for example, seeks social security benefits for retirees, NOW lobbies for higher wages for working women, and the NRA supports a strong economic market for the purchase and sale of guns. One could even argue that the Sierra Club, often considered a quintessential example of a public interest group, seeks benefits that materially benefit its members by lobbying for the protection of wilderness areas that provide hiking opportunities for its members who otherwise could not afford to purchase and protect hiking areas on their own.

Citizen groups are the newest and fastest growing category of political interest group. Technological and social changes fueled the rapid growth of these organizations during the 1960s and 1970s, as improvements in techniques of mass communication—television, WATTS long-distance telephone lines, and computerized mailing capabilities—and the rise of political activism in the racial and war protests of the 1960s provided both the leadership and the technical means by which citizens could be organized at the grassroots level. Also figuring prominently in the formation of citizen groups during this period were grants and gifts from individuals, foundations, other associations, and even the government.[37] The Students for a Democratic Society (SDS), for example, a liberal student organization of the 1960s, received its principal source of funds from the United Auto Workers. When the SDS leadership began advocating revolutionary positions in the late 1960s, however, the UAW withdrew its support, eventually leading to the disintegration of the organization.[38]

Intergovernmental Groups

One important, but often unrecognized, sector of interest group activity is what is often referred to as the "intergovernmental lobby."

---

[37]See Jack L. Walker, "The Origins and Maintenance of Interest Groups in America," *American Political Science Review* 77 (1983): 390–406.
[38]Ibid., p. 403.

The intergovernmental lobby consists of states, counties, cities, towns and townships, irrigation districts, and other local political jurisdictions, together with governors, mayors, attorneys general, state legislators, and city managers. All are active participants in Washington politics. They frequently testify before congressional committees, participate in rule making by federal agencies, and submit briefs and participate as parties in judicial proceedings. State and local governments seek regulatory relief from the federal government, and they compete with one another for federal aid administered through categorical and block grants.

Listed in the *Encyclopedia of Associations* are 267 governmental organizations.[39] Some of the better-known groups are the National Governors' Association, the National League of Cities, the National Association of Counties, the U.S. Conference of Mayors, the National Conference of State Legislators, and the National Association of Towns and Townships. Some of the lesser-known organizations are the American Association of Airport Executives, the National Association of Housing and Redevelopment Officials, and the National Association of Smaller Communities. In 1988 the six better-known organizations listed above had a combined budget of more than $30 million, and between 1983 and 1986 they participated in more than 500 congressional hearings.[40] More than 40 percent of all governmental organizations in existence today were established between 1960 and 1979, a period of dramatic growth in the federal government and expanded federal aid to state and local governments.

Charitable and Religious Groups

The final category of groups listed in Table 2.2—religious, charitable, and community groups—are frequent participants in the polit-

---

[39]This count is provided in Patrick Donnay, *Politics and Professionals: The Demand for Participation in the Intergovernmental Lobby*, Ph.D. dissertation, The University of Iowa, 1991, p. 84.

[40]Ibid., p. 92.

ical process, even though their primary organizational purpose is nonpolitical. Organizations like the Epilepsy Foundation of America, the Anti-Defamation League of B'nai B'rith, the Girl Scouts of America (GSA), the YMCA, the Salvation Army, and the University of California have political agendas ranging from tax policy on charitable contributions to the distribution of federal research grants. Like corporations, these organizations do not attempt to attract or maintain members on the basis of the political positions they advocate. Robert Salisbury refers to such organizations as "institutional" interests and notes that unlike membership groups, "institutions have interests that are politically and analytically independent of the interests of particular institutionalized members."[41] The political interests of university students, therefore, are not what compel universities to seek federal research grants, and the political preferences of Girl Scouts do not lead the GSA to seek special tax benefits. Rather, these institutions pursue political goals only as a means of enhancing the economic or social standing of the organization itself.

One form of political interest group not listed in Table 2.2 is that of the political action committee. PACs, which raise and contribute money to congressional candidates, certainly fit the definition of a political interest group; nevertheless, they are, for the most part, subsidiaries of organizations already listed in Table 2.2, and so I have elected not to classify them separately. As I explain shortly, federal election campaign laws require corporations, unions, and other organizations that want to make financial contributions to candidates' campaigns to do so through separate organizational entities generally known as PACs. Hence, PACs themselves are typically classified by the type of organization (e.g., corporation, labor union, trade association) with which they are affiliated. The one exception is the category of PACs generally known as a *nonconnected* PACs, which have no affiliation with a standing organization. However, roughly 90 percent of all of the money contributed to federal con-

---

[41]Robert H. Salisbury, "Interest Representation: The Dominance of Institutions," *American Political Science Review* 78 (1984): pp. 67–68.

gressional candidates through political action committees is contributed through PACs that are affiliated with an organization in one of the basic categories listed in Table 2.2, and thus I chose to treat all types of PACs separately and at greater length in Chapter 5.

Political Organization and the Legal Environment

Political action committees are but one of several different types of subsidiary organizations connected with contemporary political interest groups. Many groups have not only PACs as affiliated organizations but also legal defense funds and foundations for the purposes of litigation and public education. Affiliated with the Sierra Club, for example, are the Sierra Club Committee on Political Education, the Sierra Club's political action committee; the Sierra Club Legal Defense Fund, a public interest law firm representing the organization in environmental litigation and related matters; and the Sierra Club Foundation, which supports research and public education programs. Affiliated with the National Organization for Women are the NOW Foundation and NOW/PAC. The National Rifle Association has several affiliates, including the Firearms Civil Rights Legal Defense Fund, its litigation arm; the Institute for Legislative Action, its legislative arm; and the NRA Political Victory Fund, its political action committee. The National Association of Wholesaler-Distributors has the Distribution Research and Education Foundation and the Wholesaler-Distributor Political Action Committee.

This atomization of interest groups—that is, the breaking up of groups into various subsidiaries—is largely a consequence of groups' complying with, or else reacting strategically to, provisions of the federal tax code that regulate their political activities. The fundamental issue is whether individuals' dues and contributions to an organization can be deducted from federal income taxes. The Internal Revenue Code classifies the tax status of organizations in four ways: charitable organizations, defined under section 501(c)(3); social welfare organizations, section 501(c)(4); labor unions, section 501(c)(5); and trade or professional organizations, section 501(c)(6). Only charitable groups, groups with 501(c)(3) status, are allowed to let individuals deduct their dues and contributions. The catch, however, is that charitable organizations are greatly restricted in the amount of lobbying in which they can legally engage.[42]

Naturally, organizations prefer tax-exempt status in order to encourage individuals to join the organization and to contribute money, but because a tax exemption for individual dues and contributions limits their lobbying activities, many organizations have adopted a bifurcated organizational structure where one part operates as a tax-exempt organization and the other operates as a full-fledged lobbying organization. The Sierra Club, for example, changed its tax status from 501(c)(3) to 501(c)(4) in 1965 after coming under pressure from the IRS for its lobbying activities. Leaders of the Sierra Club had been reluctant to give-up their tax-exempt status for fear that they would lose members, but as it turned out, the change to 501(c)(4) status resulted in no decline in membership.[43] As a result, the Sierra Club has actually been able to expand its activities by establishing the Sierra Club Legal Defense Fund and

---

[42]In the Revenue Act of 1939, Congress amended the Internal Revenue Code so that certain nonprofit organizations would *lose* their tax exempt status if a "substantial" part of their activities consisted of "carrying on propaganda, or otherwise attempting, to influence legislation." The limits on lobbying by charitable organizations were later clarified by Congress in the Tax Reform Act of 1976. Allowable lobbying expenditures were set at 20 percent of an organization's first $500,000 of general, tax-exempt expenditures; 15 percent of the second $500,000; 10 percent of the third $500,000; and 5 percent of each additional $500,000. (See Congressional Quarterly, Inc., *The Washington Lobby*, Fourth Edition (Washington, DC: Congressional Quarterly, Inc., 1982), p. 39.) In addition, Congress set a total limit of one million dollars per year for lobbying expenditures by 501(c)(3) organizations and provided for an excise tax of 25 percent of excess lobbying expenditures as penalty for exceeding the limits. Under the new provisions, organizations exceeding spending limits by 50 percent over a four year period would lose tax-exempt status. Tax-exempt status also restricted grassroots lobbying expenditures, defined as attempts to influence general public opinion on legislation, to no more than one-fourth of lobbying expenditures. Churches and church-related organizations were excluded, however, so as not to interfere with separation of church and state.
[43]For details and analysis, see Robert Cameron Mitchell, "National Environmental Lobbies and the Apparent Illogic of Collective Action," in Clifford Russell (ed.), *Collective Decision Making: Applications from Public Choice Theory* (Baltimore, MD: Johns Hopkins University Press, 1979).

the Sierra Club Foundation, both tax-exempt affiliates that carry out the litigation and educational activities of the organization.

In general, the federal tax code has not proven to be an impediment to the effective maintenance and operation of organized interests. In fact, it could be argued that the atomized organizational structures that have developed in response to tax regulations have actually lead to greater specialization within groups of their basic functions and activities. With clear separation of funds and clear division of labor, the various activities and functions of organizations have become institutionalized in a way that assures continuity and encourages professional specialization. The overall effect is probably to make groups more efficient and effective at what they do rather than to limit or curtail their activities in any significant way.

Controlling Factions: Regulation and the Endurance of Political Interests

The response of political interest groups to the federal tax code is but one instance of their ability to adapt to changes in the external legal environment. Organizational adaptability is essential to the endurance of organized interests, for historically there have been numerous efforts to regulate their activities, either through manipulations of the tax code or through other statutory means. In general, however, efforts to control interest groups through legal means have been rather weak and ineffective. The reason is partly because interest groups are good at adapting to new circumstances and partly because it has proven to be very difficult for Congress and the courts to write and enforce statutes that on the one hand effectively regulate political activity and on the other hand protect First Amendment freedoms of speech, assembly, and the right to petition the government for redress of grievances. The ultimate result is that the organization of political interests in the United States has been affected only marginally by regulatory efforts.

There is no better illustration of this point than the complications involved in legally defining lobbying activity, and thus enforcing the registration and reporting of lobbying activities. Although Title III of the Legislative Reorganization Act of 1946 requires individuals or groups that solicit or collect funds for the principal purpose of influencing Congress on legislation to register with the clerk of the House or the secretary of the Senate and to file for each calendar quarter a financial statement of their activities, this act has never been successfully implemented. The law is riddled with loopholes, and interest groups have been very adept at finding them. Consequently, it is often difficult, if not impossible, for the outside observer to determine which organizations actually lobby the federal government and which do not. A brief history of this legislation and its subsequent implementation illustrate the problems of regulation and the ability of interest groups to survive largely unfettered by regulatory efforts.

Known as the Federal Regulation of Lobbying Act, Title III of the Legislative Reorganization Act of 1946 requires individuals or groups that solicit or collect funds for the principal purpose of influencing Congress on legislation to register with the clerk of the House or the secretary of the Senate and to file for each calendar quarter a financial statement of their activities. Section 307 details to whom the act applies:

> The provisions of this title shall apply to any person (except a political committee as defined in the Federal Corrupt Practices Act, and duly organized State or local committees of a political party), who by himself, or through any agent or employee or other persons in any manner whatsoever, directly or indirectly, solicits, collects, or receives money or any other thing of value to be used principally to aid, or the principal purpose of which person is to aid, in the accomplishment of any of the following purposes:
>
> (a) The passage or defeat of any legislation by the Congress of the United States.
>
> (b) To influence, directly or indirectly, the passage or defeat of any legislation by the Congress of the United States.

The successful implementation of this act has been greatly hindered by its ambiguity. It did not elaborate on the clauses "principally to aid, or the principal purpose" and "directly or indirectly." Nor did it define "lobbyist" or "lobbying." Whether Congress left the language vague because of concerns about the constitutionality of more restrictive definitions or simply because it was not all that interested in regulating lobbying is unclear. Belle Zeller has suggested that one reason for the lack of precision is that the act was given only cursory debate, as members were much more concerned about other aspects of legislative reorganization at the time.[44] Whatever the reason, the ambiguities were soon an issue for litigation.

In 1952 New York cotton broker Robert M. Harriss was indicted for not reporting payments made to a Washington lobbyist who attempted to influence Congress on legislation of interest to the cotton industry. A federal appellate court dismissed the charges against Harriss, ruling that the 1946 act was unconstitutional in that it was too vague and indefinite to meet the requirements of due process, and that it violated First Amendment guarantees of freedom of speech, assembly, and petition for the redress of grievances. Upon appeal, the U.S. Supreme Court overturned the appellate court's decision and ruled 5–3 to uphold the act in *United States v. Harriss*. The Court's decision provided only lukewarm support for the regulation and reporting of lobbying activities, however. The charges against Harriss were dismissed, because even though he *paid* money to a lobbyist, he did not *solicit, collect, or receive* money for the principal purpose of lobbying. Moreover, in order to preserve the constitutionality of the act, the Court determined that lobbying entailed only "direct communication with members of Congress on pending or proposed federal legislation."[45] Part (b) of section 307, which originally included the phrase "directly or indirectly," was therefore amended significantly, excluding indirect activities such as grassroots activities from the scope of the act. The Court also interpreted the "principal purpose" clause narrowly, choosing not to expand the meaning to include political organizations whose *principal* purpose was not lobbying. The Court explained that it found it necessary to construe the act "narrowly to avoid constitutional doubts."[46] By giv-

---

[44]Belle Zeller, "The Regulation of Pressure Groups and Lobbyists," *The Annals of the American Academy of Political and Social Science* 319 (September 1958): 98.

[45]*United States v. Harriss*, 347 U.S. 1954, 620. There is some doubt about whether Congress intended the act to apply so narrowly. Based on a reading of the House and Senate committee reports and based on the "directly and indirectly" phrase, Wooton argues that the act was meant to cover telegram and letter campaigns that originated outside Washington, DC. See Graham Wooton, *Interest Group Politics in America* (Englewood Cliffs, NJ: Prentice-Hall, 1985), p. 182.

[46]Ibid.

ing up specificity in order to maintain constitutionality, the Court opened up massive loopholes for registration and reporting under the Federal Regulation of Lobbying Act. It is estimated, for example, that only one out of every six lobbyists is registered, and that only about one-tenth of all lobbying expenditures are reported.[47] For many years, the lobbyists for the National Association of Manufacturers did not register, because they maintained that the "principal purpose" of the organization was not to influence legislation.[48]

The conclusion to be drawn from this brief history is that regulating the activities of organized interests, even something as seemingly simple as identifying organizations whose principal purpose is lobbying, can entail major complications. The Congress and the Court must strike a delicate and difficult balance between holding minority factions accountable and preserving First Amendment freedoms. In addition, since any effort to regulate groups poses potential threats to their existence and effective operation, they will use all resources available either to adapt effectively or else simply to resist. The abilities of interest groups to adapt successfully by establishing more firmly their existence and mode of operation in accepted law—as they have in response to stronger restrictions in the tax code—or to resist legal efforts to regulate their activities—as they have in response to reporting and disclosure requirements—ensures their endurance and legitimacy in the political system.

I began this chapter by noting the great diversity of organized interests in American politics and their steady evolution and development over the years. I conclude by simply noting that prospects for their continued evolution are quite positive. Given that interest groups have proven adept at surviving largely untouched by federal regulations for easily more than 100 years, it is unlikely that their development will be impeded in any significant way by statutory action in the near future. Consequently, perhaps the best hope for those who wish to see the influence of organized interests checked and constrained is that groups themselves, not government, be the

---

[47]See Helen Dewar, "Major Overhaul of Lobbying Laws Clear Senate, 95-2," *Washington Post*, May 7, 1993, A, 1:5.

[48] See Richard W. Gable, "NAM: Influential Lobby or Kiss of Death?" *Journal of Politics* 15 (1953): 263.

regulators. As will become clear in ensuing chapters, competition between groups does indeed provide some degree of accountability in the information that groups present to legislators.

INTEREST GROUPS, CONGRESS, AND PUBLIC POLICY

Leaders of interest groups and members of Congress have very different perspectives on the relevant importance of each to the other. To members of Congress, interest groups are only one of several actors attempting to influence the legislative process. Legislators must consider appeals from congressional party leaders, the White House, and their own constituents in addition to those from interest groups. To interest groups, Congress is only one of several institutions with the power to determine policy outcomes. Interest groups must also contend with the judicial system, the president, and bureaucratic agencies, each of which can exercise considerable influence over the realization of their policy goals. From the perspective of Congress, what interest groups do *within* Congress matters most; but from the perspective of interest groups, what they do *outside* Congress is often as important or more important than what they do inside Congress.

As students of interest groups *and* Congress, it is important to gain some perspective on interest groups' activities outside, as well as inside, the legislative arena. This chapter provides an overview of both. The first part of the chapter examines the fundamental strategies and activities of groups within Congress. Groups must decide whether to pursue a public relations campaign, a grassroots effort, Washington lobbying, or some combination of all three. Some of these tactics are more effective at one stage of the legislative process than at another, and thus it is useful to dissect the legislative process in order to understand a group's choice of tactics and the effectiveness of those tactics at various stages of the process. The second part of the chapter briefly reviews the basic activities of interest groups in the judicial and administrative arenas. Congress may be a separate branch of government, but it is not an isolated branch. What groups accomplish or fail to accomplish in Congress often depends on their successes and failures in the other two branches of national government. The third section of the chapter presents a case study of policy making on family and medical leave to illustrate some of the key points of sections one and two; and the fourth and final part of the chapter explains how and where interest groups fit into traditional models of legislative decision making.

Interest Group Participation before Congress

Seldom does one need to worry about the U.S. Congress making hasty or quick decisions. Congress, most of the time, moves very deliberately and acts only after careful consideration of competing viewpoints and alternative courses of action. One explanation for the deliberate pace of the legislative process is that members of Congress wish to collect and process a great deal of information before making decisions. Indeed, one prominent theory of legislative organization holds that legislative procedures are designed explicitly to encourage specialization and policy expertise among members and that the goal of acquiring and sharing information motivates and explains much about the organization of legislatures.[1]

The high value that legislators apparently place on information suggests that interest groups, provided they have useful information to share, should be an integral part of the legislative process. One should expect to find them involved in virtually all major phases of decision making, beginning with the formulation and introduction of bills, proceeding through committee hearings and markup sessions, and concluding with action on the floor and the resolution of differences between chambers. The following brief overview of interest group activities at these various stages attests to their intense involvement throughout the process.

[1]See Keith Krehbiel, *Information and Legislative Organization* (Ann Arbor, University of Michigan Press, 1991).

Formulation of Bills

Some of the most active lobbying often takes place even before a specific bill is introduced. Lobbying at this very early stage of the process is important for establishing perceptions of the political, legal, and administrative viability of various policy options. By narrowing or expanding the perceived range of legislative possibilities, groups are often able to define the terms of the debate. They can squelch proposals before they receive formal consideration, and they can anticipate and deflect potential objections. The National Licensed Beverage Association, for example, began organizing and contacting members of Congress early in 1993 to head off a possible tax increase on alcoholic beverages to pay for national health insurance, even though no specific proposal had been introduced, or was even likely to be introduced, for several months.[2] Similarly, the American Medical Association bused hundreds of its members to Washington to register opposition to any proposals that might freeze physicians' fees.[3]

Early participation at the formulation stage also helps groups establish themselves as players—organizations with political resources and an economic or social stake in an issue. To be effective, lobbyists must have visibility with legislators, and one way they achieve visibility is to establish themselves and their organizations as prominent spokespersons for specific policy proposals. It is often easier to attain visibility early in the process before hundreds of other organizations join the fray, and so groups that establish early their commitment to a particular position may have an easier time gaining access to later stages of decision making.

Groups signal their involvement at the formulation stage not only to legislators but also to other groups. One technique groups use to stake out their turf is "advocacy advertising," in which groups place ads in major newspapers, periodicals, and on television as a way of informing key legislators and other interest groups that they have a serious stake in some issue. By spending money early on advertising,

---

[2] Michael Weisskopf, "Liquor Lobbying, Grass-Roots Style," *Washington Post*, March 10, 1993, A, 1:4.
[3] Michael Weisskopf, "AMA Buses Doctors to Practice Preventive Medicine at Capitol," *Washington Post*, March 26, 1993, A, 10:1.

groups signal their willingness to invest additional resources later on. One political consultant described this tactic as one in which a group says to its opponents, "We're prepared to wage a fight that could get ugly and expensive for you."[4] This strategy is typically employed inside the Washington beltway, where the objective is to impress legislators and other group leaders rather than to mobilize mass opinion. Organizations such as the American Medical Association, the Pharmaceutical Manufacturers Association, and Prudential Insurance Company employed this tactic during the initial consideration of various national health insurance proposals in 1992. By committing resources at the outset, these groups hoped to deter the opposition, or at least to give notice of their willingness to fight.

Committee Hearings and Markups

Most lobbying, like most legislative work, takes place at the committee level. The House and Senate typically hold more than 3000 committee hearings and markups each year, and virtually all interest groups are involved in these proceedings in one way or another. One recent study reports that testifying at congressional hearings is the technique groups use most frequently to exercise influence, and that 99 percent of all Washington-based organizations testify at congressional hearings.[5]

Committee hearings provide a formal opportunity for representatives of organized interests to express their preferences for or against proposed or existing policies. Kevin Leyden has identified four basic types of congressional hearings, the most common of which involves policy oversight.[6] These hearings are designed to solicit reactions from organized groups and relevant individuals about whether existing legislation is achieving its intended effects. Hearings of this type usually center around a specific bill or set of

[4]Howard Kurtz, "For Health Care Lobbies, a Major Ad Campaign," *Washington Post*, April 13, 1993, A, 1:2.
[5]Kay Lehman Schlozman and John T. Tierney, *Organized Interests and American Society* (New York: Harper and Row, 1986), pp. 150–151.
[6]Kevin M. Leyden, "Congressional Hearings, Organized Interests, and the Provision of Information," manuscript, Department of Political Science, West Virginia University, 1992.

bills proposing changes in the existing legislation. Other types of hearings are designed to elicit opinions and illuminate potential problems in unchartered policy areas, to investigate and oversee bureaucratic implementation of existing programs, and to bring attention to problems such as malnutrition or poverty at the formative stages of the policy process.

Groups participate in congressional hearings in one of two ways. They either send an official or other member of the group to testify in person, or they submit written comments to the committee, or both. Most organizations prefer to testify in person because it offers greater visibility and prestige, but they are not always able to do so. Groups must be invited, usually by the committee staff, to present oral testimony, but almost any organization or individual can submit written comments to the committee. When groups participate in person, the individual who testifies is typically not the group's Washington-based lobbyist, but rather the group's national spokesperson or president, a policy expert, or even a rank-and-file member. Organizations generally use witnesses other than Washington-based lobbyists to emphasize the broader significance of the groups' concerns outside the beltway. The typical format of a hearing is for the witness to present a brief statement describing the organization and its general position, and then for members of the committee to ask detailed questions of the witness.

One of the most important functions of committee hearings is to inform and educate members of Congress.[7] They help legislators learn about the problems or shortcomings of existing programs, and they help specify the likely consequences of newly proposed programs. Hearings help legislators determine which options are most likely to achieve the desired policy objectives, which options are politically feasible, and which can be effectively implemented. Of course, much of the information presented at hearings is not new to legislators. For most issues, legislators will have heard the same arguments presented at an earlier hearing or in another forum, and

---

[7]See Leyden, "Congressional Hearings, Organized Interests, and the Provision of Information," and Kenneth Entin, "Information Exchange in Congress: The Case of the House Armed Services Committee," *Western Political Quarterly* 26 (1973): 427–439. Also, see Christine DeGregorio, "Congressional Hearings Revisited," presented at the Midwest Political Science Association, Chicago, IL, 1990.

they will have seen the same alignments of organized interests. Congressional hearings are informative, however, even when they do not introduce new arguments or startling revelations. That there are no unexpected arguments or concerns is itself important information, as members of Congress frequently need to reassure themselves that the political winds have not shifted, that new problems have not arisen, or that groups have not changed their positions.

A second important function of congressional hearings is to force organized interests to reveal their preferences and to state them publicly. This makes it costly for groups to change their positions at some later time. Legislators must be confident that interest group alignments and preferences are accurately presented and relatively stable if they are to engage in effective bargaining, negotiation, and compromise. Without stability of preferences, agreements would break down quickly. The public visibility of hearings, together with the publication of the transcripts of hearings, makes it difficult for groups to change their positions later, and it is for this reason that arguments presented at hearings often shape the subsequent legislative debate.

The informational value of congressional hearings is sometimes questioned by those who allege that witnesses are carefully chosen by committee members and staff to emphasize one particular point of view at the exclusion of another.[8] The main purpose of congressional hearings, according to this view, is to gain media attention and to begin building political support for just one particular position. One problem with this argument is that bills reported from committees that have stacked the witness list during the hearings may be open to challenge later on the grounds that the full economic or political consequences have not been thoroughly investigated. Even legislators who are predisposed to support the committee's bill may be hesitant to cast a visible vote on the floor until all of the relevant information has been made available and until all issues have been clarified.

Although testimony at most hearings is relatively balanced on both sides of the issue, it is not the case that all groups have an equal chance of being invited to testify. According to Leyden, the invita-

---

[8]See, for example, Stephen K. Bailey, *Congress Makes a Law* (New York: Columbia University Press, 1950).

tion process is largely an "insider's game."[9] Leyden discovered that committee staffers generally take great care to assemble witness lists in a way that reflects the balance of interests they hear from *privately*.[10] Leyden found that these are generally the organizations that can afford to hire their own Washington-based lawyers and maintain professional staff support. Organizations that lack these resources are not as likely to be perceived as significant players or as groups with particular expertise worth sharing and, as a result, do not enjoy a high degree of access to committee members or staff.

Hearings are only the first step in the committee process. The real legislative work begins in markup sessions, where committee members amend and vote on particular provisions within bills. Most committee markup sessions are now open to the public, and so lobbyists are particularly attentive and vigilant at this stage of the process. During markup, a lobbyist will typically work closely with one or two members of the committee, recommending the deletion or insertion of specific provisions, offering suggestions for new language, evaluating procedures for deciding among competing bills, and generally warning of potential problems in the committee's deliberations. Committee members will often consult with lobbyists on the more technical and obscure provisions of bills to make sure that they understand the potential consequences of their decisions. It is the lobbyists' job to understand and be able to explain these provisions, and it is their general expertise on technical or complicated matters that makes them an important informational resource for legislators.

Floor and Conference Action

The relatively few bills that emerge from committee proceedings often involve significant and controversial issues, frequently resulting in divisive votes on final passage. Votes on final passage are not the only important decisions the full chamber makes, however. Votes on rules governing debate and amendment procedures, and even decisions about if and when to schedule votes, are also critically

---

[9]Leyden, "Congressional Hearings, Organized Interests, and the Provision of Information," p. 29.
[10]Leyden, "Congressional Hearings, Organized Interests, and the Provision of Information," p. 5.

important and attract a great deal of interest group participation. In the House, lobbyists attempt to gain favorable decisions from the Rules Committee for the amendment and debate procedures to be followed on the floor, and they must be able to anticipate any rules or amendments that might adversely affect their bills. During consideration of a national energy strategy in the U.S. House during the 102nd Congress, for example, a coalition of energy groups formed to fight several killer amendments they expected to be offered on the floor. Bills reported by the Interior and Merchant Marine and Fisheries Committees were to be considered under open rules, thereby inviting amendments on the floor, and the American Petroleum Institute, the National Coal Association, the American Gas Association, and other groups organized to fight amendments that would limit offshore drilling, restrict licensing of nuclear power plants, and limit carbon dioxide emissions.[11]

Two important tactical approaches distinguish lobbying during floor deliberations from lobbying during committee deliberations. One is the heightened presence and importance of broad-based coalitions of groups. Groups generally begin to band together at the very early stages of legislation, but coalitions are much more important on the floor, especially in the House, where groups must reach hundreds of members rather than just those on the committee. Most groups simply do not have broad enough contacts to reach hundreds of legislators effectively, and so it is imperative that they join forces with other groups pursuing similar interests. Although coalitions are most important during floor proceedings, they have also become important at the committee stage in recent years because of the dispersion of power in Congress brought about by reforms of the 1970s. Bills are now often sequentially or jointly referred to more than one committee, requiring that groups achieve much broader access than during the prereform period.[12]

---

[11]Thomas Lippman, "Energy Lobby Fights Unseen 'Killers'," *Washington Post*, April 1, 1992, A, 21:4.

[12]See Scholzman and Tierney, *Organized Interests and American Democracy*, Chapter 12; and Robert H. Salisbury, "The Paradox of Interest Groups in Washington: More Groups, Less Clout," in Anthony King, ed., *The New American Political System*, Second Edition, (Washington, DC: American Enterprise Institute, 1990), pp. 203–229.

In a typical coalitional lobbying effort, groups will take responsibility for lobbying those representatives with whom they have the best working relationships and the strongest constituency support. This is because one of the most effective ways for organized interests to gain the attention of legislators is to demonstrate a visible organizational presence in their electoral constituencies. John Kingdon has noted that groups with no connection to representatives' districts "have little or no influence on their decisions."[13] The logic of coalitional lobbying is then very simple. As explained by a lobbyist for a national trade association: "You just divide it [the effort] up on the basis of where each group is geographically strongest."[14]

A second, and related, tactical characteristic of interest group lobbying on the floor is that grassroots techniques are more prevalent and effective. The reason is simply that constituents are more easily mobilized on bills under consideration by the full chamber, because these bills receive greater media attention and therefore are more visible and easily understood than bills under consideration at the committee level. This makes it easier for organizations to convince their members of the importance of the bill and to encourage them to contact their representatives or senators through letters, telephone calls, telegrams, and personal visits.

One of the final phases of legislative lobbying occurs as the House and Senate attempt to reconcile any differences in their bills. Institutional and ideological differences between the two chambers often favor different kinds of interests, and, as a result, differences between the House and Senate versions of a bill are often significant, prompting extensive lobbying during deliberations by conference committees. During the 99th Congress, for example, a long and drawn-out conference fight occurred over how corporations should be taxed to pay for the environmental "superfund." The Senate's bill, favored by a relatively narrow coalition of oil and chemical interests led by the American Petroleum Institute, dispersed the tax burden across all manufacturers, not just oil and chemical producers. In contrast, the House's bill, favored by a large and diverse coalition

---

[13]John W. Kingdon, *Congressmen's Voting Decisions* (New York: Harper and Row, 1973), p. 150.
[14]Interview with the author, June 17, 1985.

of manufacturing groups led by the Grocery Manufacturers Association, placed most of the tax burden on the oil and chemical industry. A compromise was finally reached, but only after 10 months of negotiation by the conference committee.[15] In a more recent case, an extensive coalitional effort was mounted to win support in conference for the House's version of the "motor voter" bill passed during the 103rd Congress. The League of Women Voters, the American Association of Retired Persons, the National Association for the Advancement of Colored People (NAACP), and 62 other organizations successfully opposed provisions in the Senate's version of the bill that would have restricted registration at social service agencies.[16]

The legislative process is not complete until the Congress presents a bill to the president and it is signed. A presidential veto, or the anticipation of a veto, can have a significant impact on groups' lobbying strategies. Groups that both favor and expect a veto sometimes put forth little effort trying to defeat bills on final floor votes. Instead, they simply let the bill pass in a form they know the president will veto, thereby saving their resources to lobby against any override attempt by either or both chambers. Naturally, attempts to override a presidential veto often stimulate intense lobbying by organizations on both sides of the issue. Efforts to pass family and medical leave legislation, described later in this chapter, provide a good illustration.

The Defensive Advantage

The numerous procedural steps required to move a bill through Congress provide multiple opportunities for legislators to acquire and process information, but they also provide multiple opportunities for groups to forestall or block legislation antithetical to their interests. The advantage of a deliberate process, of course, is that it is information intensive; the disadvantage is that bills are easily

---

[15]Joseph A. Davis, "Senate Moves Quickly to Adopt 'Superfund,'" *Congressional Quarterly Weekly Report*, October 4, 1986, pp. 2384–2385.
[16]Helen Dewar, "Coalition Will Press Hill Conferees to Scrap 'Motor Voter' Restrictions," *Washington Post*, April 1, 1993, A, 15:1.

derailed. Change-oriented groups must win repeatedly, at each step of the process, while status quo interests have to win just once.[17] Thus, one important consequence of a legislative process with multiple decision points is a bias in favor of status quo interests. Grant McConnell has aptly noted that it often seems that "American institutions are studded with so many barriers to action that stalemate is the essential reality of politics in the United States."[18]

Given all of the possibilities for organized interests to intervene and derail proposals, it becomes extremely difficult to implement new policies or to alter existing policies when they are opposed by entrenched and well-organized interests. One illustration of the power of the status quo is the repeated failure over the years by both Republican and Democratic administrations to reduce federal support for low-interest loans to rural electric cooperatives. The Rural Electrification Act (REA) of 1935 provided federal support to electric cooperatives in rural areas, but some politicians now feel that the task of bringing electricity to rural areas has long been accomplished and federal help is no longer needed. Presidents Nixon, Reagan, and Clinton all tried unsuccessfully to reduce or eliminate funding for the program, but in each instance their efforts provoked stiff opposition from rural cooperatives and their employees. Presidential proposals to reduce funding for REA loans or to phase out the agency entirely have been rejected in both the House and the Senate at the committee level.

The leading opponent to these proposals has been the National Rural Electric Cooperative Association (NRECA), formed in 1942 for the express purpose of defending the economic and political interests of rural electric cooperatives. More than 1000 rural cooperatives employing in excess of 70,000 individuals provide dues—nearly $11 million in 1992—and grassroots support for the NRECA's lobbying efforts.[19] In addition, the NRECA's political

[17]See Truman's discussion of the advantages of "defensive groups" in David B. Truman, *The Governmental Process: Political Interests and Public Opinion* (New York: Knopf, 1955), pp. 353–362.
[18]Grant McConnell, *Private Power and American Democracy* (New York: Knopf, 1966), p. 337.
[19]Kevin Merida, "Foot Soldiers for Rural Coops Invade Hill to 'Educate' Congress," *Washington Post*, May 8, 1993, A, 3:1.

action committee contributed $714,930 to 364 congressional candidates during the 1991–1992 election cycle. With resources like these, when the NRECA informs members of Congress that serious electoral repercussions are likely to result from any reduction in federal support to rural cooperatives, they listen. Especially attentive are those members of the key House committee with jurisdiction over electricity, the Subcommittee on Energy and Power of the House Energy and Commerce Committee. Historically, many of the members of this committee have represented rural districts with strong connections to the rural electric cooperatives.

Clearly, one of the keys to the NRECA's success over the years has been its ability to confine legislative action to the committee stage, where its lobbyists have access to many of the key decision makers. In general, the number of legislators with which groups must establish access increases as a bill moves from the initial phase of formulation and introduction, to committee deliberations, and finally to floor proceedings. Since the costs of achieving access escalate throughout the legislative process, organized interests often have greater success early in the process when they have greater control over the points of access and when it is far easier to block proposals than to advance them. This is certainly true in the case of the NRECA, which by establishing access and influence at the narrow jurisdictional level of congressional committees has been able to thwart initiatives arising from the broader national constituency of the president.

Groups defending the status quo have a distinct advantage as long as the "scope of conflict" remains narrow. E. E. Schattschneider once observed that the "best point at which to manage conflict is before it starts" and that the broader the conflict, the more likely the original participants will be unhappy with the outcome.[20] One of the most effective ways that organized interests can expand the scope of conflict is by taking issues outside Congress to the courts and administrative agencies. Action in these arenas often involves additional constituencies and organizations that do not have the interests or resources to participate effectively before Congress. Their involvement outside Congress can have an important impact on the

---

[20]E. E. Schattschneider, *The Semisovereign People: A Realist's View of Democracy in America* (New York: Holt, Rinehart and Winston, 1960), p. 15.

ways that issues and problems are defined inside Congress. Much of what happens in Congress happens in *reaction* to events in the other two branches or in *anticipation* of what might happen in the judicial or executive arenas.

Interest Group Participation beyond Congress: Agencies and the Courts

Organized interests are advantageously positioned to deal with the tripartite structure of American national government. They often initiate action in one arena as a means of stimulating action in another, and when they lose in one institutional arena, they typically pursue their cause in another. Groups can sometimes use their relationship with one branch to achieve influence over another. A group might lobby Congress on behalf of an executive agency or the president in order to gain favor with the executive branch or to provide policy information to a congressional committee for use in an oversight hearing in an effort to influence an executive agency. Groups can also employ litigation strategies to nullify congressional actions or, as is the case more frequently, to shape the content of legislation so that it will pass judicial scrutiny. In short, because interest groups, unlike political parties, do not seek to control the entire government, they often have the strategic advantage of being able to play one institution against another.

Whether an interest group participates before Congress, the courts, executive agencies, or some combination of the three depends in large part on the particular resources the group controls. A resource that is essential to successful legislative participation—for example, a large and diverse membership that penetrates into numerous states and congressional districts—is not necessarily essential to judicial or administrative participation. Similarly, a resource such as legal expertise, while essential to judicial participation, is not necessarily essential to legislative participation. Groups choose their arenas of involvement carefully in terms of their organizational resources, and, as a result, the types of organizations that participate before the courts or federal agencies are often quite different from those participating before Congress.

Participation before the Courts

The most direct way that organized interests can participate before the courts is as a named party in litigation—that is, as plaintiff or defendant, as appellant or appellee in cases involving appeal, or as respondent or petitioner in cases taken to the Supreme Court. Not just any individual or organization, however, is entitled to bring a lawsuit; before courts will accept a case for review, the party bringing the suit must have standing. Prior to the 1960s and 1970s, the laws of standing—the rules governing who may bring suit and with respect to which actions—precluded most organizations from participating as parties in litigation; however, the requirements for standing have been relaxed significantly over the past couple of decades so that organizational participation as a party in a suit is now fairly commonplace.[21] Under current law, organizations such as the Sierra Club or the Consumers Union are allowed to bring suit on behalf of harm or injury inflicted on a broad collectivity of individuals.

The most familiar form of interest group participation before the courts is as amicus curiae, or, literally, friend of the court. Organizations wishing to participate as amici curiae must receive permission of the parties in the case or, if they decline, the court itself. Participation involves filing a short brief in which information or legal arguments are offered on behalf of one party or the other in addition to whatever information or arguments are presented by the parties themselves. Organizations sometimes file amicus curiae briefs for the purpose of urging the court to review a particular case, but more frequently they file briefs for the purpose of influencing the court's final opinion.[22] During the 1987 term of the Supreme Court, 80 percent of the cases decided had amicus curiae briefs filed by one or more organized interests.[23]

---

[21] For a thorough review of the legal history of standing, see Karen Orren, "Standing to Sue: Interest Group Conflict in the Federal Courts," *American Political Science Review* 70 (1976): 723–741.

[22] Information on the frequency of amicus participation by various types of organizations can be found in Gregory A. Caldeira and John R. Wright, "Amici Curiae Before the Supreme Court: Who Participates, When, and How Much?" *Journal of Politics* 52 (1990): 782–806.

[23] Thomas G. Walker and Lee Epstein, *The Supreme Court of the United States: An Introduction* (New York: St. Martin's Press, 1993), p. 135.

A third important way that organizations participate before the courts is as "direct representatives," or "sponsors" of litigation. When participating as direct representatives, groups provide legal or financial resources to one of the named parties in the case. There is usually no formal record of a group's participation of this sort, but an organization's involvement is often apparent if the attorney for one of the parties is also the attorney for an interest group.[24] By one estimate, 65 percent of the cases decided by the Supreme Court during the 1987 term were sponsored by interest groups.[25]

The most important organizational resources for participation before the courts are legal and policy expertise. Organizations such as the AFL-CIO and the U.S. Chamber of Commerce support their own internal legal staffs that prepare briefs and lend advice and support to other organizations. Public interest law groups, such as the Mountain States Legal Foundation (MSLF) or the Center for Science in the Public Interest (CSPI), typically have substantial budgets for litigation and large legal staffs.[26] Organizations that do not employ their own lawyers also sometimes participate in litigation by hiring outside law firms to do their legal work. The cost of hiring outside lawyers, however, can be quite high, as the cost of preparing a single amicus brief can run as high as $50,000.[27]

Legal expertise is crucial for preparing amicus briefs or otherwise participating in the judicial process, but the content of briefs often involves substantive matters of policy rather than technical legal arguments. As a result, groups must possess substantive expertise about policy as well as legal expertise in order to participate effectively before the courts. The information that groups present in amicus curiae briefs is usually information about the alleged conse-

---

[24]For one effort to determine sponsorship, see Lee Epstein and C. K. Rowland, "Debunking the Myth of Interest Group Invincibility in the Courts," *American Political Science Review* 85 (1991): 205–217.

[25]Walker and Epstein, p. 135.

[26]The CSPI has an annual budget of $2,200,000 and a staff of 26; the MSLF has a $1 million budget and a staff of 20. See Karen O'Connor and Lee Epstein, *Public Interest Law Groups: Institutional Profiles* (Westport, CT: Greenwood Press, 1989), pp. 43 and 122.

[27]See Gregory A. Caldeira and John R. Wright, "Why Organized Interests Participate as Amicus Curiae in the U.S. Supreme Court," presented at the annual meeting of Law and Society, Madison, WI, 1989.

quences of the court's decision. Groups typically argue that the social or economic consequences of the court's decision would be so far-reaching that the court must decide the case in a particular way.[28] Clearly, to make these arguments convincingly, groups must command broad substantive knowledge about the economic or social aspects of the issues they are contesting.

Participation before Administrative Agencies

Organized interests participate actively in bureaucratic decision making through membership on advisory committees, by attending rule-making hearings and submitting written comments on proposed agency rules, and by filing or supporting complaints in the adjudication of agency rules. Most federal agencies, at one time or another, establish advisory committees designed to provide specialized technical information or to serve as sounding boards for testing agency proposals.[29] Agencies frequently seek the involvement of groups with relevant political or policy expertise, and groups usually value such participation highly for the access it provides to agency decision making.

Agency rule-making procedures, formally spelled out in the Administrative Procedure Act of 1946, require that federal agencies provide a "commenting" period on all proposed regulations. Agencies must publish any proposed regulations in the *Federal Register* and then allow at least 30 days during which time interested individuals or organizations can submit comments for or against the proposed rule. In addition, agencies often hold one or several hearings, much like congressional hearings, at which organized interests are often invited to testify.

Once an agency regulation is established, alleged violations are brought before the agency in the form of formal complaints, which are then either dismissed as frivolous or sent before an administrative law judge for adjudication.[30] Interest groups participate actively

---

[28]See Gregory A. Caldeira and John R. Wright, "Organized Interests and Agenda-Setting in the U.S. Supreme Court," *American Political Science Review* 82 (1988): 1109–1127.

[29]See A. Lee Fritschler, *Smoking and Politics: Policymaking and the Federal Bureaucracy*, Fourth Edition (Englewood Cliffs, NJ: Prentice-Hall, 1989), pp. 36–38.

[30]For a discussion of procedures and analysis of political strategies, see Terry M. Moe, "Control and Feedback in Economic Regulation: The Case of the NLRB," *American Political Science Review* 79 (1985): 1094–1116.

in these quasi-judicial proceedings, much as they participate in actual judicial proceedings. They file briefs, act as advisers, provide financial support, and transfer services to organizations or individuals playing a formal role in the process.

One of the most important resources for participation in administrative procedures, especially adjudication, is legal expertise. Rule making also often raises difficult legal questions, and organizations frequently comment on proposed rules in terms of the legal issues they raise. A second important resource is policy expertise. In selecting organizations for advisory committees and in gauging the effects of proposed rules, agencies seek advice and counsel on the economic and social impact of their decisions. Finally, political expertise can also be an important resource in dealing with administrative agencies, as agencies must always be sensitive to congressional reactions.

Organizations that participate before the courts or administrative agencies generally have considerable policy expertise prior to their participation, or else they acquire it in the course of their participation. In either case, experience with policy issues in either the judicial or administrative arenas can be an important asset to groups when they enter the legislative arena. Groups with extensive experience with issues before the courts or agencies will be recognized not only for their expertise about technical aspects of policy but also for their knowledge of the political considerations necessary for successful implementation or adjudication of policies. The importance of interest group participation outside Congress for shaping events inside Congress is plainly illustrated by the case of family and medical leave legislation.

The Family and Medical Leave Act: A Case Study of Interest Groups and Policy Making

The Family and Medical Leave Act (FMLA), passed by Congress and signed into law by President Clinton in 1993, illustrates several important aspects of interest group participation before the courts, administrative agencies, and Congress. In addition to demonstrating the ability of status quo interests to obstruct and delay the process, it illustrates how organizations choose their arenas of participation carefully on the basis of the resources they control, and it reveals how the congressional agenda can be influenced significantly by the success or failure of organized interests and the resulting policy decisions in the courts and administrative agencies. This case also shows how interest groups acquire substantial expertise in policy matters long before they participate in congressional hearings or lobby members directly.

The FMLA represents the culmination of nearly 20 years of active interest group involvement across all three branches of national government and numerous state governments. As enacted in 1993, the FMLA allows both male and female employees of businesses with 50 workers or more to take 12 weeks of unpaid leave a year for the birth or adoption of a child; the need to care for a child, spouse, or parent with a serious health condition; or the employee's own serious illness. Employers must provide health insurance during an employee's leave of absence and must guarantee the employee the same or equivalent job upon return.

The historical roots of the FMLA extend back to Title VII of the Civil Rights Act, which made it unlawful for employers to discriminate individuals' privileges of employment because of their sex. Of course, Congress had no idea when it passed Title VII that it was laying the groundwork for family and medical leave legislation 30 years later; yet, regulation and litigation pertaining to Title VII were essential to the formulation and passage of the FMLA in 1993. When Congress first passed the Civil Rights Act in 1964, it delegated authority for implementing Title VII to the Equal Employment Opportunity Commission (EEOC), which issued its initial guidelines in 1965. Then, in what turned out to be an extremely controversial ruling in 1972, the EEOC amended its initial guidelines on Title VII to include employment policies relating to pregnancy and childbirth. Prior to 1972, most employers excluded conditions of pregnancy and childbirth from the health insurance and sick leave plans they offered to their employees, and the EEOC concluded that this practice constituted employment discrimination on the basis of sex, a clear violation of Title VII. Specifically, the EEOC ruled that

> Disabilities caused or contributed to by pregnancy, miscarriage, abortion, childbirth, and recovery therefrom are, for all job-related purposes, temporary disabilities and should be treated as such under any

health or temporary disability insurance or sick leave plan available in connection with employment.[31]

This new guideline was clearly an instance of the EEOC's exercising the administrative discretion that Congress provided it in the authorizing legislation of Title VII, and, predictably, it was immediately criticized by those who felt that the EEOC had strayed from the original congressional intent. Business interests, seeking to avoid the higher costs of employee benefit programs, challenged the EEOC's ruling in court, but failed in case after case to overturn the agency's decision. Between 1972 and 1976, the EEOC's extension of sex discrimination to pregnancy was upheld in rulings by 18 district courts and seven courts of appeal.[32]

Finally, in 1976, business interests found a successful legal vehicle for their position in *General Electric Co. v. Gilbert*, a case in which female employees of General Electric (GE) claimed that the company had violated Title VII of the Civil Rights Act of 1964 by not paying them sickness benefits while they were absent from work due to pregnancy.[33] The Supreme Court, in this instance, decided in favor of GE, ruling that discrimination on the basis of pregnancy did not constitute *general* sex discrimination, as pregnancy was just one of any number of disabilities unique to women, and employers could not be expected to cover all disabilities in any reasonable insurance plan.

The decision in *Gilbert* was not an isolated ruling by the high court. Following on the heals of *Gilbert* was *Nashville Gas Co. v. Nora Satty* in 1977, a case in which Nora Satty had taken a leave of absence because of pregnancy but was not paid sick leave during her absence and, moreover, lost her job seniority as result of her absence.[34] As in *Gilbert*, the Court ruled that denial of sick leave pay did not constitute a violation of Title VII; however, the Court did rule that any loss of job seniority was in violation of Title VII.

The losers in these cases, principally unions and women's organizations, turned their attentions to Congress in an effort to rewrite Title VII in such a way that the Court would have to rule in their

[31] 37, *FR*, 6837 (April 5, 1972).
[32] 44, *FR*, 23804 (April 20, 1979).
[33] 429 U.S. 125.
[34] 434 U.S. 136.

favor in future cases. What these interests sought was an amendment to Title VII that explicitly included discrimination on the basis of pregnancy, childbirth, or related medical conditions as unlawful sex discrimination. Eventually, the unions and women's organizations prevailed over business organizations, and in 1978 Congress passed, and President Carter signed into law, the Pregnancy Discrimination Act (PDA) as an amendment to Title VII of the Civil Rights Act. The PDA achieved for the unions and women's groups through legislation what they had failed to achieve through litigation.

A diverse set of interests participated before Congress during consideration of the Pregnancy Discrimination Act. Those organizations that testified at congressional hearings in 1977, the only formal record of interest group participation before Congress, are listed in Table 3.1.[35] Two characteristics of these participants conform with our expectations about interest group participation before Congress, and at congressional hearings in particular. First, with the exception of the nongovernmental participants, all are membership organizations of one sort or another. The Communication Workers of America has individuals as members, the Electronics Industry Association has firms as members, and the Chamber of Commerce has both firms and individuals as members. These groups have the capacity to reach members of Congress where it counts—in their districts—and are much more likely to be effective in the congressional arena than staff organizations or governmental entities. The second important characteristic of the participants in Table 3.1 is that they were relatively evenly divided in terms of their support or opposition to the PDA. Of 13 nongovernmental organizations that testified, six were business-related interests, led by the Chamber of Commerce and the National Association of Manufacturers. Hence, this hearing conforms with our expectations about most congressional hearings in that the list of witnesses is fairly balanced.

Since the PDA affirmed EEOC's 1972 guidelines on sex discrimination, passage of the PDA required only minor modifications

[35]Lobby registrations also provide some information about interest group participation before Congress, but since so many organizations manage to escape the requirements for registration, these document do not provide very complete information.

Table 3.1   Organizations Represented at Congressional Hearings on Pregnancy Discrimination Act, 1977

AFL-CIO
American Citizens Concerned for Life
American Civil Liberties Union
American Council of Life Insurance
Chamber of Commerce of the United States
Communication Workers of America
Electronics Industry Association
Equal Employment Opportunity Commission
Health Insurance Association of America
International Union of Electrical, Radio, and Machine Workers
Leadership Conference on Civil Rights
National Association of Manufacturers
New Jersey Department of Labor and Energy
Magnavox Consumer Electronics Corporation
United Steel Workers of America
U.S. Department of Justice, Civil Rights Division
U.S. Department of Labor, Women's Bureau

in the EEOC's guidelines. However, in revising its guidelines in 1979 to conform to the PDA, the EEOC took the additional and controversial step of requiring employers to make available health insurance coverage for medical expenses of pregnancy-related conditions of the *spouses of male employees.*[36] Predictably, the EEOC's action provoked considerable comment from individuals and organizations in the 30-day period following its publication in the *Federal Register.* The EEOC received a total of 79 comments from individuals and organizations. Listed in Table 3.2 are many of the organizations that submitted written comments to the commission, some protesting and others lauding the EEOC's ruling.[37]

[36]The EEOC clarified its position at 44, *FR*, 23804 (April 20, 1979).
[37]Not included in Table 3.2 are the individuals and small corporations that commented. Thanks are due to Mary Grady of the EEOC for directing me to this information in the commission's library.

Table 3.2   Organizations Commenting on EEOC
Guidelines, 1979

American Association of University Professors
American Federation of State, County and Municipal Employees
Association of Cypress, California, Teachers
Bethlehem Steel Corporation
City of Sonoma, California
City of Yuma, Arizona
Equal Employment Advisory Council
Georgia Municipal Association
International Union, UAW
Machinery and Allied Products Institute
Mobil Oil Corporation
National Association of Counties
National Association of Life Underwriters
Professional Independent Mass-Marketing Administrators
Riverside County, California
State of Illinois
Underwriters Laboratories, Inc.
University of Houston at Clear Lake City
U.S. Commission on Civil Rights
U.S. Department of Justice, Civil Rights Division
U.S. Steel Corporation
Virginia Education Association
Women's Legal Defense Fund

There is an important difference in the types of organizations
that participated before the EEOC and those that did so in the congressional hearings. Most of the organizations that commented
before the EEOC were institutional groups, not membership
groups. Only nine of the 23 organizations listed in Table 3.2 are
clearly membership organizations. More prevalent than membership
groups in Table 3.2 are institutional groups such as the State of Illinois, Bethlehem Steel Corporation, Riverside County, and the U.S.
Commission on Civil Rights. The significantly larger proportion of
institutional groups relative to membership groups participating
before the EEOC than before Congress in 1977 clearly reflects the
different resource requirements for participation in the two arenas.

Given their expertise in legal and policy matters, institutional groups commenting before the EEOC could do so credibly despite having no dues-paying members.

The EEOC's revised guidelines of 1979 were soon challenged and eventually brought before the Supreme Court in 1983 in *Newport News Shipbuilding & Dry Dock Companyv. v. EEOC.*[38] Newport News Shipping & Dry Dock had provided *less* coverage for the spouses of male employees than for the spouses of female employees, and it challenged the EEOC's guideline requiring it to extend benefits to the spouses. Here the Court sided with the EEOC by ruling that employers had to provide the same amount of disability coverage for spouses of male employees as for spouses of female employees. By establishing the constitutionality of extending benefits to spouses, this decision was an important boost for proponents of a comprehensive family and medical leave policy. The success of the unions and women's organizations in this case led them to seek a broader statute from Congress that would require all businesses, large and small, to provide medical leave for employees and their spouses. The only constitutional hurdle remaining was whether a comprehensive policy could require employers to reinstate employees' returning from a leave in the same or a similar job.

This constitutional question was resolved in *California Federal Savings & Loan Association v. Mark Guerra* in 1987.[39] This case involved a California statute, the California Fair Employment and Housing Act, which entitled employees to job-protected leaves of up to four months for pregnancy and required employers to reinstate employees returning from a pregnancy leave in the same or similar job. The case was prompted by an employee who was not reinstated in the same or similar job, and the question before the Court was whether the California statute was preempted by the PDA, which did not have such a provision. The Court upheld the California law, ruling that Title VII preempted only those laws that required or allowed acts that were unlawful under Title VII, and because the California law was not in violation of Title VII, the PDA did not preempt it. By establishing that the PDA did not preclude family

[38]462 U.S. 669.
[39]479 U.S. 272.

and medical leave legislation, the Court's decision in *Guerra* paved the way for legislative action.

The *Guerra* and *Newport News Shipping & Dry Dock Company* cases attracted a large number of amici. The organizations that participated as amici in either or both cases are listed in Table 3.3. Especially prominent among these organizations are public interest law firms such as the Child Care Law Center and the Mexican American Legal Defense and Education Fund, or membership organizations historically well-known for their litigation efforts such as the American Civil Liberties Union and the American Bar Association. The participation of other nonmembership organizations, particularly the state governments, is also prominent. Thus, like interest group participation before the EEOC, and unlike interest group participation before Congress, legal expertise and policy expertise rather than large memberships are the dominant resources of the participating organizations.

With many of the legal questions concerning family and medical leave legislation resolved, proponents of comprehensive legislation went before Congress. Family and medical leave bills were introduced into four consecutive Congresses from 1986 through 1993, but it was not until 1993, when the Democrats controlled the White House, that the FMLA finally became law. The first comprehensive bill was introduced during the 99th Congress (1986) and, although reported favorably by the House Labor and Education Committee, was opposed by the U.S. Chamber of Commerce and 42 other business organizations and never scheduled for floor consideration.[40] This original bill required businesses with 15 or more employees to provide 18 weeks of unpaid leave for the birth or adoption of a child and 26 weeks of unpaid medical leave.

Given the solid opposition of organized business to family leave during the 99th Congress, proponents were willing to compromise in the 100th Congress in order to get some form of legislation passed. The key compromises in 1988 exempted most small businesses—only businesses with 50 employees or more were required to provide leave—and the length of the leave for any reason was reduced from 18 and 26 weeks to just 15 weeks. These compromises allowed a bill to

---

[40]Julie Rovner, "House Committee Approves Guaranteed Family Leave Bill," *Congressional Quarterly Weekly Report* 44 (June 28, 1986): 1485.

Table 3.3 Organizations Participating as Amici Curiae in *Newport News Shipping & Dry Dock Company* v. *EEOC* and *California Federal Savings & Loan* v. *Mark Guerra*

AFL-CIO
American Association of University Women
American Civil Liberties Union
Americans for Democratic Action
California Women Lawyers
Child Care Law Center
Coal Employment Project
Coalition for Reproductive Equality in the Workplace:
    Betty Friedan
Coalition of Labor Union Women
Council of State Governments
Emerson Electric Company
Equal Employment Advisory Council
Equal Rights Advocates
International City Management Association
International Ladies' Garment Workers Union
Lawyers Committee for Urban Affairs
League of Women Voters of the U.S.
Mexican American Legal Defense and Education Fund
National Association of Counties
National Bar Association—Women Lawyers Division
National Conference of State Legislatures
National League of Cities
National Organization for Women
National Railway Labor Conference
National Women's Law Center
National Women's Political Caucus
9 to 5, National Association of Working Women
NOW Legal Defense and Education Fund
Planned Parenthood Federation of America, Inc.
State of Connecticut
State of Hawaii
State of Montana
State of Washington
U.S. Chamber of Commerce
U.S. Conference of Mayors
United Steel Workers of America
United Teachers—Los Angeles
Women Employed
Women for Racial and Political Equality
Women's Equity Action Project
Women's Law Project
Women Lawyers' Association of Los Angeles
Women Lawyers of Sacramento
Women's Legal Defense Fund

reach the floor of the Senate, but Republicans then filibustered and the Democratic majority was unable to muster the necessary 60 votes for cloture. The session ended with no further action.

Family and medical leave legislation was finally passed by both House and Senate during the 101st Congress, but to no avail as President Bush vetoed the measure. Bush had made clear his intention to veto the legislation long before it reached the floor of either chamber, and thus business groups provided little resistance. A lobbyist for the National Association of Wholesaler-Distributors recounted that "I had John Sununu [President Bush's chief of staff] look me straight in the eye and say that the president would veto it."[41] Not only were business groups confident that any legislation would be vetoed, but given the absence of two-thirds majority support for the bills in either the House or the Senate, they were also confident that any override attempt would fail. They were correct.

With continued Republican control of the White House during the 102nd Congress, business groups were able once again to water down the content of family and medical leave legislation significantly. Action was stalled in the Senate until concessions were made to business groups that allowed employers to deny leave to "key employees", reduced penalties for noncompliance, raised the number of hours employees must work to obtain leave, and required employees to give 30 days advance notice for nonemergency leave. However, in September of 1992, President Bush vetoed even this watered-down version, and although the Senate was able to override the veto, the House was not. Only after President Clinton took office during the following Congress, the 103rd, did family and medical leave legislation become law. The version that Clinton signed was essentially the same watered-down version that President Bush vetoed the previous year.

Several congressional hearings were held on family and medical leave between 1987 and 1993, and these attracted the participation of a diverse set of organizations, listed in Table 3.4. Some of these organizations—notably the AFL-CIO, AFSCME, Chamber of Commerce, NAM, NOW, 9 to 5, and the Women's Legal Defense Fund—had participated before Congress in 1979 or before the EEOC or the

---

[41]As quoted in Alyson Pytte, "House Passes Parental Leave; White House Promises to Veto," *Congressional Quarterly Weekly Report* 48 (May 12, 1990): 1471.

Table 3.4   Organizations Represented at Congressional Hearings
on Family and Medical Leave Act, 1987–1992

American Academy of Child and Adolescent Psychiatry
American Academy of Pediatrics
American Association of Retired Persons
American Federation of State, County, and Municipal Employees
  (AFSCME)
AFL-CIO
American Society for Personnel Administration
Chamber of Commerce of the United States
Concerned Alliance of Responsible Employers
Consortium for Citizens with Developmental Disabilities
Independent Insurance Agents of America
Families and Work Institute
Family Research Council
Georgia Department of Transportation
National Association of Manufacturers (NAM)
National Association of Women Business Owners
National Association of Wholesaler-Distributors
National Coalition for Cancer Survivorship
National Federation of Business and Professional Women's Clubs
National Federation of Independent Business
National Organization for Women (NOW)
National School Boards Association
National Small Business United
9 to 5, National Association of Working Women
North American Council on Adoptable Children
Oregon Bureau of Labor and Industries
Service Employees International Union
Small Business Council
Society for Human Resource Management
U.S. Catholic Conference
Women's Legal Defense Fund

Supreme Court. However, in contrast to the types of organizations
that generally participate before the Supreme Court and the EEOC,
most of the groups in Table 3.4 have large, national memberships.
There are some exceptions—the Georgia Department of Transportation, the Oregon Bureau of Labor and Industries, and the Women's

Legal Defense Fund—but overall, the vast majority of groups listed in Table 3.4 are membership organizations, and relatively large ones. The types of organizations Congress invited to the hearings were the types of organizations it was likely to hear from politically later during committee and floor deliberations.

The history of the FMLA illustrates several important points about interest groups and the broader policy-making process. First, organizations choose their arenas of participation carefully on the basis of the resources they control. Although only a handful of the organizations listed in Tables 3.1 through 3.4 participated in more than one institutional arena, the interests of the basic coalitions are consistent across arenas. Family and medical leave was generally supported by a coalition of labor unions and women's groups and opposed by a coalition of large and small businesses. The particular groups within these general coalitions varied from arena to arena, however, in predictable fashion. Organizations having legal expertise but few members were much more likely to participate before the EEOC or the Supreme Court, whereas organizations with large memberships were much more likely to participate in the congressional arena.

Second, the congressional agenda is influenced significantly by the success or failure of organized interests and the resulting policy decisions in the courts and administrative agencies. Had the Supreme Court ruled differently in *Gilbert* or *Satty* in 1976 and 1977, respectively, it is not at all clear that the issue of medical leave ever would have reached Congress. Had the Court sided with the EEOC in those cases, the unions and women's organizations would have had no need to seek redress from Congress; only the business organizations would have had an incentive to take the issue before Congress, and whether they would have is something we will never know. Of course, it was the EEOC's guidelines in 1972 that triggered the *Gilbert* and *Satty* cases, and thus it was really the EEOC, more than the courts or Congress, that was the policy initiator. The effect of *Guerra* on congressional action is less clear. Even if the Court had not asserted the constitutionality of medical leave in 1987, the unions and women's groups may still have appealed to Congress. Whatever the case, the important lesson is that interest groups do not appear before Congress out of thin air. They make deliberate and strategic decisions to take issues before Congress, often in response to actions that have occurred in other governmental arenas. Had interest groups not been able to expand the scope of conflict beyond the congressional arena in the case of family and medical leave, their legislative efforts may have failed altogether.

Third, the defenders of the status quo, in this case business organizations, were able to obstruct and delay the legislative process for many years, forcing those groups desiring change, in this case the unions and women's groups, to compromise on several important aspects of the legislation. Had it not been for presidential opposition to family and medical leave, it is not clear that business interests would have permitted any form of family and medical leave to pass the House and Senate during the 101st and 102nd Congresses. When opponents of family leave sensed a presidential veto would prevail, they put up only token resistance to final floor passage; when an override was attempted, they mobilized successfully. Even though a version of parental leave was passed, opposition success in defeating override attempts eventually paid off because the final version was watered down significantly from the original version.

The fourth and last lesson of the FMLA is that interest groups often acquire a great deal of experience and expertise with issues long before they appear at congressional hearings or lobby representatives in their offices. Groups acquire much of their expertise about public policy through their involvement in litigation and rule-making proceedings, and this expertise can be an extremely valuable resource in the legislative arena. The acquisition of expertise is most pronounced for those groups that participate in multiple arenas, groups such as the Chamber of Commerce or the AFL-CIO, and for this reason, organizations that have some capacity to litigate or participate in the rule-making process probably have some advantage in dealing with Congress.

Interest Group Activities and Legislators' Policy Calculations

Once groups choose to embark on a legislative strategy, they must compete with other forces for legislators' support. Several factors weigh prominently into legislators' choices of policy positions; the

preferences of their constituents, their own personal policy preferences, and the preferences of party leaders are among the most
important. These variables have formed the core of most theoretical
and statistical models of legislative decision making.[42] Lobbying by
interest groups, in contrast, has generally not been regarded by congressional scholars as one of the core variables in legislative decision
making and has instead been generally treated as a residual factor
with no clear theoretical specification of how it might fit into the
core model of decision making. Thus, the final task of this chapter,
before turning to a more detailed analysis of exactly how groups
affect legislators' choices, is to provide an overview of how and
where lobbying enters into the legislator's calculus.

When there is little or no disagreement among the preferences
of constituents, party leaders, and legislators themselves, the legislator's choice is easy. It is only when there is conflict, as is often the
case, that legislators must make difficult choices about how to weigh
the various preferences articulated to them. Should legislators exercise their own policy judgment or defer to the preferences of constituents? What should the legislator do if the pressures from the party
leadership conflict with those from the constituency?

When faced with these difficult choices, legislators frequently
receive information from organized interests, both directly and indirectly through their constituents, that can affect their policy choices.
Interest groups engage in three principal information gathering and
transmitting activities: advertising, or public relations, campaigns;
direct contacting of representatives in Washington; and citizen, or
grassroots, mobilization. These activities by no means exhaust all
interest group activities, but they are the core activities of any lobbying campaign. An experienced lobbyist once explained that any well-
orchestrated lobbying campaign is like a "three-legged stool," where
each leg corresponds to one of these three core activities.[43] *Advertising campaigns* involve the use of television, radio, and newspaper

---

[42]For some of the classic works, see Julius Turner, *Party and Constituency: Pressures on
Congress* (Baltimore: Johns Hopkins Press, 1951); Lewis A. Froman, Jr., *Congressmen
and Their Constituents* (Chicago: Rand McNally, 1963); Warren E. Miller and Donald
E. Stokes, "Constituency Influence in Congress," *American Political Science Review* 57
(1963): 45–56.
[43]Interview with the author, 1985.

advertising on a broad scale to influence citizens' beliefs about the effects of various policy options. The "Harry and Louise" television ads aired during the debate on national health insurance in 1994 and paid for by the Health Insurance Association of America are a classic example.[44] *Washington contacting* involves direct communication between lobbyists and legislators or their staff and involves activities such as testifying at congressional hearings, visiting representatives' offices, and taking legislators to lunch or playing golf with them. *Grassroots mobilization* involves carefully organized and coordinated efforts by interest groups to encourage constituents to contact their representatives by writing letters, sending telegrams, making telephone calls, and so forth.

Figure 3.1 depicts graphically the role of these interest group activities in the determination of legislators' policy choices. These basic activities can affect constituents' policy preferences, legislators' own policy preferences, and legislators' perceptions of their constituents' preferences and the electoral consequences of deferring or not deferring to constituents' preferences. None of these activities has a direct and proximate impact on legislators' choices of policy positions, but each can have an important indirect impact through its effect on the more immediate factors that influence legislators' choices.

The three basic interest group activities portrayed in Figure 3.1 certainly do not exhaust all interest group activities, nor do all interest groups engage in all three. Policy groups, or think tanks, for example, often testify at congressional hearings but typically do not engage in grassroots lobbying or advertising campaigns. Some groups, such as People for the American Way, a public interest organization founded by television producer Norman Lear, engage in extensive advertising campaigns but do little direct Washington lobbying. Other groups engage in additional activities, such as making campaign contributions or organizing get-out-the-vote drives on Election Day. These other lobbying activities are examined in greater detail in the following two chapters.

---

[44]In those ads, Harry and Louise portrayed the average American couple, distressed over how the Clinton health care proposal would detract from their freedom to choose physicians and overwhelm them with bureaucratic red tape.

Figure 3.1 Interest Group Activities and the Determinations of Legislators' Policy Positions

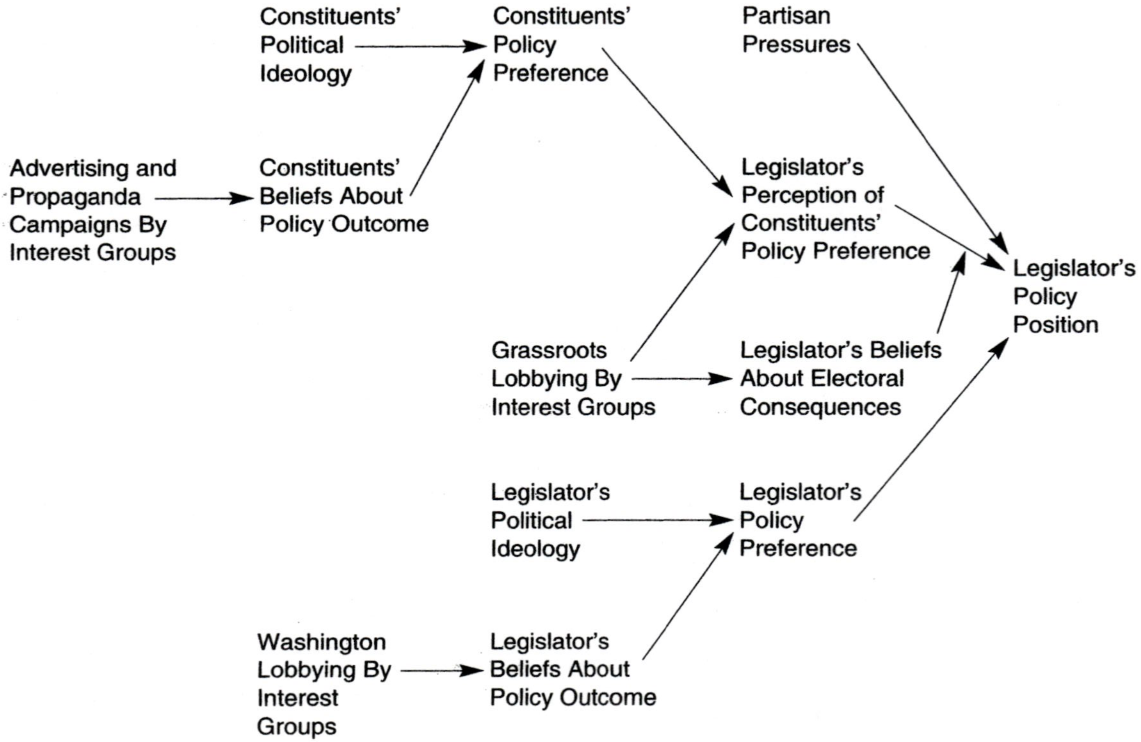

Advertising Campaigns

As indicated by the arrows in the upper-left portion of Figure 3.1, advertising and propaganda campaigns influence constituents' beliefs about policy outcomes, which in combination with citizens' broad political ideologies—for example, basic preferences for more or less governmental intervention in the economy—determine their policy preferences. In the debate over a national health care policy, for example, constituents' preferences for or against a system of universal coverage would by the logic of Figure 3.1 depend on their basic ideological predilections plus their beliefs about how a system of universal coverage would work. Citizens who ideologically preferred minimal government, for example, might have supported a system of universal coverage if they believed that it would not result in an unmanageable bureaucracy, but citizens with the same ideological preference who believed that universal coverage would lead to massive governmental bureaucracy would have opposed the policy.

Since citizens' beliefs about the likely outcomes of proposed policies depend largely on the information they receive about those proposals, interest groups can play an important role in the development of citizens' policy preferences through advertising campaigns. In 1987, for example, groups opposing Robert Bork's nomination to the U.S. Supreme Court used extensive print, radio, and television advertising to inform citizens about what they believed to be Bork's liabilities as a Supreme Court justice. This campaign, which is described more fully in the next chapter, was regarded by both supporters and opponents of Bork to have been a critical factor in the defeat of Bork's nomination.

Washington Contacting

Legislators, like constituents, develop individual policy preferences based in part on information provided by organized interests. As depicted in the lower portion of Figure 3.1, interest groups provide detailed information to legislators on the merits of policy proposals through Washington lobbying activities. Legislators then use this information to form their beliefs about how different policy options will work, and these, together with their basic ideological beliefs, determine their policy preferences. Legislators' policy *preferences* are distinct from their policy *positions*, of course, in that they sometimes follow the preferences of their constituents or party leaders instead of their own personal preferences.[45] Washington contacts are extremely important to groups, because direct contact is one of the most important and effective ways that groups can communicate information to legislators.

In the example of national health care, suppose a legislator ideologically prefers an active federal government in order to bring about equality in health care, thus favoring universal coverage in principle, but, on the basis of information provided by business groups, concludes that the economic consequences to small businesses of having to provide health insurance to all of their employees would outweigh the benefits. On the issue of whether and how much the federal government should subsidize the health care costs of small businesses, such a legislator might prefer that the health care costs of small businesses be heavily subsidized. During the health care debate in 1994, organizations such as the National Federation of Independent Business expended tremendous effort to make just such a case to lawmakers or else convince them to exempt small businesses from covering their employees at all.

In general, then, legislators' policy preferences are not simply a function of their ideological predilections; their preferences depend also on policy-relevant information, and interest groups are one important source of such information. Interest groups routinely collect specialized information and conduct technical analyses; write and distribute reports of their research to members of Congress; and call upon members and their staffs to answer questions, make clarifications, and counter any opposing information or concerns that might arise. By combining the information they receive from interest groups with information from their committee staffs, the Congressional Research Service, and the General Accounting Office, legislators have ample opportunity to develop a thorough understanding of the technical aspects of policy proposals and their implications. They can then gauge the extent to which specific proposals will achieve results that are consistent with their general ideological

---

[45]For evidence, see Roger H. Davidson, *The Role of the Congressman* (New York: Pegasus, 1969).

beliefs, and if they choose, can form their preferences in terms of the perceived merits of the proposals. Ultimately, the preferences they adopt will depend on which information they choose to believe and which to ignore.

Grassroots Mobilization

Before legislators can act on either their own policy preferences or those of their constituents, they must first know what their constituents want. Determining exactly what constituents want, however, and how badly they want it, is not always easy.[46] Information about constituents' preferences does not come automatically to legislators. They cannot simply infer citizens' policy preferences from knowledge about constituents' basic ideological orientations, because ideology does not correspond perfectly with preferences on particular policies, and they cannot simply conduct opinion polls on every issue, because not only are polls expensive, but they also convey little or no information about intensities of preferences. To decipher the direction and intensity of constituents' preferences, legislators need additional sources of information. For starters, they must visit their districts regularly, talk with constituents and opinion leaders, and pay close attention to their mail. For additional information, they can observe grassroots lobbying campaigns in their districts.

Grassroots lobbying campaigns, which are essentially miniexperiments in political mobilization, reveal important information to legislators about how constituents might react to their policy stands on Election Day. An estimate of the electoral consequences of one's policy stand is one of the most important aspects of the legislator's decision process, and the information contained in grassroots mobilization efforts can be very important to legislators when forming their estimates of the likely electoral consequences of their actions.[47] As indicated in Figure 3.1, grassroots lobbying by interest groups

---

[46]For a discussion of the difficulty legislators have determining their constituents' preferences, see John W. Kingdon, "Ideas, Politics, and Public Policies." Paper presented at the annual meeting of the American Political Science Association, Washington, DC, 1988, p. 21.

[47]See Morris P. Fiorina, *Representatives, Roll Calls, and Constituencies* (Lexington, MA: D. C. Heath and Company, 1974).

affects legislators' perceptions of their constituents' preferences and beliefs about the electoral consequences of their actions.

How spontaneous constituency reactions are to groups' mobilization efforts is never entirely clear. Interest group leaders typically like to portray constituency reactions as spontaneous; legislators sometimes choose to discount the importance of form letters, postcards, and computer-generated mail. Nevertheless, even these expressions of preference contain some useful information about the true direction and intensity of constituents' policy preferences, and few legislators disregard this information totally.

The Legislator's Policy Position

When legislators eventually take a stand on important policy questions, they must weigh carefully their own policy preferences, those of their constituents, and those of their party leaders. From the standpoint of legislators' political careers, one of the crucial questions concerns the weight that should be placed on constituents' preferences. The greater the anticipated electoral consequences of taking one position versus another, the greater the weight that legislators must attach to constituents' preferences. This is reflected in Figure 3.1 by the arrow leading from "Legislators' Beliefs About Electoral Consequences" and that intersects the arrow from "Legislator's Perception of Constituents' Policy Preference."

Naturally, as legislators place greater weight on constituents' preferences, they will place less weight on their own preferences or the preferences of party leaders. For example, when the expected electoral consequences of their actions are considerable and when the position of their party conflicts with the preference of their constituency, legislators are likely to ignore the appeals of party leaders and side with their constituents. Alternatively, when the expected electoral consequences of their actions are negligible, legislators are free to follow their own policy preferences or those of party leaders.

To influence legislators' policy positions, interest groups must coordinate carefully their grassroots and Washington lobbying efforts. It is essential that representatives hear the same messages from their constituents as they hear from Washington lobbyists. When the constituency and Washington information is consistent, then legislators' own policy preferences are more likely to be aligned with their beliefs about the electoral importance of their positions to constituents. The combination of these forces is likely to be decisive in determining the legislator's final policy position.

In summary, interest group activities play a very important role in the determination of legislators' policy positions, but they do so indirectly, not directly. Through advertising campaigns and the provision of information through grassroots and Washington lobbying, interest groups can influence both citizens' and legislators' preferences and they can influence legislators' perceptions of the direction and importance of constituents' preferences. Some or all of this information may eventually come to bear upon the legislator's choice of a policy position. Influencing legislators' decisions, however, is not a straightforward matter of applying pressure or making a campaign contribution. Whatever influence interest groups achieve results from the acquisition and transmission of information, not from electoral threats, arm-twisting, or other overt forms of pressure. Interest group lobbying typically enters into the legislator's decision calculus only *indirectly* through its influence on other important factors, not directly through a quid pro quo or other explicit bargain.

An interest group's decision to lobby a member of Congress involves strategic choices at several levels of generality. This chapter has touched upon some of the considerations involved at several of the most general levels—participation in the congressional arena in relation to participation in the judicial and administrative arenas, participation at various stages of the legislative process, and the relationship of interest group lobbying to other important forces that bear on legislators' policy choices. The next chapter focuses on the some of the more specific aspects of lobbying itself—access, the acquisition of information, the content of lobbying messages, and decisions about when and whom to lobby.

C H A P T E R 4

LEGISLATIVE LOBBYING

Organizations attempt to influence legislative decisions through a broad range of activities. These include efforts at cultivating and maintaining good working relationships with legislators; engaging in public relations and advertising campaigns; organizing and mobilizing constituents at the grassroots; making campaign contributions, researching policy issues; gathering information about legislators' voting intentions and the legislative agenda; testifying before congressional committees; and communicating directly with legislators, their personal staff, or committee staff. All of these activities constitute what is generally referred to as *lobbying*.[1] It is through these various lobbying activities that organized interests acquire and transmit information to legislators.

The argument of this chapter is that interest groups achieve influence in the legislative process by strategically providing information to change or reinforce legislators' beliefs about legislative outcomes, the operational effects of policies, and the electoral ramifications of their actions. The key components of this argument are developed in four sections of the chapter. The first discusses the two fundamental goals of all interest groups—access and influence. A distinction is drawn between access and influence that highlights the differences between how lobbyists *position* themselves to present information and how they *persuade* legislators through the presenta-

---

[1] There is no simple definition of *legislative lobbying*. The Lobby Disclosure Act of 1992, perhaps the most comprehensive effort ever undertaken to define *lobbying*, uses more than 1000 words to define terms such as *lobbyist, lobbying contact,* and *lobbying activity. Congressional Record*, 102nd Cong., 2d sess., 1992, pp. S2547–2548.

tion of information. The second section identifies the major sources of uncertainty in the legislative process. It explains how uncertainty makes it difficult for representatives to achieve their legislative and political goals and, consequently, why legislators seek information. The third section describes how groups specialize in the types of information legislators seek, and the fourth describes how interest groups strategically use information to achieve influence. Because of the importance generally attributed to campaign contributions, decisions about how they are allocated and their role in the lobbying process are treated at length in the next chapter.

The Objectives of Organized Interests: Access and Influence

All lobbying begins with access. Access is absolutely critical to any successful lobbying campaign and, along with influence, is one of the principal objectives of organized interests. Yet, exactly what access is and how it differs from influence is seldom made clear by the politicians, journalists, and academics who frequently talk and write about access and influence. Unfortunately, when the concepts are used interchangeably, as they often are, typical explanations for access— for example, making campaign contributions or hiring high-profile lobbyists in Washington—can incorrectly be construed as explanations for influence. Some clarification is needed.

Access

The concept of access is one of the most ubiquitous, and also one of the most ambiguous, in all of the lobbying literature. To some, access means nothing more than establishing contact with a member of Congress or a staff person. One specific measure of access in this sense is the number of minutes a member of Congress spends in his or her office with representatives from organized interests.[2] To oth-

---

[2]For an analysis of the relationship between this measure of access and campaign contributions, see Laura I. Langbein, "Money and Access: Some Empirical Evidence," *Journal of Politics* 48 (1986): 1052–1062. For a similar definition, see Jeffrey M. Berry, *The Interest Group Society* (Boston: Little, Brown, 1984), p. 169.

ers, however, access means not only establishing contact but also achieving influence—getting legislators or staff to give serious consideration to particular arguments, perhaps even to act on them. John Hansen, for example, defines *access* as a "close working relationship between members of Congress and privileged outsiders."[3] Presumably, it is influence in some form that provides for a "close" working relationship or makes one outsider more "privileged" than another. Another scholar notes at least four meanings of the term *access:* (1) convincing a policy maker to listen to arguments; (2) establishing a "regular relationship" with a policy maker for the exchange of information; (3) becoming "institutionalized" into the policy process by, for example, acquiring formal representation on governing boards of agencies; and (4) gaining influence.[4] Appropriately, Schlozman and Tierney observe that the concepts of *access* and *influence* are not always "fully separable."[5]

One way to conceptualize the differences between access and influence is to imagine a continuum ranging from no access on one end to influence on the other. Such a continuum for any given interest group and legislator is depicted graphically in Figure 4.1. Although the divisions on this continuum are arbitrarily located, they represent qualitatively different relationships between a legislator and group. At the far left of the continuum is the lobbyist who has no access whatsoever with a given legislator. A lobbyist with no access is one who is unable, or else makes no effort, to communicate with the legislator in any fashion—either through social interaction, staff contacts, personal business meetings, or telephone or fax communications. Lobbyists sometimes fail to achieve access, or else choose not to seek it, because they are not well known individually or employed by a well known group, because the lobbyist's group is one with which the legislator does not wish to be associated for political reasons, or because they are perceived as unreliable or untrustworthy.

[3]John Mark Hansen, *Gaining Access: Congress and the Farm Lobby, 1919–1981* (Chicago: University of Chicago Press, 1991), p. 22.
[4]S. J. Makielski, *Pressure Politics in America* (Lanham, MD: University Press of America, 1980).
[5]Kay Lehman Schlozman and John T. Tierney, *Organized Interests and American Society* (New York: Harper and Row, 1986), p. 165.

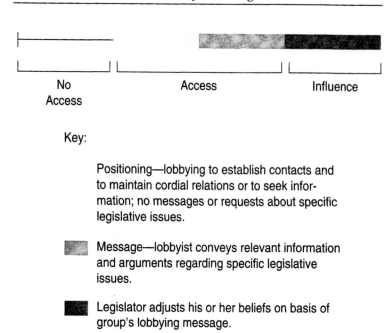

Key:

Positioning—lobbying to establish contacts and
to maintain cordial relations or to seek information; no messages or requests about specific
legislative issues.

Message—lobbyist conveys relevant information
and arguments regarding specific legislative
issues.

Legislator adjusts his or her beliefs on basis of
group's lobbying message.

Figure 4.1   Access—Influence Continuum

Access to legislators can be achieved at two different levels. The
first and most basic level of access is represented by the most lightly
shaded region in Figure 4.1. At this level, lobbyists try to *position*
themselves favorably in order to send a particular message or make a
specific appeal at some later time. Positioning involves efforts to
attain recognition as a regular participant or "player" in a policy
area, to establish cordial working relationships with legislators, and
generally to demonstrate that one has something worthwhile to say.
Groups and their lobbyists position themselves by opening Washington offices, inviting legislators to social functions, assisting them
with constituency requests for information, and making campaign
contributions. The distinguishing feature of contacts at this basic
level is that they are very generalized. Lobbyists may discuss broad
policy interests of the organization, but the objective of access at this
level is not to try and persuade the legislator to support or oppose
any particular legislative issues. The purpose instead is simply to

establish visibility and good relations with legislators through professional and social courtesies.[6]

Being favorably positioned with a legislator can be beneficial to an organization even if it leads to no specific legislative favors or victories. Interest groups routinely seek information about bills that might be introduced, the scheduling of hearings or votes, and the policy positions of legislators. Gathering information about the political process is a large part of what lobbyists do, and those lobbyists who are favorably positioned with legislators are most likely to acquire this information. One lobbyist explained the logic and importance of the positioning aspect of lobbying as follows:

> We're talking to everybody we can about what the general mood of the Congress is. What issues are they going to deem important? How are the members lining up? How strongly they feel, for example, about new taxes to deal with the deficit problem. That is what we do, it's a network, it's a game. All the people that we know, and we've done favors for, gotten jobs for, sent them business, are part of it. What you know and your ability to interpret it—your ability to understand what's important and what's not—is what it's all about.[7]

A second level of access is depicted in Figure 4.1 by the second most heavily shaded region. Access at this level is much more specific in nature than access at the first level. Here access typically involves a scheduled meeting with the legislator or staff person, and it is at this time that the lobbyist conveys a specific *message* designed to gain the legislator's support. Jeffrey Birnbaum has observed that relative to the first level of lobbying, this second level constitutes a relatively small part of the overall process.

> Only the smallest part of lobbying, at the very end of the process, entails directly asking members of Congress for specific favors. The

---

[6]Lester Milbrath recognized the importance of these activities for "keeping communication channels open." He noted that it is just as important to keep communication channels open as it is to transmit the communications themselves. See Lester W. Milbrath, *The Washington Lobbyists* (Chicago: Rand McNally, 1963), pp. 255–294; and "Lobbying as a Communication Process," *Public Opinion Quarterly* 24 (1960): 32–53.

[7]From Jeffrey H. Birnbaum, *The Lobbyists: How Influence Peddlers Get Their Way in Washington* (New York: Times Books, 1992), p. 31.

Greenbrier event [a weekend retreat held in West Virginia in 1989 for lobbyists and Democratic House members], with its socializing and camaraderie, was more what lobbying is about most of the time: becoming part of the Washington network and, through it, learning the lay of the legislative landscape.[8]

Although the cost to the legislator of granting either type of access is not trivial, it is still relatively low. While it is true that legislators have enormous demands on their time, it is also true that Congress is by design an accessible institution. Each member commands a large personal staff and usually several district offices. Legislators frequently assign staff, and occasionally even interns, to meet with lobbyists. Moreover, most meetings with lobbyists are short, as lobbyists usually understand the constraints on a legislator's time. Somewhat surprisingly, a survey of 92 House members from the 95th Congress revealed that the average legislator spends only 37 minutes each week in face-to-face contact with representatives of organized groups.[9] Based on a reported average week of 54 hours of work, meetings with lobbyists consume only 1 percent of the average legislator's time. Clearly, the popular image of representatives having their offices overrun with lobbyists is more fiction than fact.

One reason that legislators do not spend more of their time in face-to-face meetings with lobbyists is that there are numerous other ways for organized interests to present information to members of Congress. Organizations write letters, stage demonstrations, present their case to the media, and participate in committee hearings. Naturally, lobbyists prefer face-to-face meetings in order to ensure that their messages are presented and interpreted accurately, but getting messages delivered is not the ultimate concern of lobbyists. Their main problem is getting legislators to consider their arguments carefully and to give weight to their claims.

Influence

Even before talking to lobbyists, legislators usually have fairly well-formed beliefs about whether proposed policies will be economically

---

[8]Birnbaum, *The Lobbyists*, p. 25.
[9]Langbein, "Money and Access: Some Empirical Evidence," p. 1057.

efficient, socially equitable, and politically viable. They also generally have well-formed beliefs about the importance of these policies to their constituents and the likely electoral consequences of the positions they take. Importantly, however, legislators may *revise* their beliefs when new information becomes available. Ultimately, interest groups hope to determine legislators' policy stands, but, as was indicated in Figure 3.1, to do so they must first manipulate the beliefs that determine legislators' policy preferences and their perceptions of the electoral implications of the positions they take. The purpose of a lobbying message is to introduce information that will alter or affect these beliefs. Sometimes legislators dismiss lobbyists' claims, but other times they accept the claims and adjust their beliefs accordingly.

The point at which access ends and influence begins is the point at which legislators adjust their beliefs on the basis of lobbying information. This point is depicted in Figure 4.1 by the darkly shaded region. Upon receiving lobbying information, legislators can either dismiss it, in which case they are not influenced, or revise their beliefs, in which case they are influenced. Thus, lobbying information can affect legislators' beliefs in two basic ways: it can *maintain* or *reinforce* their beliefs—that is, prevent their beliefs from changing in response to alternative information; or information can alter the *direction* of legislators' beliefs held prior to any lobbying—that is, change their beliefs about whether a policy will work as claimed or whether their constituents support or oppose a given proposal.

Influence differs from access, therefore, in that access implies only that lobbyists are in a *position* to affect legislators' beliefs, not that beliefs have actually been altered, maintained, or reinforced. Since influence involves the impact of lobbying information on beliefs, not behavior, influence will not always be readily observable. Legislators may change their beliefs without altering their policy preferences or their perceptions of their constituents' preferences. Consequently, the distinction between access and influence is much easier to make at a conceptual level than at an empirical one, and this may explain why access is frequently taken as the standard measure of a lobbyist's success. Relative to influence, access is tangible. Interest groups can easily be observed making campaign contributions, playing golf with legislators, participating in congressional hearings, and so forth, and thus any apparent influence that lobbyists achieve is often attributed to these sorts of activities.

That new information can change the way legislators think, and, therefore, act presumes that legislators are often uncertain about what course of action to take. This assumption is critical to an information-based explanation of interest group influence, for unless legislators are uncertain about what to do, there is no need for them to seek the counsel of professional lobbyists. Hence, it is important to establish clearly the various sources of uncertainty in legislative decision making.

The Uncertainty of Legislative Decision Making

Legislators are motivated by three basic goals: reelection, good public policy, and influence within the legislature.[10] To most Americans, the success of legislators in making good public policy or achieving legislative success is not as apparent as their success in getting reelected. Nonetheless, many legislators do espouse these as central goals. The three goals are interdependent: legislators must have some influence within the legislature if they are to enact good policies, and they must hold onto their jobs in order to pursue their legislative objectives. The attainment of these goals is complicated by the fact that legislators cannot be certain about how voters will react to their policy decisions, how policies will actually work once implemented, or what kinds of political complications might arise during the legislative process.

There are, then, at least three important sources of uncertainty that affect legislators' decisions.[11] Perhaps the most important of

[10]See Richard F. Fenno, Jr., *Congressmen in Committees* (Boston: Little, Brown, 1973), p. 1.

[11]David Truman identifies two basic types of uncertainty, or as he puts it, "knowledge required by the politician." The two types are "technical knowledge that defines the content of a policy issue; and political knowledge of the relative strength of competing claims and of the consequences of alternative decisions on a policy issue." To these two basic types, I add a third: knowledge about the legislative process. See David B. Truman, *The Governmental Process: Political Interests and Public Opinion* (New York: Knopf, 1951), p. 334.

these is uncertainty about *reelection*. Legislators must know which issues are important to their constituents and which positions to take on those issues. Legislators who seriously misjudge the direction or intensity of constituents' preferences often experience stiff electoral competition and sometimes even defeat. The *legislative process* is a second important source of uncertainty. Questions about how other legislators will react to a bill, what kinds of trade-offs will be necessary to gain majority support, and what kinds of procedural roadblocks lie ahead can weigh importantly into legislators' decisions about what actions to take. Uncertainty about the legislative process is of particular concern to those legislators whose primary goal is influence within the legislature. A third source of uncertainty concerns *policy performance*. The technical and substantive aspects of policy proposals must be fully understood in order to determine whether a policy will truly produce the outcomes that are intended. Uncertainty about policy performance affects all legislators seeking to make good public policy.

Uncertainty about Reelection

Legislators must constantly evaluate the electoral ramifications of the positions they take. They must discern the prevailing direction of opinion among constituents, and they must assess whether or not the position they take will become an issue during the next election campaign. Although most constituents pay little attention to what Congress is doing, there is always a possibility that they will *become* attentive. Douglas Arnold suggests that latent preferences among inattentive constituents "can quickly be transformed into intense and very real opinions with enormous political repercussions." He argues that members of Congress ignore inattentive constituents "at their peril."[12].

Given the high reelection rate for members of Congress, it is not immediately clear that uncertainty about reelection is one of their main concerns. More than 90 percent of incumbent members of the U.S. House of Representatives seeking reelection have won in 21 of the 24 congressional elections since 1950. Moreover, more

---

[12]R. Douglas Arnold, *The Logic of Congressional Action* (New Haven: Yale University Press, 1990), p. 68.

than 70 percent of all incumbents seeking reelection have won with 60 percent of the vote or more on average over the past 20 elections.[13] With these success rates, how can members of Congress be uncertain about reelection?

The answer is that these statistics are not appropriate indicators of uncertainty. Reelection rates are statistical averages, but uncertainty must be measured by variation around these averages. It is the variation around the reelection rates that indicates the tendency for incumbents to win easily in one election but then to either lose or win by a small margin in the next. Gary Jacobson has computed the change in incumbents' vote percentages between successive elections from the 1940s through the 1980s and discovered that the *variance* in interelection vote swings for incumbents not only is surprisingly high but also has been increasing over the years.[14] In other words, even though incumbents have been winning at high rates on average over the years, the probability that incumbents' vote margins will deviate from what they were in the last election has also been increasing. Electorates, it seems, have become more volatile over time.

According to Jacobson's calculations, one in every six incumbents who won with 63 percent of the vote in 1988, for example, would be expected to win with just under 55 percent of the vote in 1990. Also, one in every six incumbents who won with 58 percent or less of the vote in 1988 would be expected to lose in 1990. Thus, it is with some regularity that incumbents win very easily in one election and marginally in the next or that they make a solid showing in one election and lose in the next. To make the point more specifically, 15 U.S. House incumbents were defeated in 1990; yet, these same 15 won election in 1988 with an average of 61.4 percent of the vote. Similarly, the 17 House incumbents who were defeated in 1992 won in 1990 with an average of 64.1 percent of the vote. The 36 House

---

[13]See Norman J. Ornstein, Thomas E. Mann, and Michael J. Malbin, *Vital Statistics on Congress, 1991–1992* (Washington, DC: Congressional Quarterly Press, 1992), pp. 50–60.

[14]Gary C. Jacobson, "The Marginals Never Vanished: Incumbency and Competition in Elections to the U.S. House of Representatives, 1952–82," *American Journal of Political Science* 31 (1987): 126–141.

incumbents who lost in 1994 won with an average of 55 percent of the vote in 1992.

Congressional scholar Richard Fenno aptly describes the uncertainty that incumbents harbor about their electoral prospects:

> Though last time's reelection constituency will have been ample, electoral trouble may be only a couple of elections away. In sum, knowing or sensing or fearing these several unhappy electoral possibilities, House members will continue to be a lot more uncertain than the statistics of their last election would warrant.[15]

Uncertainty about the Legislative Process and Policy Performance

To realize their policy objectives, legislators must ensure that their favored proposals not only receive legislative support but also that the content of their proposals lead to the desired outcomes. They must deal with the variability of the legislative process *and* with questions about how policies will actually perform once implemented.

Legislators who take or share responsibility for managing a bill must confront a host of difficult questions. What are the personal and political agendas of other lawmakers? How will national economic or political factors affect the viability of the bill? How much interest group support or opposition does the bill have or is it likely to have? Is there majority support in committee or on the floor? If not, how can a majority coalition be fashioned? How should the bill be handled procedurally in the House and in the Senate? Should it be rolled into and buried in an omnibus bill? Should it be considered under a suspension of the rules in the House, or can it be tabled in the Senate? Questions such as these have no quick and easy answers.

Even legislators who have no responsibility for managing a bill must still confront difficult questions about the bill's legislative life. Will the bill proceed far enough into the legislative process that it will demand their attention? If the bill gains the attention of constituents or relevant interest groups, will it be stalled in committee or

---

[15]Richard F. Fenno, Jr., *Home Style: House Members in Their Districts* (Boston: Little, Brown, 1978), p. 14.

will it require a roll call vote? When will it be necessary to stake out a position? Most legislators simply do not have the time or the resources to answer these questions for each bill that comes before them.

In their quest to make good public policy, legislators must also judge whether a bill will produce desirable economic, social, or environmental outcomes. What outcomes legislators judge desirable or undesirable depend, of course, on their individual ideological predilections, but, even so, it is often difficult to ascertain whether policies will actually operate consistently with those predilections. Bureaucratic agencies, for example, must be given specific enough instructions to carry out policies as designed yet have sufficient flexibility to respond to unforeseen economic or political circumstances. Policies must also be designed to anticipate demographic changes and legal loopholes or challenges that could affect the distribution of benefits or costs.

Accurately forecasting the impact of policy proposals is a constant challenge for professional policy analysts. In early 1993, for example, the country's leading economic experts disagreed over the likely consequences of President Clinton's budget proposal. Some thought his proposed tax increases would stifle the emerging economic recovery at the time, while others thought that increased consumer confidence and lower interest rates resulting from a smaller federal budget deficit would offset the dampening effects of the tax increases. President Clinton's health care reform proposals in 1993 offer another example of uncertainty over policy performance, as experts disagreed about whether a plan of "managed competition" would produce significant savings in comparison to a market-based approach. Even a study by the Congressional Budget Office was unable to conclude that one approach would clearly lead to greater savings than another.[16] Debate over ratification of the North American Free Trade Agreement (NAFTA) during the fall of 1993 provides yet another example of policy uncertainty. What the net economic benefits or costs to the nation from NAFTA would be

---

[16]Dana Priest, "Key House Democrat Attacks 'Managed Competition' Health Plan," *Washington Post*, May 14, 1993, A, 18:1.

were unclear. While there was general agreement that some American jobs would be lost if NAFTA was enacted, it was unclear whether removing trade barriers would stimulate the economy sufficiently to offset those losses.[17]

Uncertainty about policy performance and electoral circumstances are often connected. If one does not know the operational effects of policies, for example, it may be difficult to judge the electoral ramifications. However, even when the operational effects are known with certainty, the electoral consequences may not be. A legislator might know that by voting in favor of stronger pollution controls on industries in his or her district will cost 300 jobs, but to know the electoral consequences of these job losses requires additional information. To assess the electoral implications, one must know how well organized the unemployed workers are and to what extent they will hold the legislator responsible for their job losses at election time. Conversely, even when legislators have little or no uncertainty about electoral consequences, they may still not know which decision is economically most efficient or socially most equitable.

Legislators do not necessarily encounter uncertainty about reelection, the legislative process, and policy performance on each and every bill that comes before them. They may be absolutely sure that some bills will or will not become salient, that constituents will rebel or remain silent in response to their positions on others, and that some bills will never produce the effects that are intended. Yet, it seems likely that legislators encounter at least one and perhaps several kinds of uncertainty for many of the issues on which they must take positions. Since the existence of any uncertainty is potentially an obstacle to the achievement of representatives' legislative and political goals, their demand for good political and policy information is quite high. Predictably, interest groups specialize in the kinds of information legislators need most. The specialized information they acquire is probably their most valuable asset in their quest to influence legislators' policy choices.

---

[17]For additional examples, see Keith Krehbiel, *Information and Legislative Organization* (Ann Arbor: University of Michigan Press, 1991), pp. 66–70.

The Information Specialties of Organized Interests

Interest groups specialize in three basic types of information. They collect and disseminate information about the status and prospect of bills under active consideration; they provide information about the electoral implications of legislators' support for or opposition to those bills; and they analyze and report on the likely economic, social, or environmental consequences of proposed policies. It is no coincidence that these three types of information correspond to the three types of uncertainty that beset lawmakers. The informational relationship between legislators and lobbyists has a marketlike quality to it: legislators demand information to reduce uncertainty, and lobbyists supply it.

The special role that interest groups play in the acquisition and transmission of information is recognized by representatives, lobbyists, and academics alike. Former representative Tony Coelho once remarked that lobbyists sometimes "know more about the subject than the staff or the committee members. The Cotton Council will be writing legislation for the cotton industry in the cotton subcommittee."[18] Representative Michael Synar expressed concern about the power that interest groups can wield on the basis of their expertise: "They have become such a dominant force in politics, financially and informationwise. They have better grassroots organizations than most congressmen."[19] Lobbyists understand their informational roles quite well. One lobbyist explained to journalist Hedrick Smith: "A good lobbyist is simply an extension of a congressional member's staff...if they want information and they trust you, they'll call *you* for that information."[20] Academics also recognize the informational roles that groups play in the legislative process. Political scientist John Hansen claims that interest groups "provide political counsel" for members of Congress. He argues that groups provide "political intelligence about the preferences of con-

[18]Hedrick Smith, *The Power Game: How Washington Works* (New York: Ballantine Books, 1988), p. 234.

[19]*New York Times*, January 11, 1981. Stephen V. Roberts, "An Angry Young Congressman Criticizes Special Interest Groups," *The New York Times*, January 11, 1981, A, 24:3.

[20]Smith, *The Power Game*, p. 234.

gressional constituents" in exchange for representatives' consideration of their policy concerns.[21]

While there is widespread agreement that interest groups have useful information to offer legislators, it is not entirely clear how groups actually acquire their information. If the acquisition of information is easy or relatively costless, then information provides little strategic advantage for groups, for legislators can acquire the same information without relying on interest groups. Consequently, for information to be a source of influence for groups, it must be the case that information is scarce *and* that groups can acquire or provide it more efficiently than members of Congress, political parties, or private individuals.

Constituency Preferences and Reelection

Short of holding a special election, the only way representatives or interest group leaders can really be sure of the extent to which voters are concerned about a particular issue, and the extent to which it might eventually affect their voting decisions at election time, is to observe the extent to which constituents are willing to register their concerns through some costly political activity. Costly political activities include writing letters or sending telegrams to members of Congress, calling representatives' offices, raising money, contributing money, passing out leaflets, registering others to vote, attending informational meetings, writing editorial letters to local newspapers, and so forth. Political activities that are costly to undertake require voters to put their money where their mouth is, so to speak, and thus costly activities are the best indicators of the electoral significance of voters' preferences. Not all expressions of political preference are costly, however, and those that are not yield little information. Consider opinion polls, for example. Since virtually no effort is required for poll respondents to tell an interviewer that they care about an issue very strongly, or even that a representative's position on that issue will determine their vote, there is no necessary reason to believe that respondents in public opinion polls will back up their rhetoric with action.

---

[21]John Mark Hansen, *Gaining Access: Congress and the Farm Lobby, 1919–1981* (Chicago: University of Chicago Press, 1991), p. 5.

Much more informative than opinion polls are grassroots lobbying campaigns in which groups mobilize citizens to write or call their members of Congress and engage in other costly activities.[22] The principal value of grassroots mobilization, and one of the reasons that grassroots campaigning has become increasingly common and important, is that it *simulates* electoral mobilization. Larry Sabato notes that grassroots lobbying campaigns and election campaigns typically employ some of the same basic technology. Political consultants, observes Sabato, "have been active in equipping PACs and single-issue groups with the tools of the new campaign technology—survey research and polling, sophisticated television and radio advertising, and direct mail for fundraising and voter persuasion."[23] If these techniques fail to mobilize voters to phone or write their representatives on an important congressional issue, then it is also unlikely that these same techniques will succeed in mobilizing voters over the same issue at election time.

One might think of grassroots lobbying campaigns as field experiments in electoral mobilization. Even though grassroots lobbying campaigns lack the control group comparisons of true experiments, they do provide a treatment, or stimulus—an "action alert" or other request from an organization to write a letter or make a telephone call—and they provide a measurable response—the actual number of phone calls or letters generated. Groups that engage in these quasi experiments can determine exactly the level of response that results from each unit of organizational effort expended.

Practically speaking, lobbyists and other group officials do not always develop precise estimates of the effects of organizational effort on the success of grassroots campaigns. They do, however, gauge the overall spontaneity of grassroots campaigns, and this

---

[22]Burdette Loomis has reported the following definition of *grassroots* taken from the *Random House Dictionary of the English Language:* "of, pertaining to, or involving the common people, esp. as contrasted to or separable from an elite." See Burdette A. Loomis, "A New Era: Groups and the Grass Roots," in Allan J. Cigler and Burdette A. Loomis (eds.), *Interest Group Politics* (Washington, DC: Congressional Quarterly Press, 1983), p. 270.

[23]Larry Sabato, "Political Consultants and the New Campaign Technology," in Allan J. Cigler and Burdette A. Loomis (eds.), *Interest Group Politics* (Washington, DC: Congressional Quarterly Press, 1983), p. 146.

information has considerable value because of its scarcity. Since organizations are not required to disclose publicly how much they spend overall on grassroots mobilization, it is difficult for outsiders, even legislators, to judge accurately the spontaneity of the effort. Legislators observe the actual output of the mobilization campaign—the number of letters, telegrams, phone calls, and so forth—but without information about the group's actual expenditure of time and money, they cannot be certain how easy or difficult it was for the group to mobilize constituents. This is information legislators would like to have, however, as spontaneous constituency reaction is often much more compelling politically than constituency reaction that is forced or manufactured, even if both result in the same number of letters and phone calls. Many representatives place much greater weight on original, handwritten letters than on form letters, postcards, or other mass-produced mail. Thus, it is not always the total volume of mail that counts, but the ease or difficulty in generating responses that is important, and in this regard interest groups have a distinct informational advantage over legislators.

Interest groups not only provide important electoral information to members of Congress, but they also *create* it. In addition to mobilizing citizens to contact their representatives, organizations also monitor, evaluate, and even shape perceptions of how well incumbents are doing their jobs. Many organizations tabulate and publicize voting scores for legislators as a way of alerting and informing constituents about the voting trends of their representatives. Some organizations encourage their members to write editorials for local newspapers in the district, criticizing or praising their representatives. Other organizations actively recruit candidates to run against incumbents. Groups that participate in these activities, especially groups with politically active members in a representative's district, tend to know the political trends in the district because they create the trends. For this reason, representatives often make it a point to meet with officials or members of politically organized groups when they visit their districts.[24]

Most importantly, though, to make credible claims about electoral consequences, groups must recruit members and activists, invest

[24]Fenno, *Home Style*, Chapter 1.

in mobilization technology such as direct mail, or perhaps even form a political action committee. These are all costly investments and commitments, which serve to differentiate groups with credible electoral information from those without credible information. Think tanks and policy institutes, for example, can make credible claims about the economic or social ramifications of various policy choices, but lacking mass memberships, such organizations cannot credibly make claims about the electoral ramifications of policy choices.

Legislative Process and Policy Performance

Lobbyists can acquire a great deal of institution-specific information through regular contacts with legislators. In the normal course of establishing and maintaining access to legislators, they may learn about the scheduling of hearings, markups, floor debates, and votes; procedural strategies that committee or subcommittee chairmen will employ in markup sessions; positions that legislators have taken or are thinking about taking; and amendments that other legislators or groups might offer. In short, by simply making their routine legislative rounds—lunch or dinner, golf, or a chance meeting in the hallway—lobbyists learn about what legislators are thinking and planning on doing. It is for this reason that access is of critical importance to lobbyists, for it is primarily through access that they gather information about the legislative process.

One piece of information that lobbyists collect systematically is information on legislators' voting predispositions on particular bills. To make efficient decisions about how to allocate their lobbying efforts, organizations must keep track of legislators' positions, monitoring constantly changes in their expected support or opposition. Lobbyists assemble their head counts from analysis of prior voting patterns, from personal meetings and conversations with legislators and their staffs, and from secondary reports by other organizations or legislators. The ability to conduct a thorough head count, and a reputation for conducting accurate ones, is an important informational resource for lobbyists.

Lobbyists who accumulate information about legislators' positions and plans gain an important informational advantage in the legislative process. In a large body like the U.S. House of Representatives with its 435 members, it is not always easy for legislators to know what their colleagues are thinking or planning. Lobbyists, particularly those who have broad access, can play an important role in facilitating the exchange and dissemination of information throughout the legislature. Lobbyists obviously do not have a monopoly on such information, but a large portion of their job is devoted to acquiring it, and many seem to do so with relative efficiency. Their knowledge about what legislators are planning and thinking is an important resource that can be used to shape perceptions about the viability of various policy options.

Like electoral information, information about the legislative process that is easy to acquire is of little value. The lobbyists with the most valuable legislative information are typically those who are best known for their ability to obtain access and to understand the legislative process. It is no accident that the lobbying profession is full of people who earlier had careers as legislative or committee staffers, or who were elected representatives. These are individuals who have invested significant portions of their lives in developing the skills needed to understand the legislative process and to know where and how to acquire information. Lawyer-lobbyists, or "hired guns," earn high salaries precisely because of their reputations for being able to gain access to key decision makers. Their ability to gain access broadly to key members of Congress virtually assures that they have valuable legislative information to share.

A group's expertise about policy performance—the economic, social, or environmental consequences of existing policies as well as proposed policies—derives from two basic sources. One is the organization's professional research staff. For example, the National Association of Realtors employs professional economists to assess the impact of tax policies and other economic policies on the real estate market; the Environmental Defense Fund employs engineers to assess the impact of various land use policies on the environment; and the National Association of Life Underwriters employs accountants and legal experts to monitor the complex and arcane tax laws relating to insurance companies. The second source of technical information, although not available to all organizations, is the group's rank-and-file membership. Individual group members, whether insurance agents, farmers, small and large businesses, or elderly citizens, are the ones who are affected economically and socially by tax laws, welfare programs, and other public policies. Individuals directly involved with government programs and policies are a natural and credible firsthand source of information about how existing policies are actually working or not working, and it is for this reason that organizations often call upon their members to testify at congressional hearings and to submit written comments to congressional committees.

Not all organizations claiming policy expertise have members to draw upon as a source of expertise. Organizations such as the Food Research and Action Center, the National Women's Law Center, the Health Research Group, and the Children's Defense Fund have no dues-paying members. Sometimes called staff groups, these organizations are funded largely by foundation grants, proceeds from publications and conferences, and private donations. Lacking a large membership base, these organizations and others like them achieve their reputations for technical expertise because of their singular focus, their professional staffs, and their research orientation. Naturally, these organizations are much better known for their technical expertise than for their political expertise. As mentioned in Chapter 3, these organizations often gain considerable policy expertise through their participation before the courts or administrative agencies.

One example of the kind of technical information that groups often provide was revealed during consideration of the 1994 budget reconciliation in the U.S. House. Consisting of more than 1500 pages of legal prose, the reconciliation bill was not a document that was easily or thoroughly absorbed by even the most diligent legislators. Representative John Bryant observed that "No lawmaker could profitably use his time by thumbing through a 1500-page document."[25] Nevertheless, the bill contained numerous provisions of great economic consequence to millions of Americans. One such provision stated simply that "Section 306(b) of the Consolidated Farm and Rural Development Act shall apply to a borrower of a loan under this Act in the same manner in which such section applies to an association referred to in such section."[26] Despite its innocuous

[25]Ibid.
[26]Kevin Merida, "Obscure Item in Huge Bill Sparks a Lobbying War," *Washington Post*, May 26, 1993, A, 7:1.

appearance, this obscure paragraph carried important implications for the competition between rural and municipal utilities. The purpose of the provision was to prevent municipal electric utilities companies, represented by the American Public Power Association (APPA), from taking over customers of rural electric utilities, represented by the National Rural Electric Cooperative Association (NRECA), whenever a city expanded its boundaries. Both organizations fully understood the implications and significance of the provision, though most members of Congress initially did not. Only after extensive lobbying by both organizations did most members of the House of Representatives fully understand the economic consequences of the provision.

In general, whether information is about reelection, policy outcomes, or the legislative process, the only expedient information in lobbying is information that is difficult and costly to acquire. The costliness, or scarcity, of information, tends to screen organizations that do not have the resources to acquire relevant information out of the lobbying game. Scott Ainsworth has shown that if the informational costs of lobbying are too low, legislators cannot distinguish between good information and bad information, as all groups will appear informed.[27] Any organization can claim to be an expert if the costs of becoming an expert are relatively low, but as the costs to interest groups of acquiring information increase, legislators can begin to distinguish between the organizations that truly have the capability of acquiring the relevant information and those that do not.

The Strategic Use of Information

The preceding sections of this chapter have emphasized the uncertainty of legislative decision making and the ability of organized interests to acquire and transmit information through lobbying activities. What remains is to discuss how groups strategically use their information to achieve their legislative objectives. As discussed

---

[27]Scott Ainsworth, "Regulating Lobbyists and Interest Group Influence," *Journal of Politics* 55 (1993).

earlier, legislators hold prior beliefs—prior to any lobbying, that is—about how policies work or about the electoral ramifications of their positions and support for bills. These beliefs are usually predicated on experience with similar bills or on general knowledge about their constituencies. Legislators stake out their a priori policy positions on the basis of these beliefs. The strategic objectives of lobbying are to change legislators' beliefs, and hence positions, or else to prevent these beliefs from being changed, by presenting accurate, or sometimes, misleading information.

Groups' lobbying strategies can be characterized generally as either *proactive* or *counteractive*. Under a proactive strategy, a group presents information in an effort to *change* a legislator's policy position; under a counteractive strategy, it presents information in an effort to *prevent* an opposing group from changing the legislator's position. Groups use proactive strategies, therefore, for legislators whose a priori policy positions are opposite their own, and they use counteractive strategies for legislators whose a priori positions are the same as their own.

When a group chooses its lobbying strategy, it must anticipate what opposing groups will do. A group will use a counteractive strategy only when it anticipates that an opposing group will lobby proactively and, if not countered, successfully. In the event that no potentially successful proactive effort is expected, it makes little sense for a group to expend valuable resources lobbying a legislator whose a priori agrees with the group's position. Similarly, a group will use a proactive strategy only when it anticipates that it will not encounter a successful counteractive effort.

The notion that interest groups will strategically attempt to *change* a legislator's position is alien to the model of interest group politics that became popular during the 1960s. Bauer, Pool, and Dexter, for example, argued that groups would lobby only those legislators who were already convinced and who agreed with them. Their reasoning was that lobbyists would avoid the pressure of trying to change legislators' minds because of the human tendency to take the "easy path."[28] The argument here is that groups will

---

[28]Raymond A. Bauer, Ithiel de Sola Pool, and Lewis Anthony Dexter, *American Business and Public Policy*, (New York: Atherton, 1963), p. 353.

actively and strategically attempt to change the beliefs of legislators who *disagree* with them, and that groups will lobby their friends only in an effort to counter the efforts of groups employing proactive strategies.

Presented next are two examples of lobbying campaigns. The first involves a successful proactive, but unsuccessful counteractive, strategy; the other involves a successful counteractive, but unsuccessful proactive, strategy. Both examples involve efforts by groups to change legislators' a priori positions, and both involve information that was allegedly misleading. In the first example, a counteractive lobbying effort failed to convince legislators that proactive groups had misrepresented Judge Robert Bork's ideological views and likely judicial positions if confirmed as a justice of the U.S. Supreme Court. In the second example, however, a spontaneous counteractive grassroots lobbying effort proved successful in convincing legislators that the political strength of the gay and lesbian movement was not strong enough to support President Clinton's proposal to remove the ban on gays in the U.S. military.

Lobbying on Robert Bork's Nomination to the Supreme Court

On July 1, 1987, just four days after Justice Lewis Powell announced his retirement from the U.S. Supreme Court, President Ronald Reagan nominated Judge Robert Bork to be the next justice. Robert Bork was well known in Washington and in the legal community. He had been a member of the faculty of Yale Law School for 15 years, U.S. Solicitor General under Presidents Nixon and Ford, and a judge for the U.S. Circuit Court of Appeals for the District of Columbia since 1982. While on the faculty at Yale, Bork's academic writings clearly reflected his legal philosophy of strict adherence to the Constitution.

Of the possible replacements for Justice Powell, Robert Bork was the clear favorite among conservative interest groups. Conservative groups had been active in the selection and appointment of conservative judges since the early 1980s, and their support for Judge Bork was well known in Washington. Working through the Judicial Reform Project, formed in the early 1980s under the aegis of the

Free Congress Research and Education Foundation, conservative groups had lobbied the Reagan Administration for Bork's appointment. Liberal groups, however, had also monitored judicial nominations within the Reagan Administration, and to them Bork was neither stranger nor friend.[29]

According to the initial head counts by both pro-Bork and anti-Bork forces, a majority of the Senate was expected to vote to confirm Robert Bork as the next Supreme Court justice.[30] Any effort to oppose Bork's nomination, therefore, clearly required a proactive effort. Several liberal organizations decided almost immediately to pursue such a strategy and began coordinating their efforts within days of the nomination. Among the groups that organized early to oppose Bork's nomination were the Alliance for Justice, People for the American Way, the National Association for the Advancement of Colored People (NAACP), the National Abortion Rights Action League (NARAL), the Leadership Conference on Civil Rights, and the AFL-CIO. Leaders of these other groups met during the first week of July to form four task forces: a *lobbying task force* comprised of 30 organizations to lobby senators in Washington, a *grassroots task force* to organize coalitions and mobilize citizens at the state and local levels, a *media task force* to present information to the general public, and a *drafting task force* to formulate the basic messages and themes of the overall lobbying campaign.

The lobbying task force began contacting senators almost immediately, asking them not to take a position until after the hear-

[29]For a recent history of interest group conflict over judicial nominations, see Gregory A. Caldeira and John R. Wright, "Lobbying for Justice: The Rise of Organized Conflict in the Politics of Federal Judgeships," in Lee Epstein (ed.), *Contemplating Courts* (Washington, DC: Congressional Quarterly Press, 1995), pp. 44–71.

[30]Much of the information about this lobbying campaign can be found in Michael Pertschuk and Wendy Schaetzel, *The People Rising: The Campaign against the Bork Nomination* (New York: Thunder's Mouth Press, 1989) and in Patrick B. McGuigan and Dawn M. Weyrich, *Ninth Justice: The Fight for Bork* (Washington, DC: Free Congress Research and Education Foundation, 1990). I have verified these accounts and, in some cases, supplemented them with information contained in the private files and records of both the liberal and conservative groups that were active in this campaign. Both sides were generous and gracious in allowing Greg Caldeira and myself access to this information.

ings. This effort to "freeze the Senate" was designed to give the coalition time to mobilize at the grassroots and to avoid giving the appearance that opponents of Bork were taking positions without first carefully examining the nominee's qualifications. The task force also began to identify those senators and states that would comprise their primary and secondary lobbying targets. As would be expected with a proactive effort, among the primary targets were nearly a dozen senators who had generally supported previous judicial nominations put forward by President Reagan and therefore were expected to support the nomination of Robert Bork.

The grassroots task force planned for three stages of action: a pre-hearing stage, a committee stage, and a floor stage. The main objectives during the prehearing stage were to organize as many different groups as possible at the statewide level and to begin to shape public sentiment by organizing meetings and rallies, distributing literature, sending editorials to local newspapers, sponsoring ads in local papers, establishing speakers' bureaus to send prominent local individuals to speak before large group meetings, and identifying key people at the local level who opposed the nomination and who knew the senator. The main objective during the committee and floor periods was to initiate a "far-reaching, massive grassroots effort." Letter-writing campaigns were conducted through churches, unions, and social clubs, and advance authorization of mailgrams was arranged through large group meetings.

The media campaign against Bork's nomination was organized and funded primarily by People for the American Way, (PAW); NARAL; Planned Parenthood Federation of America, Inc.; and the American Federation of State, County, and Municipal Employees (AFSCME). Together, these organizations spent more than $1 million dollars on print, radio, and television advertising between the beginning of August and the middle of October. The first ads were run in early August and designed to convince citizens that an active Senate role in the confirmation process was appropriate and that as part of the process of advice and consent, the Senate legitimately could and should consider the ideology of the nominee. Later ads emphasized the basic themes worked out by the drafting task force.

The drafting task force worked throughout the month of August perfecting the basic themes and messages of the lobbying campaign.

The objective was to develop themes that were relatively simple and straightforward, yet emotionally powerful enough to move citizens to action. In addition, it was necessary to find themes that would appeal to the diverse interests of the coalition. Essential to the development of a general message strategy was background research conducted by organizations such as the National Women's Law Center, which in mid-August issued a 40-page analysis of Bork's opinions and writings.

During the last week of August, the anti-Bork lobbying message was finally perfected. The general message consisted of three basic themes: (1) Bork was not a fair-minded person, (2) he lacked sensitivity to civil rights and equal justice for women and minorities, and (3) he was an extremist whose views were out of the mainstream. These three themes formed the basis of the grassroots communications with senators, the Washington lobbyists' communications with senators, and the media ads. One 60-second television spot narrated by Gregory Peck alleged that Bork "has a strange idea of what justice is," that he "defended poll taxes and literacy tests which kept many Americans from voting," and that he "doesn't believe the Constitution protects your right to privacy." A newspaper ad paid for by PAW claimed that Bork's "views are so extreme that over the last 25 years he has consistently taken positions against the Constitutional rights of average Americans;" and a radio ad sponsored by AFSCME asserted that "Bork is the wrong man for the job, not because his views are partisan, but because they are extreme."

Conservative, pro-Bork interest groups such as the American Conservative Union, Concerned Women of America, and the Fraternal Order of Police lobbied hard to counteract the anti-Bork lobbying information. Leaders of these organizations fully understood that theirs was largely a counteractive lobbying campaign. In one memorandum distributed late in the campaign to conservative coalition members and outlining the final lobbying strategy, 11 senators were identified as "get backs"—senators who conservative lobbyists believed would ordinarily have supported Bork, but who had been lobbied extensively by liberals and taken positions against Bork. In the end, however, the conservative groups failed to convince a majority of the U.S. Senate that the liberals were wrong about Bork's policy views or that politically their members could offset any loss of electoral support that the liberals might inflict during the 1988 elections. On October 23, 1987, the U.S. Senate rejected Robert Bork's nomination to the Supreme Court by a 58–42 majority.

The most notable failure of the conservative groups was their inability to counter the charge that Bork was an ideological extremist. Throughout the lobbying campaign, conservatives protested that liberals had distorted and lied about Bork's judicial views; yet, they were never able to remove the doubts in senators' minds that Bork was indeed an extremist who would upset the balance of the Supreme Court. One reason for their failure was that the Reagan White House never fully mobilized its resources behind Bork. The consequence was that many moderate groups—corporations, public affairs groups, and so forth—that the White House was expected to mobilize were never heard from. Only the conservative groups of the far right visibly and vocally came out in support of Bork, a fact that signaled Bork's philosophy was indeed beyond the ideological mainstream.

The early strategy of the White House—at least according to conservatives on the far right—was essentially not to lobby. It is not entirely clear whether White House officials simply believed Bork would win nomination easily and that liberal groups would not successfully mobilize against him or whether they realized the impossibility of defending Bork's ideological views as mainstream. Senator Charles Grassley of Iowa, however, believed that the White House was simply "caught asleep at the switch" and placed full blame for Bork's defeat on the White House:

> This may be the last opportunity to change the Court and instead he [Reagan] was riding horses in California in August. It [Bork's defeat] was very definitely the fault of the White House, which went on vacation in August while the opposition was working.[31]

Eventually, late in the lobbying campaign, the White House did try to portray Bork as a moderate, and even Bork himself attempted to present himself as a moderate in hearings before the Senate Judiciary Committee; however, given that the conservative right was clearly associated with Bork's nomination from the very beginning,

---

[31]*Washington Times*, October 7, 1987, p. A1.

none of these claims proved credible. Their effect was only to create further uncertainty and doubt in senators' minds about Bork's true views.

The conservatives also lost the political battle. The mobilization efforts of the liberal groups ultimately proved more compelling, not because they generated more mail or phone calls—in fact, the conservatives probably won the mail battle—but because the political information of the liberal groups was more focused and informed. Whereas the liberal strategy called for just three basic themes, the conservative strategy was to articulate 19 different themes over the final weeks of the campaign. Many of these themes were directed not at Bork, but at the liberal groups opposing Bork. Arguing that the left was engaging in "raw politics," imposing "litmus tests" on judges, and attempting to portray the battle as the "radical left vs. America," the conservatives focused much of their effort against liberals themselves rather than on the messages that the liberals were sending to Congress.

Not only was the liberal message more focused, but the liberal groups did a better job of getting their message across to the general public. The conservatives never succeeded in matching the liberals in media spending, a fact that proved to have important consequences for the credibility of the grassroots communications. In a grassroots lobbying campaign, each citizen is in effect a lobbyist, and just as Washington lobbyists must be informed to be credible, so must citizen lobbyists. Given the imbalance in media advertising, citizens who wrote to their senators in protest of Bork's nomination appeared much more informed than citizens who contacted their senators in support of Bork. In one embarrassing incident for the conservatives, a pro-Bork group distributed a form letter to grassroots activists in which Bork's name had been misspelled, resulting in a deluge of letters to Senator Howell Heflin's office urging him to "vote for Bark." Clearly, such communications are not very effective in convincing senators that constituents will hold them accountable for their actions at election time. To be perceived as having credible information requires some costly expenditure of effort, and the conservatives, given their lack of media advertising, were unable to convince a majority of senators that their constituents were truly informed about the issues and stakes involved. In the final analysis, then, no amount of constituency mail and phone calls could disguise the fact that Bork's supporters were not nearly as committed as Bork's opponents.

Finally, the political campaign of the liberals proved more compelling than that of the conservatives because the liberal grassroots effort included a much broader and more diverse political base. The anti-Bork coalition ultimately included more than 300 different organizations, where as the pro-Bork coalition involved roughly 100 organizations. More importantly, though, the liberal coalition included many more moderate and middle-of-the-road groups. Opposition to Bork by groups such as the National Federation of Business and Professional Women's Clubs—an organization with many Republicans as members—and small business groups such as the Service Station Dealers of America added credibility to the liberal lobbying message and strengthened the political standing of the anti-Bork coalition.

Whether the liberal groups did in fact misrepresent Bork's policy positions to the American public is an issue about which both the supporters and opponents of Bork have long made up their minds and need not be decided here. The important lesson here is simply that proactive lobbying information, whether true or false, can be quite compelling when there is little or no credible information to the contrary. In employing a proactive strategy, the liberals calculated correctly that they had a reasonable chance of getting their message across and having it believed. That Bork had written extensively about a number of controversial issues no doubt contributed to their decision to oppose his nomination. Bork's supporters ultimately failed to counter the anti-Bork message, in part because there simply was little counteractive effort from moderate groups and in part because the conservative support at the grassroots level appeared less informed and less committed than the liberal opposition.

The next case provides an example of how proactive lobbying information *can* be countered effectively. In the case of policy over gays in the military, the political strength of those groups that wanted to remove the ban was greatly exaggerated in the minds of some decision makers when the policy change was initially proposed, but countermobilization proved effective, causing many of the policy initiators to change their original positions.

Lobbying on Gays in the Military

As a presidential candidate in 1992, Bill Clinton had promised to remove the ban on gays in the military, and after his victory and inauguration in 1993, gay rights organizations pressed him hard to follow through on his promise. Gay rights organizations were perceived to be an influential political force in the 1992 campaign. They not only voted cohesively as a bloc—one national poll showed that 89 percent of all gays and lesbians voted Democratic in the 1992 presidential campaign[32]—but they also contributed more than $3 million to Clinton's presidential effort.[33]

Apparently believing that gays and lesbians were strong enough organizationally to provide him with the necessary political support to remove the ban, Clinton reiterated his pledge to lift the ban just five days after his inauguration. The negative popular reaction that followed this announcement was overwhelming, indicating that Clinton may have seriously misjudged the political situation. On January 26, the capitol switchboard reported 434,101 incoming calls, more than five times the normal volume.[34] As much as 90 percent of the callers expressed opposition to lifting the ban.[35] Many of the calls were organized by the fundamentalist Christian movement, but many others were evidently spontaneous.

Fearful that organized opposition would force Clinton to back down from his campaign pledge, gay rights activists tried to reaffirm the president's belief in their organizational strength by announcing on February 25 that they expected more than 1 million participants for their march on Washington scheduled for late April. Since the march had been in the planning process long before the presidential election of 1992 and because significant financial resources had been pledged to the march, this claim was plausible. Also adding plausibility to the claim was the fact it was sure to be verified on April 25,

---

[32] Jean Latz Griffin, "Most Gays Voted for Clinton, Polls Show," *Chicago Tribune*, November 6, 1992, 1, 18:1.

[33] Paul Cellupica, "The Political Dawn Arrives for Gays," *New York Times*, November 7, 1992, A, 21:2.

[34] Michael Kranish and John W. Mashek, "Capitol Deluged with Calls on Gay Service Ban," *Boston Globe*, January 27, 1993, A, 1:5.

[35] Ibid.

the scheduled date of the march. Clinton maintained a wait-and-see attitude.

Any doubts about the ability of the gay and lesbian movement to mobilize 1 million marchers were quickly confirmed, as the number of individuals who marched on April 25 was far lower than advertised. The U.S. Park Service estimated that the march drew only 300,000 participants instead of the anticipated 1 million.[36] March organizers bitterly disputed the Park Service's estimates, but a second estimate convinced most observers that participation did indeed fall far short of the million mark. Not only did participation fall short of the million mark, but it was also failed to match the number of calls to the capitol switchboard opposing the ban on the day after Clinton's announcement in January that the ban would be lifted. Faced with these facts, Representative Barney Frank, one of the congressional leaders of the gay rights movement, acknowledged that the "grassroots organization hasn't been there.... The fact is that members of Congress have heard far more from opponents than from supporters."[37] President Clinton then backed down from his original pledge to remove the ban and settled instead for a policy of "don't ask; don't tell."

As outside observers, it is impossible to know whether the gay rights leaders deliberately misled President Clinton. The most charitable explanation is that they simply had inaccurate information themselves about their true organizational strength, or else that they did not anticipate the countermobilization. Whatever the case, the organizational capacity of the movement was eventually revealed to be considerably less than what President Clinton or various members of Congress had believed. Gay activists were able to secure policy commitments from these politicians when there was uncertainty about the true strength of the movement, but once the strength of the movement was unambiguously juxtaposed against the strength of the opposition, political support vanished quickly. Full information was revealed in this case only through the counteractive grassroots lobbying effort of opponents of the ban.

[36]Charles W. Hall, "The Clash Over Crowd Estimates," *Washington Post*, April 26, 1993, A, 1:3.
[37]John Lancaster, "Rep. Frank Urges Deal on Gay Ban," *Washington Post*, May 19, 1993, p. A13.

Misrepresentation as a Lobbying Strategy

One common feature of these two cases is that both involved disputes about the accuracy of the information presented by one side or the other. The existence of such disputes is an essential and predictable feature of an information-based theory of interest group lobbying. Indeed, if there were no conflicts over the veracity of lobbying information, then one could explain interest group behavior simply in terms of "service bureaus" or as extended staff for legislators. Legislators could always trust lobbyists, and lobbyists would never violate this trust, even if they could get away with it and gain important economic and political benefits. Moreover, one should never find lobbying messages from opposing groups to be in conflict. If lobbyists are always telling the entire truth and if lobbyists are well informed, then there should be no disagreement in the information they present. Thus, disputes about the veracity of lobbying information or other evidence of misrepresentation of the facts pose a substantial challenge to the traditional view of interest group politics.

Some might question the extent to which groups deliberately attempt to mislead legislators. After all, a reputation for accuracy is frequently noted as one of the essential qualities of a successful lobbyist.[38] Yet, lobbyists who always divulge everything they know, who do not provide information selectively so as to present their case in the most favorable light, and who refuse to play up the amount of grassroots support for their position may miss important strategic opportunities to exercise influence. This is not to say the lobbyists regularly abuse whatever confidence legislators have in them; nevertheless, the *possibility* of misrepresentation by interest groups, especially in the transmission of information about political strength, is very real.

One classic example of a group's deliberate misrepresentation of its political strength involves the efforts of Coca-Cola and Hershey to defeat the sugar tariff in 1930.[39] Since neither Coca-Cola nor

[38]See, for example, Lewis Anthony Dexter, *How Organizations Are Represented in Washington*, (Indianapolis: Bobbs-Merrill, 1969).

[39]Scott Ainsworth presents these examples in "Regulating Lobbyists and Interest Group Influence." They are drawn from E. E. Schattschneider, *Politics, Pressures, and the Tariff* (Englewood Cliffs, NJ: Prentice-Hall, 1935), p. 274.

Hershey were membership organizations capable of demonstrating electoral strength in representatives' districts, the two companies funded a lobbying effort by the American Bottlers of Carbonated Beverages, which boasted 12,000 members. Lobbyists for Coca-Cola and Hershey then claimed to represent the interests of 12,000 individuals nationally.

Another classic historical example involves the efforts of the public utilities in 1933 to defeat the Wheeler-Rayburn bill, which called for substantial reform and reorganization of public utility holding companies. Opponents of the bill generated a massive telegram campaign in which telegrams were sent to members of Congress at the rate of as many as 4000 per hour. Subsequent investigation, however, revealed that most of the telegrams were signed with names taken at random and without authorization from telephone books.[40]

Examples of misrepresentation in recent years are also common.[41] One alleged instance in 1993 involved the Student Loan Funding Corporation (SLFC), which manages the secondary market for student loans. The SLFC opposed President Clinton's proposal for revamping the student loan program, because under the president's proposal the program was to be administered directly by the federal government, which would have eliminated the need for a secondary market. Although the SLFC has no individual dues-paying members, it clearly understood the importance of demonstrating broad political support in legislators' constituencies. Consequently, the organization spent $25,000 on advertising directed at college students in Ohio, encouraging them to call their senators through an 800 number. Senator Paul Simon, sponsor of the direct loan program in the Senate, criticized the lobbying effort as a "sham," even though the SLFC claimed it did not attempt to disguise the source of the grassroots response.[42] Evidently, what upset Simon and others was the implication that grassroots opposition to

---

[40]See Karl Schriftgiesser, *The Lobbyists: The Art and Business of Influencing Lawmakers* (Boston: Little, Brown, 1951), p. 71.
[41]See Ainsworth, "Regulating Lobbyists and Interest Group Influence," 41–56.
[42]Michael Weisskopf, "Simon Attacks Lobbying by Student Loan Industry," *Washington Post*, May 26, 1993, A, 2:4.

the president's proposal was spontaneous and independent when in fact it was not.

In another recent case, Citizens for a Sound Economy (CSE) attempted to build opposition to a tariff on foreign minivans by contacting individuals in local chapters of organizations such as the Boy Scouts of America and the March of Dimes. When an individual was identified who agreed with CSE's position on the tariff and agreed to contact his or her member of Congress, CSE allegedly added the organization's name to its coalition, even if the organization had not officially taken a position on the issue. This effort, and others like it, are sometimes referred to by pundits as "astroturf" campaigns.[43]

One can surely uncover many other examples of misleading claims—or at least allegations of misleading claims—in lobbying campaigns both past and present. Perhaps more important than the actual number of such instances, however, is the fact that some of these cases appear to involve deliberate misrepresentation. Groups do sometimes knowingly and strategically encourage or allow legislators to believe information that does not perfectly represent the facts. This should not be too surprising whenever the political stakes are high. Political scientist E. E. Schattschneider recognized the importance to interest groups of a strategy of misrepresentation as early as 1942:

> Claims as to the size, enthusiasm, and unanimity of their membership are subject to no verification by the objective public process of an election contest. The very fact that claims are not subject to verification is one of the principal sources of the influence of pressure groups.... The first rule of successful pressure politics therefore is to make a noise like the clamor of millions but never allow an investigation of the claims. Exaggeration is the life of pressure politics. The more realistically it can be done the more apt it is to worry timid congressmen, and that is enough.[44]

[43]Arsa Q. Nomani, "Critics Say Antitariff Activists in Washington Have Grass-Roots Base That's Made of Astroturf," *Wall Street Journal*, March 17, 1993, A, 16:2.
[44]E. E. Schattschneider, *Party Government* (New York: Holt, Rinehart and Winston, 1942), pp. 199–201.

Schattschneider was surely correct in observing that misrepresentation can be an important source of interest group influence. Indeed, that is a central claim of this book. It is unclear, however, whether exaggeration is as common and widespread as he suggests, and exactly when groups elect to employ a strategy of misrepresentation. One very important consideration in the strategic decision to misrepresent the facts is the likelihood of being discovered and punished, for as the possibility of discovery increases, the likelihood of successful misrepresentation decreases. Ultimately, the likelihood of discovery depends on the legislator's ability to verify the lobbying claims made by groups.

Checking Misrepresentation

Legislators have numerous sources they can turn to for information about the legislative or political outlook on any given issue, and the possibility that they will turn to these sources provides a strong inducement for lobbyists to report information accurately. To appreciate the importance of legislators' own resources for encouraging groups to provide accurate information, suppose for the moment that legislators could never determine when lobbyists were telling the truth and when they were not, so that all groups could misrepresent the facts with impunity. Under these conditions, legislators could never trust any information provided by groups. In fact, in a world where all lobbying information was unreliable, legislators would have no reason to listen to groups, for groups could never be relied upon to provide accurate information. However, if legislators never believed anything they heard from interest groups, interest groups would have little incentive to lobby. Their claims would always fall on deaf ears, and thus there would be no reason to incur the costs of lobbying.

Yet, interest groups do lobby, and they lobby extensively. This fact alone suggests that some reliable information must be transmitted through lobbying. Evidently, legislators trust lobbyists—at least some of the time—and thus it follows that legislators must have some way of determining when lobbyists are misrepresenting the facts. What makes informational lobbying possible, then, is that legislators have sources of their own, independent of groups, that they can turn to for information.

Of the three basic types of information provided by interest groups—information about the legislative process, information about the policy process, and information about the political situation in the constituency—the easiest for legislators to verify is information about the legislative process. Legislators talk to other legislators, and members of their staffs talk to members of other staffs. Legislators can also turn to the party whips for head counts or other information about levels of support or opposition within the chamber. Although relying on lobbyists for some of this information may be a convenient shortcut, legislators do not have to rely entirely on lobbyists to learn when hearings or votes might be scheduled, what amendments or rules might be proposed, and other information relevant to the legislative process. When necessary, they can acquire the relevant information through their own resources and use it to verify what lobbyists tell them.

Some electoral information is also within the reach of legislators. Members of Congress have budgets for essentially an unlimited number of trips back to their districts each year, and most visit their constituencies every weekend. They also have ample allowances for district offices and staff—the average House member employs six to eight staff persons in the district; the average senator employs roughly 12—and these resources help them keep abreast of political situations in the district even when they are in Washington. Supplementing these travel and staff benefits is 15,000 minutes of long-distance telephone time from Washington to the district each year. All of these resources help legislators stay in touch with their districts, and even though they cannot simulate electoral mobilization as effectively as interest groups can through grassroots campaigns, they can and do gain a good sense of where their constituents stand on most issues.

Legislators also have various resources to draw upon to understand the operational effects of policies. Not to be underestimated is their own experience and expertise in specific policy areas. The House Ways and Means Committee, for example, regularly deals with accounting and tax rules for corporations, and the House Agriculture Committee writes a major farm bill every five years.

Through repeated exposure to complex issues, legislators often acquire sufficient expertise that do not have to rely on lobbyists to understand how "nonrecourse loans" work, for example, or how tax rules apply to capital gains arising from the conversion of "C corporations" to "S corporations."

In addition, legislators can turn to their own personal staff and to committee staffs for technical expertise, and when more intensive study or analysis of a particular problem is called for, they can turn to the Congressional Research Service, the Congressional Budget Office, the General Accounting Office, and the Office of Technology Assessment. These agencies can provide general reference assistance or conduct analytical studies in areas such as economics, education, environmental policy, and foreign affairs. Reports from these agencies often play an important role in buttressing or refuting arguments and claims of competing interests. The GAO, for example, gave legislators ammunition for attacking sugar subsidies when it reported that subsidies to U.S. sugar producers cost consumers 11.4 billion dollars a year.[45] An analysis by the Congressional Research Service (CRS) reinforced claims by those defending the administration of student loans through private banks when it reported that the government could not administer loans as efficiently as the private sector.[46] The CRS also analyzed advertising by the National Rifle Association in 1988, which claimed that citizens would have to pay a $200 tax for shotguns and semiautomatic weapons under two bills then before the Senate. The CRS analysis found that the claim was untrue.[47]

Despite the considerable array of resources available to legislators, the acquisition of any kind of information is still costly. Representatives cannot travel to the district prior to each and every important vote, and there are only so many hours they and their staff can spend on the telephone each day speaking with constituents or colleagues. The resources of committee staff and the research agen-

[45]Sharon LaFraniere, "U.S. Keeps Sugar Prices High, GAO Says," *Washington Post*, May 17, 1993, A, 5:1.

[46]Mary Jordan, "Student Loan Proposal May Increase U.S. Debt, Report Warns Congress," *Washington Post*, February 24, 1993, A, 12:1.

[47]*Congressional Quarterly Almanac*, 101st Congress, 1st Session, 1989, Volume XLV (Washington, DC: Congressional Quarterly, Inc.), p. 265.

cies are also limited, and studies cannot always be generated as quickly as they are needed. The significance of the informational resources available to legislators, therefore, is not that they satisfy all of their informational needs all of the time, but that they make it possible for legislators occasionally to *verify* information from organized interests.

When legislators have their own resources for verifying lobbyists' claims, the proclivity for lobbyists to provide misleading information is greatly reduced, for it is always possible that inaccurate information will be discovered and the fabricator revealed. Legislators can then punish the fabricator in a variety of ways. They can vote against the group on subsequent issues, they can deny access, and they can use their contacts with the media to generate negative publicity for the group.

The ability of legislators to at least occasionally verify lobbying information is a crucial part of the lobbying process. Their resources are not so extensive that they can prevent misrepresentation entirely, but they do impose an important deterrent, and as a result legislators do not need to verify each and every claim that is presented to them. In some cases, groups hoping to present misleading information will simply resist, anticipating that they might be discovered; in other cases, opposing groups might lobby counteractively. As illustrated by the example of lobbying over lifting the ban on gays in the military, when the facts are wrong, opposing interests have a strong incentive to make sure the truth is revealed. The incentive for any group to lobby counteractively, therefore, is greater the more difficult it is for legislators to verify information through their own resources. Thus, even when legislators' own resources are scarce, they can rely to some extent on interest groups to check misrepresentation.

E. E. Schattschneider was correct, then, in his observation that interest groups sometimes exaggerate the facts, but he was incorrect in his claim that "one of the principal sources of the influence of pressure groups" is the fact that "claims are not subject to verification." To the contrary, it is the fact that interest groups' claims *are* subject to verification that makes them potentially useful to legislators, and thus potentially influential.

Lobbying and Influence in American Politics

While there can be no denying that groups do occasionally present misleading information or else knowingly allow legislators to base their decisions on misleading information, groups are limited in their ability to manipulate legislators' beliefs with inaccurate information. Legislators themselves can verify lobbying information by relying on advisors and their own experience, and opposing groups can always counter with accurate information. Interest group influence in American politics, therefore, takes a rather subtle form. Influence derives as much, or even perhaps more, from counteractive lobbying—that is, preventing an opposing group from changing a legislator's position—than from proactive lobbying.

Preventing legislators from changing their positions, however, is just as important a form of influence as *persuading* them to change. Were it not for the fact that groups lobby counteractively, legislators would surely change their positions in response to lobbying much more often than they do, and they would also surely be misled by groups much more often than they are. There is a bit of irony in all of this: the possibility and threat of successful proactive lobbying inspires counteractive lobbying, which in turn reduces the effectiveness of proactive lobbying. Still, proactive lobbying is sometimes successful, as illustrated by the case of lobbying on the Bork nomination, and thus the possibility of proactive lobbying is always present.

Finally, it is worth emphasizing once again that one xsource of interest group influence in American politics is the possibility that facts will be misrepresented. Groups do sometimes achieve influence by knowingly misrepresenting the facts, but this is not the only route to influence. A more common route is that groups present accurate information in order to discourage opponents from presenting inaccurate information. The possibility that misrepresentation will be successful, however, is what motivates both proactive and counteractive lobbying efforts, and thus interest group influence cannot be understood and explained apart from misrepresentation. Although deliberate misrepresentation may not occur all that often in American politics, the threat of misrepresentation is always present, and so is interest group influence.

C H A P T E R   5

POLITICAL ACTION COMMITTEES

The world of interest group politics is continually changing, but no change in recent years has been more significant than the increased visibility of their financial activities. Since 1974, special interests have been required to report publicly the amounts of money they contribute to congressional candidates, and this activity, which largely escaped notice in earlier years, is now a source of considerable interest and concern. Thanks to campaign-finance reforms during the early 1970s, groups no longer need to launder their contributions through foreign bank accounts or distribute money in brown paper bags; now it is perfectly legal for groups to make direct cash contributions to members of Congress through political action committees (PACs), and thousands of PACs are now affiliated with corporations, labor unions, and other organized interests.

PACs are probably the primary source of cynicism and distrust of politics in the United States today. Many journalists, reformers, and even some politicians are highly skeptical of PACs, and voters, increasingly frustrated with a system of campaign financing heavily dependent on the money of special interests, hold Congress in lower and lower esteem each year. The problem, according to journalist Brooks Jackson, "isn't corruption; it is more serious than that." He contends that money can "twist the behavior of ordinary legislators. The system of money-based elections and lobbying rewards those who cater to well-funded interests, ... and it also punishes those who challenge the status quo."[1]

---

[1]Brooks Jackson, *Honest Graft: Money and the American Political Process* (New York: Knopf, 1988), p. 295.

Indeed, the visibility of PACs and their connections to special interests raise many important questions about their influence and place in the political process. Where did PACs come from? What is their connection to lobbying organizations? What are the legal restrictions on them? How much money do interest groups contribute through their PACs? How many groups have PACs? Do PACs buy legislative favors or roll call votes? To what extent have PACs changed the nature of representation in American politics? After two decades of growth in the number and visibility of political action committees, these questions have never been more relevant.

The History and Characteristics of PACs

An appropriate place to begin understanding PACs is at the beginning: Where did they come from, and what are their connections to lobbying organizations? One of the most common confusions about PACs is that they are no different from lobbying organizations—that is, groups such as corporations, unions, and professional associations that lobby members of Congress. PACs and lobbying groups, however, are distinct organizational entities. Organizations such as corporations, unions, or professional associations are not allowed under federal law to make campaign contributions directly out of their general treasuries. All campaign contributions must be made from a separate organizational entity. The American Medical Association (AMA), for example, can lobby members of Congress, but it cannot make campaign contributions. Campaign contributions in the case of the AMA are made through the American Medical Political Action Committee (AMPAC), the sole purpose of which is to collect money from rank-and-file members of the AMA and distribute it among federal candidates. The roots of this crucial distinction extend back to the 1940s.

A Bit of History

From the turn of the century until the 1940s, corporations, but not labor unions, had been prohibited by law from making campaign contributions. Labor unions, even though they were politically active since the early 1900s, did not contribute any substantial amount of money to political campaigns until 1936, and thus regulation of contribution activities was restricted to corporations, which had been quite active in campaign financing since the 1880s.[2] In 1936, however, organized labor contributed more than $1 million to federal campaigns through Labor's Non-Partisan League (LNPL). The LNPL was an early prototype of a political action committee established by John Lewis to ensure Roosevelt's reelection and the election of a prolabor Congress in 1936.[3] Although the LNPL received cooperation and support from 59 different unions in 1936, it was effectively under the control of Lewis, and it operated as the political arm of the CIO until Lewis resigned as president of the CIO in 1940.[4]

Concerned about the growing campaign influence of organized labor, particularly the more leftist, aggressive CIO, as well as a series of strikes during wartime, Congress passed the War Labor Disputes Act (Smith-Connally), overriding Roosevelt's veto on June 12, 1943. Smith-Connally not only prohibited strikes for the duration of the war but also banned labor campaign contributions for the duration of the war, subjecting them to the same prohibition as corporate contributions under the Tillman Act of 1907 and the Federal Corrupt Practices Act of 1925.

Following the passage of Smith-Connally and reeling from the congressional elections of 1942 in which the CIO lost 42 allies in the

[2]Most of the money contributed by unions was raised and spent by the Committee for Progressive Political Action (CPPA), founded by the Railroad Brotherhood in 1922. This committee operated very much like a modern-day political committee. It educated members about issues and the labor records of candidates, and it raised and contributed money to candidates. An interesting, but subjective, account of early union campaign financing practices can be found in Joseph Gaer, *The First Round: The Story of the CIO Political Action Committee* (New York: Duell, Sloan and Pearce, 1944).
[3]See James Caldwell Foster, *The Union Politic: The CIO Political Action Committee* (Columbia: University of Missouri Press, 1975), p. 8; and Walter Galenson, *The CIO Challenge to the AFL: A History of the American Labor Movement* (Cambridge, MA: Harvard University Press, 1960), p. 606.
[4]Unhappy with Roosevelt's lukewarm support for the unions during the General Motors strike of 1937 and the bituminous coal strike of 1939, Lewis endorsed Wilkie in 1940 and pledged to resign the presidency of the CIO if Wilkie lost. Lewis kept his word.

House, the CIO took action. On July 7, 1943, less than a month after Smith-Connally took effect, the CIO formed the CIO-PAC. The CIO-PAC was designed explicitly to circumvent the restrictions of Smith-Connally.[5] Although unions per se could not make contributions from their general treasuries under Smith-Connally, the act did not prohibit the union's PAC, which technically was not a labor union, from contributing to candidates. The CIO established what it called the "dollar drive" to raise money for the PAC voluntarily from union members, and this money was then contributed directly from the PAC to federal candidates. In 1944 the PAC contributed an estimated $2 million.

The ban on union contributions imposed by Smith-Connally was made permanent by the Labor Management Relations Act (Taft-Hartley) of 1947. In addition, Taft-Hartley banned both campaign contributions and direct expenditures from corporate and union treasuries in primary elections and nominating conventions. Despite these restrictions, campaign money from corporations and unions continued to flow unabated. Corporations continued to funnel contributions indirectly through their employees, CIO-PAC continued in operation, and both unions and corporations used money from their general treasuries to pay their employees for time spent or expenses incurred while working for federal candidates. These practices were challenged, but in six different cases reaching the Supreme Court following passage of Taft-Hartley, the Court refused to rule directly on the constitutionality of the ban on corporate and union contributions. The Court's general reluctance to rule squarely on the constitutionality question made federal officials reluctant to prosecute and sent a signal that as long as contributions were made from a separate fund such as the CIO-PAC, they would be tolerated. Hesitantly, other labor organizations and some professional and trade associations established PACs. Kevin McKeough reported that for the 1964 election, 31 labor PACs and 26 nonlabor PACs were registered with the clerk of the house.[6] Among them were the Committee on Political Education (COPE), formed in

[5]See Foster, *The Union Politic,* pp. 24–25.
[6]Kevin L. McKeough, *Financing Campaigns for Congress: Contribution Patterns of National-Level Party and Non-Party Committees, 1964* (Princeton, NJ: Citizens' Research Foundation, 1970).

1955 when the AFL and CIO merged; the Business and Industry Political Action Committee (BIPAC) a PAC supporting business generally; and the American Medical Political Action Committee (AMPAC), affiliated with the American Medical Association.

The most serious legal challenge to PACs came in 1968, when three officials of the Plumbers and Pipefitters Union No. 562 of St. Louis were indicted for making political contributions in the 1964 and 1966 elections in violation of Taft-Hartley. The officials were found guilty, fined, and sentenced to jail. In 1970 the Court of Appeals for the Eighth Circuit upheld the convictions, and the case was appealed to the U.S. Supreme Court as *Pipefitters Local Union No. 562 v. United States.* Two issues were central to the case: one concerned the voluntary nature of contributions (it was alleged that union officials had coerced members to contribute to the union's PAC), and the second was whether the union's PAC was exempt from the restrictions on union campaign activities as specified by Taft-Hartley (union members had been solicited by union employees on the job site, which called into question the separability of the union and the PAC).

Fearful that the Court might uphold the decision of the appellate court, organized labor sought legislative action that would ensure the legality of union political committees. Their vehicle was Senate Bill 382, the Federal Election Campaign Act (FECA) of 1971, then before Congress. The proposed FECA of 1971 had a life of its own, propelled by the rising costs of campaigns resulting from the introduction of television into the electoral process. The Federal Communications Commission estimated that nonpresidential radio and television spending had doubled from $30 million to $60 million between 1966 and 1970 and had tripled since 1962.[7] As a response to these rapidly escalating costs, the FECA of 1971 proposed limits on expenditures for media communications by candidates, ceilings on the amounts that candidates or their families could contribute to their own campaigns, and reporting of contributions and expenditures. Also motivating the FECA in 1971 was the fact that the Democratic Party, then the majority party in Congress, found itself in debt going into the 1972 campaign and hoped to narrow the finan-

---

[7]Congressional Quarterly, *Dollar Politics: The Issue of Campaign Spending* (Washington, DC: Congressional Quarterly, Inc., 1971), p. 27.

cial disparity with the Republicans by placing restrictions on media advertising.

In terms of the evolution of PACs, the key aspect of the FECA of 1971 was an amendment offered by Orval Hansen, Republican from Idaho, at the request of organized labor. The amendment provided for "the establishment, administration, and solicitation of contributions to a separate segregated fund to be utilized for political purposes." A separate segregated fund was to be one that did not contain membership dues or other money as a condition of employment or membership or any money obtained through a commercial transaction. Labor's intent clearly was to legitimize their political contribution activities by enacting legislation that would fend off a possible negative decision by the Supreme Court on the constitutionality of their PAC operations.

The Hansen amendment was passed and included in the final version of the FECA, which was passed and signed into law before the Supreme Court handed down its decision on *Pipefitters*. The Court's decision was still of great importance, though, for it would determine the constitutionality of the Hansen provision. In June 1972 the Supreme Court reversed the decision of the appellate court. The Court upheld the right of unions to make campaign contributions so long as (1) the contributions came from political funds that were financed by voluntary contributions of members and (2) the funds were strictly segregated from any funds emanating from union dues. The Court emphasized, moreover, that union officials were not prohibited from soliciting contributions to the segregated fund (i.e., the PAC) or from determining how the funds were to be spent.

The Hansen amendment achieved what the unions wanted: constitutional legitimacy for their PAC operations. What applied to unions, however, also applied to corporations and other organizations. The unions recognized that corporations could benefit from the same legal provisions but, when pushing for the Hansen amendment, were willing to risk that corporations would not take full advantage of a clear and direct ruling on the constitutionality of PACs. As it turned out, they were greatly mistaken.

The FECA of 1971 and the Court's decision in *Pipefitters* paved the way for unprecedented development of political action committees. Prior to 1971, labor PACs greatly outnumbered corporate PACs, as only 10 corporations had registered political action committees. By 1974, however, 89 corporations had PACs, and by 1976, 433 corporations had formed PACs.[8] The number of corporate PACs currently stands in excess of 2000, while the total number of union PACs totals less than 500. This sudden and dramatic growth in the number of political action committees during the 1970s is directly attributable to the Hansen amendment and the Court's ruling in *Pipefitters*. The significant, but unintended, consequence of the 1971 FECA, however, is the ascendancy of business over labor in the realm of campaign financing.

Important amendments to the 1971 FECA were passed in 1974, 1976, and 1979. In short, these amendments established contribution limits for PACs, individuals, and political parties. Furthermore, they provided for the reporting and regulation of campaign contribution activity through the Federal Election Commission (FEC).[9] These amendments, however, like the legislation that preceded them, have not been immune from abuses and loopholes. One example is the practice of "bundling." Even though PACs are allowed by law to contribute no more than $5000 to any given candidate during a primary, general, or runoff election, some organizations circumvent this limit by tacitly agreeing with other PACs or individuals to coordinate, or "bundle" together, several contributions to a single candidate. EMILY's List, for example, is an organization that, as a condition of membership, requires a contribution of at least $100 to at least two congressional candidates on its list of recommended candidates. With this practice, EMILY's List is able to raise hundreds of thousands of dollars for a single candidate.[10]

The legal distinction between lobbying groups and their PACs has been defined not only in the FECA of 1971 but also in advisory opinions issued by the Federal Election Commission. In the FEC's

---

[8]See Edwin Epstein, "The Emergence of Political Action Committees," in Herbert E. Alexander (ed.), *Political Finance* (Beverly Hills: Sage, 1979), p. 165.

[9]A good discussion of these later reforms can be found in Frank J. Sorauf, *Money in American Elections* (Glenview, IL: Scott, Foresman, 1988), pp. 38–43.

[10]See Candice J. Nelson, "Women's PACs in the Year of the Woman," in Elizabeth Adell Cook, Sue Thomas, and Clyde Wilcox (eds.), *The Year of the Woman: Myths and Realities* (Boulder: Westview Press, 1994).

opinion, however, the distinction between PACs and their parent organizations need not be absolute. In an advisory opinion concerning the Sun Oil Company in 1975, the Federal Election Commission ruled that parent organizations could pay the fund-raising and administrative costs of operating their PACs.[11] This decision has blurred the line somewhat between PACs and lobbies. Professional lobbyists, for example, who are employed by the parent organization can, and often do, assist the PAC in fund-raising efforts and other administrative decisions, particularly those involving the allocation of campaign contributions to congressional candidates.[12] For this reason, PACs are sometimes closely connected with the legislative objectives of lobbying organizations, but the strength and nature of this connection tends to vary considerably across organizations.

An appreciation of how PACs came about is an important first step in understanding the connection between PACs and their parent organizations, and thus the role that PACs play in the lobbying process. PACs, however, like their parents, are not monolithic. Some are quite large, but most are extremely modest operations, and thus not all have the same impact on the legislative process. To recognize PACs for what they are, and perhaps more importantly for what they are not, it is important to draw some distinctions among PACs in terms of their organizational structures and the size and scope of their financial activities.

The Types, Number, and Size of PACs

Political action committees vary greatly in size and organizational structure. Many of the PACs registered with the Federal Election

---

[11]FEC Advisory Opinion 1975–23, December 3, 1975.

[12]Little is known about the actual operating costs of PACs, as parent organizations are not required to report this information to the FEC. What information does exist, however, suggests that the costs are generally quite small. In a survey of 107 PACs of Fortune 500 companies during the mid-1980s, Ann Matasar found that nearly one-third of the PACs reported that their administrative costs were nominal, involving only the costs of postage and printing, and another one-fourth of the corporations reported that their administrative costs amounted to less than $1000 per year. Only three companies reported administrative costs exceeding $25,000 per year. See Ann B. Matasar, *Corporate PACs and Federal Campaign Financing Laws* (Westport, CT: Greenwood Press, 1986), pp. 31–32.

Commission are dormant, raising and contributing no money at all, while others raise and contribute millions of dollars each election period. Most PACs are affiliated with some parent organization such as a corporation or labor union, but others have no organizational affiliation at all. Based on characteristics of the committees' affiliated organizations, the FEC recognizes six broad types of PACs: those connected with corporations, those affiliated with labor unions, those connected with trade/health/membership groups, those linked with cooperatives, those affiliated with corporations without stock, and those that are totally nonconnected.[13] Included among the corporate PACs are EastPAC of the Eastman Kodak Company, the Occidental Petroleum Corporation PAC, and American Airlines PAC. Among the labor unions are the PACs of the Phoenix Firefighters Local 493, the American Federation of Musicians, and the National Treasury Employees Union. The trade/ health/membership category includes the PACs of the Air Conditioning Contractors of America, the American Optometric Association, the National Association of Social Workers, and the National Organization for Women. The cooperatives are comprised mostly of agricultural interests such as the Michigan Blueberry Growers Association and the PACs of the Dairymen, Inc., but also include some PACs affiliated with health or electric cooperatives. The PACs of corporations without stock are primarily those of banking, insurance, and savings and loans but also include the Handgun Control Voter Education Fund of Handgun Control, Inc., and the Aircraft Owners and Pilots Association. Finally, in the nonconnected category are the National Right to Life Committee, and Fund for a Democratic Majority, and the Whimsical Alternative Coalition PAC (WACPAC).

Table 5.1 presents the number of PACs registered in each of the FEC's six categories during the 1991–1992 election cycle, together with a percentage of total PAC expenditures by committees in each

---

[13]The explicit connection between political action committees and corporations, labor unions, and other organizations was established legally by the "separate, segregated fund" clause of the 1971 FECA. Federal law defines a *connected organization* as "any organization which is not a political committee but which directly or indirectly establishes, administers, or financially supports a political committee." (Title II, U.S.C., Section 431(7)).

Table 5.1   Distribution of PACs by FEC's
Organizational Classes, 1992

FEC Classification	Number of PACs	Percent	Total Contributions	Percent
Corporations	1930	40.8	$68,232,429	36.3
Labor unions	372	7.9	41,005,448	21.8
Trade association, membership organization, or health-related organization	835	17.7	53,762,268	28.6
Cooperative	61	1.3	2,941,640	1.5
Corporation without stock	153	3.2	3,960,765	2.1
Nonconnected organizations	1376	29.1	18,208,003	9.7
Total	4727	100.0	$188,110,553	100.0

category.[14] Corporate PACs are by far the most common variety, accounting for 40.8 percent of all 4727 PACs registered with the FEC. Second to corporations in abundance are nonconnected PACs, followed by trade/health/membership PACs, and then labor PACs. Together, the PACs of cooperatives and corporations without stock account for less than 5 percent of all PACs. Labor PACs and trade/health/membership PACs account for a far larger portion of total PAC contributions than their numbers would suggest. Labor PACs account for only 7.9 percent of all PACs, but 21.8 percent of all PAC contributions; and trade/health/membership PACs account for 28.6 percent of all contributions, but only 17.7 percent of all PACs. Thus, labor and trade/health/membership PACs, while relatively few in

[14]An election cycle is an accounting period created by the FEC. A cycle begins on January 1 of the odd-numbered year and ends on December 31 of the even-numbered year. Unless noted otherwise, all data on PAC expenditures are taken from the Federal Election Commission's data tapes on financial activity of nonparty committees.

number, are often among the largest of all PACs. In contrast, corporations are copious in number but generally small, as they account for a larger share of total PACs than total dollars contributed.

The greatest disparity between the share of total PACs and the share of total contributions is within the category of nonconnected PACs. Nonconnected PACs account for 29.1 percent of all PACs, but less than 10 percent of all money contributed by PACs. The principal reason for this disparity is that fund-raising costs are much higher for nonconnected PACs than for their connected counterparts. As a result of the FEC's *Sun Oil* decision in 1975, nonconnected PACs are at a distinct disadvantage relative to connected PACs, since they must pay all of their fund-raising and overhead costs directly out of the money they raise. These expenses typically amount to three-quarters of all money raised, which leaves nonconnected PACs with much less money to contribute.[15]

The discrepancies between shares of PACs and shares of contributions are also apparent in Table 5.2, which lists the 20 largest PACs during the 1991–1992 election cycle. Ten of the largest 20 PACs are labor PACs (L), nine are trade or membership PACs (T), and only one is a corporate PAC (C). None of the largest PACs is a nonconnected PAC. Thus, even though corporate PACs greatly outnumber labor PACs in general, labor is by far the dominant player among the very largest PACs. Despite their success at forming small and medium-sized PACs, corporations simply do not have the membership or organizational capacity to rank among the largest PACs.

The total number of PACs registered with the FEC—4727 as of December 1992—belies the true extent of PAC organization and financial activity. Table 5.3 presents a distribution of all PACs according to 11 different levels of total contributions given during the 1991–1992 election cycle to major party congressional candidates. One of the most striking aspects of this distribution is that 1651, or 34.9 percent, of all PACs registered with the FEC spent *zero* dollars during the 1991–1992 election cycle. In fact, the cate-

---

[15]Margaret Ann Latus, "Assessing Ideological PACs: From Outrage to Understanding," in Michael J. Malbin (ed.), *Money and Politics in the United States: Financing Elections in the 1980s* (Chatham, NJ: Chatham House Publishers, 1984), p. 144.

Table 5.2   The Top 20 PACs, 1992

	Committee (Type)	Contributions
1	Realtors Political Action Committee (T)	$2,950,138
2	American Medical Association Political Action Committee (T)	2,936,558
3	Democratic, Republican, Independent Voter Education Committee (L)	2,432,552
4	Association of Trial Lawyers of America PAC (T)	2,361,136
5	National Education Association Political Action Committee (L)	2,329,622
6	UAW Voluntary Community Action Program (L)	2,226,917
7	American Federation of State, County & Municipal Employees PAC (L)	1,940,365
8	Dealers Election Action Committee of the National Automobile Dealers Association (T)	1,779,375
9	National Rifle Association Political Victory Fund (T)	1,735,946
10	Letter Carriers Political Action Committee (L)	1,624,277
11	Machinists Non-Partisan Political League (L)	1,601,296
12	American Institute of Certified Public Accountants Effective Legislation Committee (T)	1,542,851
13	International Brotherhood of Electrical Workers (L) Committee on Political Education	1,507,592
14	American Bankers Association BankPAC (T)	1,498,388
15	Active Ballot Club of the United Food & Commercial Workers International Union (L)	1,478,961
16	United Parcel Service Political Action Committee (C)	1,454,487
17	National Association of Retired Federal Employees PAC (L)	1,437,250
18	American Dental Political Action Committee (T)	1,414,958
19	Laborers' Political League of Laborers' International Union (L)	1,377,406
20	National Association of Life Underwriters PAC (T)	1,371,600

gory of zero expenditures is by far the largest of all of the categories in Table 5.3. Also striking is the fact that at the high end of the distribution, only 155, or 3.3 percent of all PACs, spent more than $250,000 on congressional campaigns, and only 8.4 percent spent more than $100,000. The vast majority of PACs, therefore, are very modest operations. Among the 3076 PACs that contributed any money at all during the 1991–1992 cycle, 2013, or roughly 65 percent, contributed less than $25,000.

The general shape of the distribution in Table 5.3 has not changed dramatically over the years, although there has been noticeable change among the smallest categories of PACs. In Figure 5.1, the distribution in Table 5.3 is compared with the corresponding distribution in 1980, adjusted for differences in the costs of campaigning between 1980 and 1992.[16] The number of PACs making contributions of $1000 or less in 1990 has more than doubled since 1980, and the numbers of PACs in the $1000 to $5000 and $5000 to $10,000 categories have also increased markedly. Evidently, not only do many existing PACs go out of business, but also many newly formed PACs fail to generate much financial activity. The more important point, however, is that the dramatic growth in the sheer number of PACs since 1980 is a bit deceiving. Much of the growth that has occurred is accounted for by very small PACs, or else by inactive PACs.

One of the most obvious characteristics of PACs, but one that receives little discussion by journalists and proponents of reform, is that the typical PAC is an extremely modest operation. Overall, among active PACs—that is, among the 3076 PACs that spent any money at all in 1992—the median PAC contributed a total of just $10,795 to major party congressional candidates. This number hardly seems large enough to raise serious concerns about the corrupting influence of PACs on the American political process. If there

---

[16]Contributions were adjusted on the basis of the mean campaign expenditures of House incumbents in 1980 ($164,453) and 1992 ($584,730). Specifically, PACs' 1980 contributions were multiplied by the ratio (584,730/164,453). For data on mean expenditures for house candidates from 1978 to 1990, see Frank J. Sorauf, *Inside Campaign Finance: Myths and Realities* (New Haven: Yale University Press, 1992), Table 3.2, p. 67. For 1992 data, see "1992 Congressional Election Spending Jumps 52% to $678 Million," press release, The Federal Election Commission, March 4, 1992.

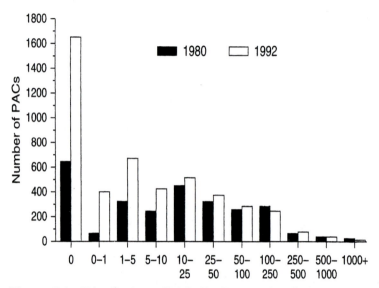

Figure 5.1   Distribution of PACs By Size, 1980 and 1992

are justifiable concerns about the undue influence of PACs, those concerns are relevant only for the few hundred or so largest PACs, not the average PAC.

The Allocation of PAC Money

Perhaps the most widely recognized characteristic of PACs is their preference for contributing to incumbents, especially Democratic incumbents in the U.S. House. Displayed in Table 5.4 are the total dollar amounts and percentages of those totals that PACs contributed to various types of candidates in 1980 and 1992.[17] House Democratic incumbents are increasingly the clear favorite of PACs, followed by House Republican incumbents and then Senate Democratic incumbents. In 1992 52.6 percent of all PAC funds

[17]Total contributions for 1992 ($188,543,690) in Table 5.4 exclude refunded contributions. The comparable number in Table 5.1 includes refunded contributions and therefore is slightly smaller.

Table 5.3　PACs Classified by Total Contributions in 1991–1992

Total Contributions 1991–1992		Distribution of PACs and Total PAC Contributions By Size of PAC			
More Than	Not More Than	Number of PACs	Percent of all PACs	Total Contributions	Percent of Total Spending
	$0	1651	34.9	$0	0.0
$0	$1000	405	8.6	230,626	0.1
$1000	$5000	676	14.3	1,893,120	1.0
$5000	$10,000	414	8.8	2,992,861	1.6
$10,000	$25,000	518	10.9	8,347,218	4.4
$25,000	$50,000	372	7.9	13,206,692	7.0
$50,000	$100,000	293	6.2	29,689,712	11.0
$100,000	$250,000	243	5.1	37,911,353	20.2
$250,000	$500,000	87	1.8	29,551,577	15.7
$500,000	$1,000,000	41	0.9	27,783,797	14.8
$1,000,000		27	0.6	45,427,662	24.2

went to House incumbents, and another 19.4 percent to Senate incumbents. Only 6.6 percent of all PAC money was contributed to House challengers, and only 5.1 percent was given to Senate challengers. Although PACs have traditionally favored Democrats because of their majority status, this has begun to change following the 1994 elections.

Favoritism toward incumbents, especially House incumbents, has increased over the years. Between 1980 and 1992, total PAC contributions to House incumbents increased by 283 percent, from roughly $25.9 million to roughly $99.1 million. At the same time, however, total PAC contributions to House challengers between 1980 and 1992 increased by only 53 percent, from $8.1 million to $12.4 million. A similar, but not so dramatic, change has occurred among Senate candidates. Total PAC contributions to Senate incum-

Table 5.4   Distribution of PAC Contributions among
Candidates, 1992

Candidate	Total PAC Contributions, 1980	Percent	Total PAC Contributions 1992	Percent
House Democrats				
Incumbents	$16,934,165	29.0	$67,106,187	35.6
Challengers	2,342,807	4.0	7,866,490	4.2
Open seats	2,071,601	3.6	13,407,388	7.1
House Republicans				
Incumbents	$9,054,494	15.5	$31,978,807	17.0
Challengers	5,784,253	9.9	4,564,352	2.4
Open seats	3,004,611	5.1	7,394,537	3.9
Senate Democrats				
Incumbents	$7,459,436	12.8	$20,027,952	10.6
Challengers	1,011,366	1.7	6,455,164	3.4
Open seats	816,199	1.4	5,695,317	3.0
Senate Republicans				
Incumbents	$2,862,646	4.9	$16,598,062	8.8
Challengers	5,690,944	9.8	3,176,774	1.7
Open Seats	1,319,888	2.3	4,272,660	2.3
Total	$58,352,410	100.0	$188,543,690	100.0

bents increased by 263 percent from 1980 to 1992, but PAC contributions to Senate challengers increased by only 44 percent.

What accounts for these differences in the percentage changes in contributions to incumbents and challengers? Are PACs contributing to fewer challengers and to more incumbents now than in 1980, or are they making smaller contributions to challengers and larger ones to incumbents? Or is it a combination of both? To answer these questions, it is necessary to compare the number of contributions, the size of the average contribution, and the total

Table 5.5 Average Contributions by the Typical PAC to House
Candidates, 1980–1992

| | House Incumbents | | House Challengers | | |
Year	Size of Contribution	Number of Contributions	Size of Contribution	Number of Contributions	Percent to Incumbent
1980	$365	7.7	$466	2.0	75.1
1982	424	8.3	452	1.6	82.9
1984	509	7.3	609	1.4	81.3
1986	536	6.5	632	0.8	87.3
1988	624	6.7	596	0.9	88.6
1990	765	6.2	801	0.7	89.4
1992	876	6.5	999	0.7	88.8

contributions made by PACs to incumbents and challengers over
time. These comparisons are presented in Tables 5.5 and 5.6.

The average contribution from the typical PAC in Tables 5.5
and 5.6 is defined as the average contribution among those PACs
contributing within $1000 of the median expenditures of all PACs in
a given election cycle.[18] During the 1979–1980 election cycle, for
example, the median PAC among all active PACs contributed a total
of $6445 to all House and Senate candidates, and 168 PACs contrib-
uted between $5445 and $7445. These 168 PACs constitute the
sample of "typical" PACs on which the figures for 1980 in Tables 5.5
and 5.6 are based. These 168 typical PACs contributed a total of
$472,789 to House incumbents in 1979–1980, yielding an average of
total contributions per PAC to House incumbents of $2814. The
average number of contributions to House incumbents among these
typical PACs in 1979–1980 was 7.7. Dividing $2814 by 7.7 gives
$365, the average contribution from the typical PAC to House
incumbents in 1979–1980.

One of the most important aspects of Table 5.5 is how *small* the
typical PAC's average contribution is to House incumbents. Even by

---

[18]It is important to use the median rather than the mean, because the distribution of
PACs by total contributions is not symmetric. Like the distribution of income, a few
very large PACs makes the mean an unrepresentative measure of the center of the
distribution.

1992, with no adjustments made for inflation, the typical PAC gave on average only $876 to House incumbents. Also important is the relatively small number of contributions to House incumbents by the typical PAC—only about six in 1992. These numbers simply confirm what Table 5.3 already revealed: the typical PAC is a small operation.

The trends over time in Table 5.5 are especially noteworthy. Among House candidates, the average *size* of contributions to both challengers and incumbents has *increased* over time, while the average *number* of contributions to both challengers and incumbents has *declined*. For example, between 1980 and 1992, the average contribution to a House incumbent from the typical PAC *grew* from $365 to only $876, while the average number of contributions declined from 7.7 to 6.5.[19] Similarly, the average contribution to challengers grew from a trifling $466 in 1980 to $999 in 1992, but the average number of contributions from the typical PAC to House challengers *declined* from 2.0 to 0.7. There is a noticeable trend, therefore, toward slightly larger contributions, but also slightly fewer contributions.

Although similar trends have occurred for both incumbents and challengers, these trends have occurred at differential *rates* for challengers and incumbents. The average contribution to House incumbents increased by 140 percent between 1980 and 1992, while the average contribution to House challengers grew by only 114 percent; and the average number of contributions to House incumbents decreased by 17 percent, but the average number of contributions to House challengers decreased by 65 percent. The net effect of these differential rates for challengers and incumbents is that *total contributions to House incumbents increased* between 1980 and 1992, while *total contributions to House challengers decreased.*

Average contributions to Senate candidates (Table 5.6) also increased between 1980 and 1992; however, the average number of contributions to incumbents remained roughly constant, while the number of contributions to challengers decreased. Nevertheless, the overall trends for Senate candidates are the same as they are for House candidates. Total contributions to incumbents increased, but total contributions to challengers decreased, resulting in an increase from 58.9 percent to 79 percent in the incumbents' share of contributions.

[19]The number of PACs within $1000 on either side of the median for each campaign year ranged from 121 to 197.

Table 5.6   Average Contributions by the Typical PAC to Senate
Candidates, 1980–1992

| | Senate Incumbents | | Senate Challengers | | |
Year	Size of Contribution	Number of Contributions	Size of Contribution	Number of Contributions	Percent to Incumbent
1980	$573	1.9	$543	1.4	58.9
1982	590	2.4	604	0.6	79.6
1984	762	2.1	674	0.6	79.8
1986	933	2.1	1012	0.8	70.8
1988	1052	2.3	755	0.5	86.5
1990	1186	2.0	1250	0.5	78.8
1992	1298	1.9	1219	0.5	79.0

Overall, Tables 5.4 through 5.6 present unmistakable evidence of a shift in PAC contributions away from challengers and toward incumbents. PACs have been making fewer, but larger contributions to both challengers and incumbents over time; however, the net shift in contributions to incumbents and away from challengers is the result of differential rates in the increase in size and decrease in number of contributions to incumbents and challengers.

One reason that PACs have been concentrating their contributions on fewer candidates, both challengers and incumbents, is that growth in their budgets has not kept pace with the rising costs of campaigning. Displayed in Figure 5.2 are the average contributions of the typical PAC in campaign-adjusted dollars—that is, contributions adjusted for increases in the costs of campaigning as measured by the average expenditures of House and Senate incumbents.[20] Even though the average contributions to both challengers and incumbents have roughly doubled over time, PAC contributions have actually declined in their real value. Adjusted to the costs of campaigning, an $876 contribution in 1992 is comparable to only a $246 contribution in 1980. Even though the average contribution to House incumbents

[20]The adjusted average contributions were computed by weighting (i.e., multiplying) the actual average contribution in year *t* by (mean spending of incumbent in 1980/ mean spending of incumbent in year *t*).

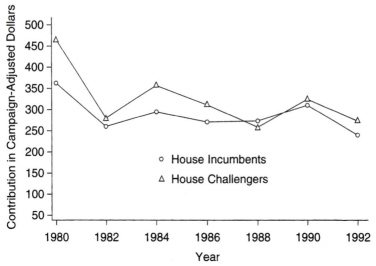

Figure 5.2   Average Contributions of the Typical PAC in
Campaign-Adjusted Dollars, 1980–1992

increased nominally by 140 percent between 1980 and 1992, in real
terms it decreased by 33 percent. This effect has occurred even in
spite of the constant $5000 limit on the allowable contribution from a
PAC to a candidate in a given election, because the average PAC contribution does not approach the maximum allowed by law.

Frank Sorauf has suggested that the shift in PAC investments
away from challengers and toward incumbents was "'forced' on
PACs when it became increasingly difficult for them to influence
policy by affecting the outcomes of House elections."[21] He argues
that in the 1970s many PACs believed they could influence the outcomes of elections, but they learned during the 1980s that their contributions yielded a higher and more certain return when invested in
incumbents and the purchase of access. This realization came about,
argues Sorauf, as incumbents became more aggressive in their fund-
raising. Incumbents began actively soliciting money from PACs,
openly communicating their displeasure when money was not forth-

[21]Sorauf, *Inside Campaign Finance*, p. 68.

coming and thus impressing upon PACs that it was wiser to keep them happy than to invest in their challengers.

Sorauf's argument is consistent with the evidence of a shift in contributions away from challengers and toward incumbents. There is also no doubt that incumbents sometimes pressure PACs for contributions, although we have no firm evidence of how often this occurs. Yet, one can explain the shift in contributions to incumbents without resorting to arguments about the increasing aggressiveness with which incumbents seek PAC money. PACs have had a clear economic incentive to shift spending toward incumbents and away from challengers without having it "forced" on them by incumbents. As the costs of campaigning have skyrocketed, the costs of contributing to affect election outcomes have almost certainly increased at a greater rate than the costs of contributing to gain access. Thus, as PAC budgets have shrunk in real terms, a plausible economic response by PACs is to decrease their demand for electoral outcomes relative to access and shift their investment away from challengers and toward incumbents.[22] Evidence that the shift in spending toward incumbents is associated with the increasing costs of campaigning is reflected in the correlation over time between these variables. The correlation over time between the average campaign expenditures of House incumbents and the incumbents' share of PAC contributions relative to challengers is almost perfect—0.98.[23]

In summary, several important characteristics and trends about PACs are important for placing them in proper perspective. First, the vast majority of political action committees are very modest financial operations. The myth that thousands of PACs regularly funnel huge contributions to congressional incumbents is exactly that—a myth.

---

[22]Electoral and access strategies can be thought of as substitutes in that they are alternative means to the same end. The singular objective of groups is to secure favorable legislative outcomes, and this can be accomplished either by changing the composition of Congress or by influencing the decisions of the current membership. Given that access and electoral strategies are substitutes, the demand for access will increase as the price of the electoral strategy increases, but only if the income effect—that is, the change in demand for access resulting from the change in PAC income as reflected in changing real budgets—does not outweigh the substitution effect.

[23]Figures on the average expenditures of House incumbents over time are taken from Sorauf, *Inside Campaign Finance*, Table 3.2, p. 67; and the percentage of contributions to incumbents is from Table 3.5, above.

The typical PAC contribution to House incumbents is only $876, which in real terms is less than the average $365 contribution in 1980. Moreover, as long as the costs of campaigning continue to rise faster than the rate at which PACs can raise additional money, the relative value of PAC contributions will continue to decline. Second, although PACs have exhibited an increasing preference for giving to incumbents rather than to challengers, the fundamental relationships between incumbents and PACs may be little different today than they were more than a decade ago. PACs may be no more vulnerable, and in fact even less vulnerable, to incumbents' exhortations for money than in the past. The real costs of campaigning have increased over the years to the point that PACs simply get more for their money by investing in incumbents to secure access than investing in challengers to affect election outcomes. Incumbents do not have to pressure PACs for contributions; PACs have a natural economic incentive to invest in them instead of challengers, and this trend is likely to continue until the costs of campaigning are brought under control.

The nature of the relationship between PACs and incumbents has important implications for the connection between PAC contributions and legislative votes or favors. If incumbents threaten and cajole PACs into contributing to their campaigns, then there is in effect a quid pro quo between legislators and PACs: when PACs contribute to their campaigns, incumbents provide legislative favors for them; when PACs do not contribute, incumbents do not provide favors. However, if PACs contribute to incumbents independently of any pressure they might apply, then it is much less likely that PACs exchange contributions for legislative votes or favors.

PAC Contributions and the Exchange of Votes and Favors

Ironically, the availability of public data on campaign financing has probably done more to intensify than to dispel concerns about campaign money and the legislative process. Thanks to public reporting requirements, it is now a relatively simple exercise to compare campaign contributions from specific PACs or groups of PACs and the roll call voting records of members of Congress. Those who engage in such exercises often find and report sizable positive correlations.

The implication that members of Congress exchange their votes for campaign cash undoubtedly contributes to the erosion of public confidence in the political process generally and in the institution of Congress in particular. For this reason alone, it is important to understand why positive correlations between money and votes sometimes exist and what they imply.

The Statistical Relationship between Contributions and Votes

A fact that is widely acknowledged in the scholarly community, but seldom reported by the media, is that the apparent connections between money and voting are generally *spurious*—that is, they result not from selling and buying of votes on the part of PACs and legislators, but instead from more basic partisan and ideological behavior. This point is illustrated by the following celebrated case.

Congressional votes were allegedly exchanged for PAC contributions in 1982 when Congress vetoed a ruling by the Federal Trade Commission (FTC) that would have required car dealers to list "known defects" in used cars on a sticker affixed to the window. The House voted 286–133 on May 26, 1982, to overturn the FTC ruling, but only after the Automobile Dealers Election Action Committee, the PAC of the National Automobile Dealers Association (NADA), contributed $606,976 to incumbent members of the U.S. House of Representatives in 1979–1980 and $433,095 during the 1981–1982 election cycle. The correlation between money and voting was obvious to all. House members who voted against the FTC ruling received almost six times as much money from the PAC of the NADA as supporters of the rule. Moreover, 87 percent of those who received money from the PAC of the NADA voted against the rule, whereas only 34 percent of those who did not receive money voted against the rule.

The strong correlation between contributions from the PAC of the NADA and voting on the FTC rule fueled assertions by interest groups, journalists, and politicians that Congress had been bought. Congress Watch, an affiliate of Ralph Nader's Public Citizen, Inc., released a report linking NADA campaign contributions to cosponsorship of the legislation.[24] Journalist Elizabeth Drew asserted that

[24]See Caroline Mayer, "Study Links Funds, Legislation," *Washington Post*, November 25, 1982, p. D9.

this was one issue where the automobile dealers "bought their way to happiness," and *The New York Times* proclaimed that there was no clearer example of special interests "buying laws they like."[25] Even some members of the House suspected that more than one of their colleagues had been manipulated by the automobile dealers. Representative Thomas Downey, for example, asserted that the outcome of the vote would have been entirely different had there been no PAC contributions.[26] Representative Mickey Edwards of Oklahoma was singled out as one legislator who appeared to have helped the NADA in return for campaign money.[27] Edwards received $2500 from the NADA's PAC in 1981 and then cosponsored the bill to overturn the FTC ruling in 1982. As an apparent reward for his actions, just four months after voting to overturn the FTC rule, Edwards received an additional $2000 contribution from the PAC of the NADA. Edwards himself denied that his behavior was influenced by money from NADA.

Are these assertions of vote buying correct? Before concluding that they are, it is necessary to consider alternative explanations for why the House voted as it did. As it turns out, the House's vote on the FTC ruling coincides not only with PAC contributions from the NADA but also with traditional philosophical differences over governmental regulation of business and the economy. The FTC ruling was plainly one involving governmental regulation of business, pitting probusiness conservatives against consumer-oriented liberals. The ideological division between conservatives and liberals in Congress over the FTC's regulatory decisions intensified generally during the 1970s as the FTC issued consumer-oriented rulings that provoked opposition from the tobacco, insurance, savings and loan, and soft drink industries.[28] To many probusiness conservatives in Congress, the FTC had been exceeding its regulatory authority for

[25]Elizabeth Drew, "Politics and Money—I," *The New Yorker*, December 6, 1982, p. 131; and "Laws for Sale," *New York Times*, May 7, 1982, p. 30.
[26]*Congressional Record*, 97th Congress, 2nd Session (May 26, 1982): H2875.
[27]See Philip M. Stern, *The Best Congress Money Can Buy* (New York: Pantheon Books, 1988), pp. 43–45.
[28]See A. Lee Fritschler, *Smoking and Politics: Policy Making and the Federal Bureaucracy*, Fourth Edition (Englewood Cliffs, NJ: Prentice-Hall, 1989); and Michael Wines, "Doctors, Dairymen Join in Effort to Clip the Talons of the FTC," *National Journal*, September 18, 1982, p. 1592.

years, and the ruling on used cars was the kind of action that convinced them it was time to assert control over the agency. To the liberals in Congress, the used-car ruling was more than just another regulatory safeguard for consumers; it reflected in addition the FTC's broad regulatory authority over consumer affairs, and as such the ruling was an important political test case.

The ideological component to the congressional voting is unmistakable in Table 5.7. Displayed there are the percentages of conservatives, moderates, and liberals who voted for and against the FTC ruling. Conservatives strongly opposed the FTC regulation and liberals supported it. At the extremes of the ideological groupings, 98 percent of all conservatives voted to overturn the FTC's ruling, and 91.9 percent of all liberals voted to maintain it. In between, 87.4 percent of moderate conservatives, but only 60.9 percent of moderates and 31.6 percent of moderate liberals voted to overturn the ruling. Ideology, therefore, is as plausible as campaign contributions for explaining the House's vote on the FTC's ruling.

The reason that ideology and PAC contributions both seem to explain congressional voting is that ideology and PAC contributions are themselves highly correlated. The NADA contributed far more heavily to conservatives than to liberals during the 1979–1980 and 1981–1982 election cycles. Table 5.8 presents the numbers. During 1979–1980, 78.1 percent of all of the NADA's contributions to House candidates went to conservatives or moderate conservatives, and during 1981–1982, 79.1 percent went to conservatives or moderate conservatives. In both election cycles, the NADA's PAC gave only roughly 10 to 12 percent of its money to liberals and moderate liberals, and the average contribution to liberals was eight to nine times less than the average contribution to conservatives. This pattern of NADA giving reflects the generally conservative, probusiness philosophy of most members of the NADA. The close connection between legislators' ideological preferences and their campaign contributions leaves it unclear as to whether money exerts an independent influence on congressional voting or whether its apparent effect is merely a consequence of its association with ideology.

To observe the independent effects of money on voting it is necessary to *control* for the effects of ideology—that is, hold ideology constant—while letting contributions vary. Only if contributions are systematically related to voting after ideological preferences have been

Table 5.7 Percentage of House Members Voting for and against the FTC's Used-Car Ruling by Ideological Position[a]

	Ideology of House Members				
Vote	Conservative	Moderate Conservative	Moderate	Moderate Liberal	Liberal
For FTC Rule	2	12.6	39.1	68.4	91.9
Against FTC Rule	98	87.4	60.9	31.6	8.1
Total	100.0	100.0	100.0	100.0	100.0
N	101	87	46	79	37

[a]The data include only members of both the 96th and 97th Congresses who voted on the rule ($N = 350$). Ideological categories were established using voting scores compiled by the Americans for Democratic Action from 19 votes during 1979. Conservatives were defined as those representatives having ADA scores of 15 or lower, moderate conservatives as those with scores between 15 and 40, moderates with scores between and including 40 and 60, moderate liberals with scores between 60 and 85, and liberals as those having scores equal to or greater than 85.

taken into account would it be appropriate to conclude that contributions influence voting. One way to evaluate the independent relationship between contributions and voting is to assess the relationship *within* different ideological groups of representatives. If moderate conservatives, for example, who receive contributions behave no differently than moderate conservatives who do not receive contributions, then it is more likely that ideology, not contributions, accounts for any behavioral differences among representatives.

Table 5.9 reports the relationship between contributions and voting within ideological groups of representatives. The entries in the table represent the estimated probabilities of a representative's voting to overturn the FTC's ruling under two situations: one corresponds to the hypothetical situation in which the representative received no contributions from the NADA—the voting probabilities

Table 5.8 PAC Contributions by the NADA and Ideology of
U.S. House Members

PAC Money	Ideology of House Members				
	Conservative	Moderate Conservative	Moderate	Moderate Liberal	Liberal
Average NADA Contribution in 1979–1980	$2261	$2235	$1123	$723	$256
Percentage of all NADA Contributions, 1979–1980	42.0	36.1	9.6	10.5	1.8
Average NADA Contribution in 1981–1982	$1916	$1634	$960	$454	$218
Percentage of all NADA Contributions, 1981–1982	45.4	33.7	10.5	8.4	2.0
N	102	89	47	80	39

are estimated solely on the basis of representatives' ideological positions—and the other corresponds to the amount of contributions
the representative actually received from the NADA.[29] The larger
the difference between this probability estimate and the first, the
larger the influence of campaign contributions.

The estimated effects of PAC contributions on voting within any
of the groups in Table 5.9 are not very large. Even in the absence of

[29]These probabilities were estimated from a probit analysis in which legislators' roll
call votes were regressed on their ADA scores and campaign contributions from the
NADA in 1989–1980. The estimation process yielded the following results: Vote =
1.85 + 0.00016 (NADA dollars) −0.0338 (ADA score). The estimated *t*-statistics were
8.39, 2.93, and −9.88 for the coefficients, respectively.

Table 5.9 Estimated Probabilities of Voting against the FTC's Used-Car Ruling with and without Campaign Contributions

Representative's Ideological Position	Estimated Probabilities of Voting to Overturn FTC's Used-Car Ruling	
	No NADA Contributions (Hypothetical)	Actual NADA Contributions
Conservative	0.95	0.97
Moderate Conservative	0.83	0.89
Moderate	0.56	0.62
Moderate Liberal	0.26	0.30
Liberal	0.09	0.10

contributions from the NADA's PAC, conservatives are predicted to vote against, and liberals for, the FTC's ruling with near certainty. The average marginal increase in the probability of opposing the ruling is only 0.02 for conservatives and 0.01 for liberals. The largest effect of campaign contributions is among moderates, who are predicted to increase their probability of opposing the used-car rule from 0.56 to 0.62 as a result of the contributions they received from the NADA. Across the entire sample of representatives, the average marginal increase in the probability of opposing the FTC because of the NADA's contributions is 0.04. In other words, the percentage of representatives voting to overturn the FTC's ruling because of the PAC money they received is four points higher than what one would predict on the basis of ideological preferences alone.[30] In the partic-

[30]This implies that campaign contributions may have changed the votes of roughly 14 representatives (0.04 times 350 members of both the 96th and 97th Congresses). Even this number of vote changes is probably higher than what actually occurred, because these predicted changes are based on statistical estimates that have not been purged of constituency or lobbying effects.

ular case of Representative Edwards, PAC contributions from the NADA increased his opposition to the FTC rule by a factor of 0.06, from 0.93 to 0.98. With an ADA score of only 11, Mr. Edwards was easily and correctly predicted to oppose the FTC rule even without the financial incentives provided by the NADA. Implications that the car dealers purchased his vote is therefore a classic case of spurious reasoning.

Overall, then, there is little basis for concluding that the car dealers "bought their way to happiness" on this issue or that the outcome of the voting in the House was determined by PAC contributions from the NADA. The vast majority of representatives voted with their ideological predispositions. Although campaign money may have changed a handful of voting decisions, and perhaps solidified a few others, the House would have voted overwhelmingly against the FTC's ruling even if the NADA had contributed no money whatsoever to representatives' election campaigns.

The lack of any clear evidence of vote buying in this one celebrated case is consistent with many other empirical studies of PAC contributions and voting. Employing sophisticated statistical techniques and large numbers of cases, scholars have generally failed to turn up consistent and substantial evidence that representatives' campaign contributions directly affect their roll call decisions.[31] Only when scholars aggregate together all of a representative's labor PAC contributions, or all of his or her corporate PAC contributions, and relate these to broad indexes of support for labor or business is

---

[31]The following studies report very weak or else no support for the hypothesis that PAC contributions determine roll call voting: Henry W. Chappell, "Campaign Contributions and Congressional Voting: A Simultaneous Probit-Tobit Model," *Review of Economics and Statistics* 62 (1982): 77–83; William P. Welch, "Campaign Contributions and Legislative Voting: Milk Money and Dairy Price Supports," *Western Political Quarterly* 35 (1982): 478–495; John R. Wright, "PACs, Contributions, and Roll Calls: An Organizational Perspective," *American Political Science Review* 79 (1985): 400–414; Jonathan Barry Forman, "PAC Contributions and Effective Corporate Tax Rates: An Empirical Study," *Akron Tax Journal* 5 (1988): 65–74; Janet Grenzke, "Shopping in the Congressional Supermarket: The Currency is Complex," *American Journal of Political Science* 33 (1989): 1–24; and John R. Wright, "Contributions, Lobbying, and Committee Voting in the U.S. House of Representatives," *American Political Science Review* 84 (1990): 417–438.

money found to have statistically significant effects.[32] At such high levels of aggregation, however, money becomes a proxy for other important interest group activities, principally Washington and grassroots lobbying. It is not clear, therefore, whether the observed effects in these cases are due to contributions or to lobbying.[33] Finally, several studies have suggested that PAC contributions are most likely to have large effects on roll call votes that have low public visibility.[34] Although these results are suggestive, a systematic analysis of a large number of both high and low visibility issues is yet to be conducted.

The general absence of any direct connection between PAC contributions and roll call voting does not lay the entire issue of money and influence to rest, however. Even though PAC contributions do not seem to influence roll call voting, they might affect other important legislative behavior such as withholding an amendment during a committee markup, providing information about procedural plans for considering amendments to a bill, or

[32]See, for example, James B. Kau and Paul H. Rubin, *Congressmen, Constituents, and Contributors* (Boston: Martinus Nijhoff, 1982); Gregory M. Saltzman, "Congressional Voting on Labor Issues: The Role of PACs," *Industrial and Labor Relations Review* 40 (1987): 163–179; Allen Wilhite and John Theilmann, "Labor PAC Contributions and Labor Legislation: A Simultaneous Logit Approach," *Public Choice* 53 (1987): 267–276; and Al Wilhite and Chris Paul, "Corporate Campaign Contributions and Legislative Voting," *Quarterly Review of Economics and Business* 29 (1989): 73–83.

[33]Although the estimated effects of money on voting are generally quite weak, several analyses have found substantial statistical effects of lobbying on voting. See Lawrence S. Rothenberg, *Linking Citizens to Government: Interest Group Politics at Common Cause* (New York: Cambridge University Press, 1992); Laura I. Langbein and Mark A. Lotwis, "The Political Efficacy of Lobbying and Money: Gun Control in the U.S. House," *Legislative Studies Quarterly* 14 (1990): 414–440; Wright, "Contributions, Lobbying, and Committee Voting in the U.S. House of Representatives"; and Gregory A. Caldeira and John R. Wright, "Lobbying for Justice: Organized Interests and the Bork Nomination in the United States Senate," Paper presented at the annual meeting of the American Political Science Association, Chicago, IL, September 1992.

[34]See Diana M. Evans, "PAC Contributions and Roll Call Voting: Conditional Power," in Allan J. Cigler and Burdette A. Loomis, *Interest Group Politics*, Second Edition (Washington, DC: Congressional Quarterly Press, 1986); Woodrow Jones and K. Robert Keiser, "Issue Visibility and the Effects of PAC Money," *Social Science Quarterly* 68 (1987): 170–176.; and Jean Reith Schroedel, "Campaign Contributions and Legislative Outcomes," *Western Political Quarterly* 40 (1987): 371–389.

even access.[35] Unfortunately, it is virtually impossible to obtain systematic data on these sorts of favors, and thus one cannot rule out the possibility of these types of exchanges on strictly empirical grounds. For this reason it is important to consider the relationship between money and influence on purely theoretical grounds.

Theoretical Models of Money and Influence

A variety of problems inherent in statistical analyses of contributions and voting cast some doubt on the validity of empirical findings. There is, of course, the problem of measurement. Some of the most important aspects of congressional behavior are not easily quantified. The extent to which representatives work behind the scenes with lobbyists to draft bills or amendments, the extent to which representatives lobby their colleagues on behalf of interest groups, and the amount of access that legislators grant to lobbyists are, for all practical purposes, unobservable. All of these activities might be closely connected to campaign contributions, but there is no way to tell for sure. There is also the problem of correctly isolating and estimating the statistical effects of money. A group's campaign contributions are often correlated with its lobbying efforts, so that what appears to be an effect of lobbying might really be an effect of contributions and vice versa. Finally, there is the problem of circular causality. Groups might give contributions to representatives as rewards for voting support in the past or as inducements for voting support in the future. In either case, money and votes will be correlated, but sorting out the direction of causality is a difficult, although not intractable, statistical problem.

For those suspicious of statistical analyses, there is fortunately an alternative: theoretical modeling. Theoretical modeling proceeds by making basic assumptions about the goals of PACs and legislators and then logically deriving propositions about how they will behave. The advantage of this approach is that because it is unfettered by data, any assumptions are possible. It can be assumed, for example,

---

[35]One important and promising effort along these lines is Richard L. Hall and Frank W. Wayman, "Buying Time: Moneyed Interests and the Mobilization of Bias in Congressional Committees," *American Political Science Review* 84 (1990): 797–820.

that legislators want to raise campaign money, that interest groups want particular bills passed, and that both PACs and legislators will agree on the size of the contribution that a particular vote or legislative favor is worth. Although these assumptions may be objectionable to some on either empirical or normative grounds, it is important to investigate their logical implications. After all, many journalists and politicians make these assumptions implicitly without rigorously analyzing whether or not they lead to plausible propositions about the actual behaviors of legislators and contributors.

Political scientists have investigated two general theoretical models. In one, groups exchange contributions for specific legislative favors; in the other, they help elect candidates whose ideological positions are closest to their own. The first is essentially a model of *legislative* influence; the second a model of *electoral* influence.[36] The legislative model assumes that candidates promise specific legislative services if elected in exchange for campaign contributions and that they honor these agreements if elected.[37] In this respect, there is an explicit quid pro quo between contributions and favors, making contributions essentially legal bribes, or what journalist Brooks Jackson has termed "honest graft."[38] The electoral model assumes that voters are uncertain about candidates' policy stands during election campaigns but that candidates can use money to advertise their positions and attract voter support.[39] To attract campaign contributions, however, candidates must establish policy platforms that are attractive to interest groups, which may involve moving away from a position most preferred by the voters. Candidates will take positions favored by interest groups in order to attract contributions only if the contributions are sufficient to offset any resulting losses in voter

[36]For an early version of these two basic approaches, see William Welch, "The Allocation of Political Monies: Economic Interest Groups," *Public Choice* 35 (1980): 97–120.

[37]For examples of these models, see David P. Baron, "Service-Induced Campaign Contributions and the Electoral Equilibrium," *Quarterly Journal of Economics* 104 (1989): 45–72; and James M. Snyder, Jr., "Campaign Contributions as Investments: The U.S. House of Representatives, 1980–1986," *Journal of Political Economy* 98 (1990): 1195–1227.

[38]Brooks Jackson, *Honest Graft* (New York: Knopf, 1988).

[39]The standard model is that of David Austen-Smith, "Interest Groups, Campaign Contributions, and Probabilistic Voting," *Public Choice* 54 (1987): 123–139.

support through additional campaign advertising. In contrast to the legislative model, there is no quid pro quo between interest groups and candidates—candidates do not *agree* to change their positions in exchange for contributions; rather, interest groups simply support the candidate who establishes the most favorable policy platform, and candidates adjust their platforms only if they can use any ensuing contributions to increase their expected vote percentage through advertising.

Some of the predictions from both the legislative and electoral models are consistent with some observable behavior of both groups and legislators. Still, there are a number of concerns with both types of models that cast doubt on whether the underlying processes are in fact occurring.[40] The electoral model assumes that campaign contributions can be converted into votes through advertising, but exactly how this occurs is not entirely clear. Also, once elected, candidates are assumed to adhere to the policy positions they took during the campaign, but whether and why candidates do so is unclear. The legislative model assumes the existence of a market and contractual agreements between candidates and contributors—candidates offer services and contributors supply money—but how such a market actually operates and how implicit contracts or agreements between groups and legislators will be honored or enforced is ambiguous. The legislative model also assumes that legislators can actually deliver the legislative favors they promise. Yet, it is not clear if or how a single legislator might settle an antitrust action for a contributor, establish an import quota, or deliver a tax break. It is assumed that legislators have monopoly power to provide legislative policy favors or else that the favors they provide are private, nonpolicy favors such as finding lost social security checks.

Another criticism of these two basic models is that the legislative model considers only the effects of money on the legislative process and the electoral model considers only how groups might distribute contributions to influence election outcomes. In reality, PACs may

---

[40]For excellent reviews of both types of models, see Rebecca Morton and Charles Cameron, "Elections and the Theory of Campaign Contributions: A Survey and Critical Analysis," *Economics and Politics* 4 (1992): 80–107; and David Austen-Smith, "Perspectives on Public Choice," in D. C. Mueller (ed.), *Handbook of Public Choice* (Oxford: Basil-Blackwell, 1996).

care about both election outcomes and legislative outcomes, and thus it is important to consider the relationship between these two objectives. One analysis that combines both concerns in a single model is that by McCarty and Rothenberg. Their conclusion is that PACs are more likely to contribute to obtain legislative access than to affect election outcomes.[41] They note that money given for access results in a private benefit to the group, whereas money given for electoral reasons provides collective benefits to all groups supporting a given candidate. Consequently, PACs must contribute to achieve access, but to achieve their electoral objectives they can free ride on the contributions of other groups. The effect of many groups behaving this way is that contributions given for access will crowd out contributions given for electoral reasons.

Despite the criticisms that have been leveled at both the electoral and the legislative models, one must remember that the purpose of these models is not to argue that there is in fact a quid pro quo relationship between campaign contributions and legislative services or that candidates do in fact adjust their electoral positions in order to attract money. The purpose of these models is simply to specify the assumptions and conditions necessary for such behaviors to occur. That neither model is fully satisfactory illustrates the difficulty of fully specifying a process whereby campaign contributions are exchanged for legislative favors or where PACs simply contribute to influence election outcomes. Clearly, it is one thing for journalists and pundits to make far-reaching claims about vote buying, honest graft, and so forth; it is quite another, however, to develop a logical structure that fully and consistently supports such claims. Although moving from the empirical world to the theoretical world avoids one set of problems, it introduces others. Given how complicated the theoretical conditions are for PACs to purchase influence, it is little wonder that empirical analyses do not find stronger effects of contributions on voting. The upshot is that no matter which approach one prefers, there still is no compelling evidence that PAC contributions

---

[41]Nolan McCarty and Lawrence Rothenberg, "The Strategic Decisions of Political Action Committees," manuscript, Carnegie Mellon University and the University of Rochester, 1994.

have any direct and independent influence on the legislative behavior of members of Congress.

PACs and Information

If PACs have no direct and independent impact on legislative behavior, then exactly what is their value? The answer is not that they determine election outcomes. Although aggregate contributions play a critical role in congressional elections, a single PAC contribution has little effect. Green and Krasno have estimated that a $1000 expenditure increases an incumbent's vote by 0.037 percent and a challenger's vote by only 0.017 percent.[42] Not even a large PAC can claim to have a substantively significant impact on election outcomes.

The answer to the question of what is the value of PACs can be summarized in a single word: access. PAC contributions help legislators determine which interest groups are most likely to provide useful lobbying information and thus which groups are worth listening to and which are not. As hackneyed as this explanation is, it is not a simple one. Legislators do not simply sell their time for money. To understand how money relates to access, it is necessary once again to turn to an informational perspective.

Political action committees complement the lobbying process through the acquisition and transmission of information in two important ways. First, group officials acquire a good deal of constituency information through the maintenance and operation of a PAC. Groups that have PACs are likely to have better electoral and constituency information than groups that do not have PACs, and thus affiliation with a PAC can enhance lobbyists' credibility when they offer information about constituents' policy preferences or electoral possibilities. Second, because a PAC contribution expresses overt support for a candidate's general policy orientation, groups can use PAC contributions to inform representatives that they share

[42]Figures are for campaigns in which challengers spend $100,000 and up. See Donald Philip Green and Jonathan S. Krasno, "Salvation for the Spendthrift Incumbent: Reestimating the Effects of Campaign Spending in House Elections," *American Journal of Political Science* 32 (1988): 884–907.

similar policy concerns. Information about similarity of preferences is important to legislators trying to decide which of many interest groups to depend on for policy or electoral information.

Information and the Operation of PACs

One informational benefit from operating a PAC is that a group's leaders and lobbyists acquire general information about the mobilizational capabilities of the organization. Through fund-raising efforts, they learn about the kinds of issues and appeals that motivate their members to contribute money to the PAC; they learn what constitutes a hot issue or an area of concern for their members; and they learn what the financial participation limits are within their organizations. Those issues that induce individuals to contribute money to a PAC are also likely to be strong motivating forces for grassroots lobbying campaigns and ultimately for election campaigns.

The repeated exercise of asking members to contribute money to the group's campaign fund helps keep individuals attuned to congressional politics and involved in the organization. Michael Malbin has argued that "forming a PAC helps a corporation or association get its members or employees active in other aspects of politics and it helps them get members of employees to respond when it is time for grassroots lobbying."[43] This is especially true for organizations that rely upon networks of activists rather than direct mail campaigns to raise money.[44] Still, no matter how fund-raising is conducted, the exercise itself helps organizational leaders stay in touch with the membership, giving them additional information on levels of activism and interest while at the same time educating and alerting the rank and file to important political developments.

Another informational benefit from operating a PAC is that group officials learn a great deal about congressional races around the country. Even though most congressional contests are not close

[43]Michael J. Malbin, "Looking Back at the Future of Campaign Finance Reform: Interest Groups and American Elections," in Michael J. Malbin (ed.), *Money and Politics in the United States* (Chatham, NJ: Chatham House Publishers, 1984), p. 264.
[44]See R. Kenneth Godwin, *One Billion Dollars of Influence: The Direct Marketing of Politics* (Chatham, NJ: Chatham House, 1988), Chapter 4.

in the final analysis, many are volatile, or potentially volatile, over the course of the campaign. A well-run PAC will stay abreast of electoral situations and know when and where to contribute money either to head off potential threats to incumbents or to spur on challengers.

PAC managers can acquire information about congressional races through a variety of sources. One source is the network of volunteers that many PACs rely upon within congressional districts to knock on doors and make telephone calls asking fellow group members to contribute money to the PAC. These activists are motivated by a variety of factors: a love of politics, the satisfaction of being involved in a cooperative effort, a desire for a sense of civic accomplishment, professional loyalty or commitment to the organization, and a desire to gain influence within the organization. Through their intense political interest and involvement, these activists are often quite knowledgeable about electoral politics at the congressional district level. They know who the likely challengers will be, they know the political strengths and weaknesses of the candidates, and they know the issues and concerns of the voters in the district.

Many of the larger, decentralized PACs employ local, state, or regional directors to coordinate the activities of the PAC, and these officials are often another important source of electoral information. AT&T PAC, for example, employs state directors who also operate as state and federal lobbyists. These officials frequently have longstanding relationships with members of Congress, sometimes dating back to state legislative races, and thus they know the electoral histories and circumstances of candidates extremely well.[45] Providing electoral information to the national PAC officers is an important aspect of the job of these state directors, and the information they acquire is a valuable asset not only in their role as PAC officials but also in their role as lobbyists.

Another source of electoral information for PAC officials is through other political groups. Corporate PACs, for example, often belong to one or several trade groups. Chemical producers may

[45]See Robert E. Mutch, "AT&T PAC: A Pragmatic Giant," in Robert Biersack, Paul S. Herrnson, and Clyde Wilcox (eds.), *Risky Business: PAC Decisionmaking in Congressional Elections* (Armonk, NY: M. E. Sharpe, 1994).

belong to the Chemical Manufacturers Association, the National Association of Manufacturers, and the National Agricultural Chemicals Association. These larger organizations help facilitate the flow of information between PAC officials and lobbyists from different smaller organizations. Information about close electoral races, especially those involving incumbents who are friends of the industry, is often useful to PAC officials from local or regional PACs who do not have the benefit of broad national memberships to inform them about key races. Corporate PAC officials can also turn to "lead" PACs such as the Business Industry Political Action Committee (BIPAC) and the Public Affairs Council, both of which collect and disseminate information on congressional races around the country. BIPAC, for example, maintains a separate Education Fund supported by corporation and trade association treasury funds, and this fund supports the publication of a newsletter that provides details on House and Senate races. This publication is available to contributors to the fund, who also are invited to monthly briefings.[46]

PACs also acquire information from political parties, candidates, candidates' staffs, and their own professional staffs.[47] The National Committee for an Effective Congress (NCEC), for example, acquires polling data from the Democratic Congressional Campaign Committee, which it then supplements with precinct-level election data. In addition, the NCEC staff visits candidates' campaign headquarters and scrutinizes their budgets, strategies, and fund-raising. The NCEC staff also consults with political aides to statewide officeholders. As Paul Herrnson explains, these aides are "considered ideal sources of information because a major portion of their time is spent keeping tabs on the activities of politicians living in the state."[48] Especially useful to the NCEC is information these aides provide on nonincumbent candidates' levels of local support, relationships with the press, and so forth.

[46]See Candice J. Nelson, "BIPAC: Trying to Lead in an Uncertain Electoral Climate," in Biersack, Herrnson, and Wilcox (eds.), *Risky Business*.

[47]Evidence and further discussion can be found in Diana Owen, "Information Resources for PAC Decision-Making," presented at the annual meeting of the American Political Science Association, Washington, DC, 1988.

[48]Paul Herrnson, "The NCEC: Liberalism, Partisanship, and Electoral Innovation," in Biersack, Herrnson, and Wilcox (eds.), *Risky Business*.

Political action committees can ill-afford to invest in candidates who have little chance of winning. Losing investments provide no legislative access and detract from the organization's reputation of electoral expertise. PACs avoid these pitfalls by continuously and assiduously collecting electoral information, and for this reason groups with PACs may have some marginal advantage in information and expertise over groups that do not. Groups with PACs are more likely to know about the specific electoral circumstances of incumbents, and they are more likely to know about the organizational capabilities and concerns of their members. A PAC constitutes a tangible and visible symbol of an organization's involvement in electoral politics and the political education and mobilization of its members, and this is an important asset when it comes to lobbying.

PACs, Information, and Access

The paramount claim about campaign contributions is that they buy access. The gist of this claim is simply that there are too many lobbyists and too little time in the day for legislators to meet with all of those who wish to see them. Legislators solve this problem, or so it is claimed, by applying a simple rule: they grant access first to lobbyists from organizations that have contributed money to their campaigns. One even hears stories from time to time about representatives who keep lists of contributors in their desk drawers and check the lists before scheduling appointments with lobbyists.

Legislators who employ this rule literally are simply selling their time for campaign cash. Although legislators desperate for money might use such a rule, a simple exchange of time for money is not the most efficient way to gather information. Provided that legislators seek information from lobbyists who are eager to provide it, their decisions to grant or deny access should be undertaken with an eye toward acquiring information, not merely exchanging time for money. The simple and direct exchange of money for access, therefore, is incompatible with an informational theory of interest group influence. An informational perspective implies that legislators grant access to contributors because contributing groups are more likely to provide useful lobbying information than noncontributors.

An informational theory linking contributions, access, and lobbying builds from the idea that legislators are more likely to receive reliable information from organizations that share their policy concerns. Other things being equal, a legislator is more likely to believe a group's information when the group's interest is the same, because it is not necessary for a group to mislead a representative with similar views in order to gain support. A prolabor legislator, for example, should not be surprised to hear a business group argue that the passage of NAFTA would not result in any long-term loss of union jobs, but knowing the business group does not share his or her same concern for union jobs, the legislator might view this claim with some suspicion. A probusiness legislator, however, upon hearing the same message would be more inclined to believe the group, for there is no need for the business group to stretch the truth in order to receive his or her vote. In general, the closer the positions of the group and the legislator, the more believable is the group's information.

Critical to an informational theory of money and access is the idea that legislators are often uncertain about groups' policy positions. If legislators always knew the policy positions of groups exactly, then campaign contributions would provide no additional information about which groups had the most reliable lobbying information. Groups would be able to receive access even without making contributions. Thus, a connection between money, access, and informational lobbying implies legislators are often uncertain about the extent to which their interests coincide with those of various interest groups.

Some fragmentary evidence suggests that legislators do often experience uncertainty about interest groups' policy positions. The sheer number of organizations located in Washington, D.C.—nearly 12,000—makes it virtually impossible for any public official to be familiar with the political agendas of most groups. In the agricultural policy domain alone, there are more than 200 active organizations and hundreds of recurring issues. The 1985 farm bill contained more than 160 major provisions and 18 titles. With so many possible combinations of groups and issue positions, even representatives of agricultural districts were not familiar with many of the organizations and their positions. William Browne interviewed members of Congress, their staffs, and agricultural policy makers to determine which agricultural organizations were most identifiable during debate over the 1985 farm bill and why. According to Browne, "The most striking point that these officials raised about the expanded universe of agricultural interests was about the confusion it creates. 'Who are these guys?' was the often-repeated question."[49]

Further evidence of the difficulty that policy makers often have in identifying the issue concerns of particular organizations is the extent to which groups attempt to establish identities, both to their members and to the Washington community, by strategically carving out "issue niches." Again, according to William Browne, organizations tend to select issues for lobbying that will have broad support among their members, can galvanize their members for grassroots action, have not already been claimed by another organization, are relatively inexpensive to research, and are winnable.[50] One consequence of all of these constraints is that the issue niches of most organizations tend to be narrow in scope. Another consequence is that it is difficult to predict exactly on which issues an organization will take a position. Groups frequently do not lobby on issues imputed to be in their interests.[51]

Legislators are most likely to be familiar with the agendas of highly visible, single-purpose organizations, but even these organizations sometimes take unpredictable positions. Many experienced politicians were surprised, for example, when the National Rifle Association (NRA) took a neutral position on Robert Bork's nomination to the Supreme Court. As a federal appellate judge, Bork had ruled favorably toward gun owners and on one occasion had even

---

[49]William P. Browne, "Issue Niches and the Limits of Interest Group Influence," in Allan J. Cigler and Burdette A. Loomis (eds.), *Interest Group Politics*, Third Edition (Washington, DC: Congressional Quarterly Press, 1991), p. 359.

[50]William P. Browne, "Organized Interests and Their Issue Niches: A Search for Pluralism in a Policy Domain," *Journal of Politics* 52 (1990): 477–509.

[51]Browne asked USDA officials, legislators, and legislative staff to identify which specific groups would take a position and lobby on range of agricultural issues. He then asked lobbyists for those groups whether they in fact took a position and lobbied on each issue. Eighty percent of the groups lobbied on less than 75 percent of the issues imputed to be in their interests, and 50 percent of the organizations lobbied on less than half of the issues imputed to be in the interests. See Browne, "Issue Niches and the Limits of Interest Group Influence, p. 350, and "Organized Interests and Their Issue Niches," p. 506.

ruled squarely in favor of the NRA. Yet, the NRA maintained a neutral position throughout the nomination campaign.[52]

Working from a premise of uncertainty about the similarity of groups' and legislators' policy positions, David Austen-Smith has formalized a model of money, access, and information.[53] He shows that under some circumstances it is perfectly rational for a legislator to conclude that a contributing group is more likely to share his or her policy concerns than a noncontributing group and, therefore, grant access only to the contributing group. By making a contribution, the contributing group in effect says to the legislator, "We have similar interests; let's work together." Believing this message to be true, the legislator grants access. As in any lobbying situation, however, there is always the possibility of misrepresentation. Groups that do *not* share the legislator's policy concerns will sometimes contribute in order to give the appearance that they share similar concerns. It is possible, therefore, for PACs occasionally to manipulate legislators' beliefs about the similarity of their interests.

In summary, an information-based theory of contributions and access involves two basic contribution strategies. Under one strategy, groups contribute to representatives with whom they already share similar interests as a way of reinforcing those representatives' beliefs about the commonality of their concerns. Under an alternative strategy, groups contribute to representatives with whom they have little in common in hopes of creating an impression of common concerns, or establishing commonality where none exists. Both strategies can be successful, but with very different implications for the representative process. The first implies that existing representational concerns of legislators will be reinforced, as groups contribute to legislators whose preferences are similar from the start. The second, when successful, implies that legislators will establish links to groups, and possibly develop representational interests, that they would not ordinarily have. A frequently cited concern in this regard is that PACs forge ties

[52]Speculation about why the NRA remained neutral can be found in Patrick B. McGuigan and Dawn M. Weyrich, *Ninth Justice: The Fight for Bork* (Free Congress Research and Education Foundation: Washington, DC, 1990), pp. 78–80.

[53]See David Austen-Smith, "Campaign Contributions and Access," *American Political Science Review*, 89 (1995).

between legislators and organized interests outside of their geographic districts. Although an informational theory of money, access, and lobbying helps answer the question of what is the value of PACs, it also raises important questions about PACs and the representative process.

PACs and Representation

The concern that many political observers and practitioners share about PACs extends beyond the issue of buying votes, favors, or access. Even more fundamental is the concern that PACs are shifting the attention of representatives away from local, electoral constituencies to broader, financial constituencies. Since much of the money representatives must raise for their election campaigns comes from outside their geographic districts, representatives must face both an electoral constituency and a financial constituency. Frank Sorauf describes this "two constituencies" problem as follows:

> [W]e have in the growth of PACs a new and developing representational system, one based on specific occupational or issue loyalties. To some extent it supplements the system of political parties. While the parties function in the local electoral constituency, the PACs work in a more national and functional constituency. Years ago the votes and the resources that elected a candidate came from the same place and the same people. They no longer do.[54]

The potential threat that PACs pose to geographic representation has been noted by others, including political scientist David Adamany, who argues that PACs "compete with local constituents;" and by Lee Ann Elliot, a former PAC staff person and member of the Federal Election Commission (FEC), who describes PACs as the "precincts of the 80s."[55]

Given legal reporting requirements, it is virtually impossible to determine precisely how much money candidates receive from PACs

---

[54]Frank J. Sorauf, "Who's in Charge? Accountability in Political Action Committees," *Political Science Quarterly* 99 (1985): 613.
[55]David Adamany, "PACs and the Democratic Financing of Politics," *Arizona Law Review* 22 (1980): 596–597; and Lee Ann Elliot, "Political Action Committees—Precincts of the 80s," *Arizona Law Review* 22 (1980): 541.

and individuals outside their geographic districts. Since 1980, only individuals who contribute more than $500 to a PAC or candidate must report their contributions to the Federal Election Commission, making it possible only to trace the geographic origins of relatively large individual contributions.[56] Analyses of these traceable contributions, however, suggest that PAC contributions flow across district boundaries frequently. On the basis of reported individual contributions to PACs, Janet Grenzke estimates that only about 2 percent of the PAC contributions to House incumbents come from PACs located within their districts and only about 16 percent come from PACs located within the incumbent's state.[57] She concludes that "it becomes less and less realistic to describe the U.S. political system using a narrow, district-based conceptualization of representation."[58]

While it may be true that PAC money is typically raised in one district and allocated in others, the threat that this poses to geographic representation is not entirely clear. When PACs move money across district boundaries, it may be into districts in which the same economic or occupational interests prevail. Consequently, the possibility that money moves fluidly across district boundaries does not necessarily imply that extradistrict concerns are being brought to the attention of legislators.

One situation in which the interests of a group and legislator intersect naturally is that in which some of the legislator's constituents belong to the interest group. For example, the AFL-CIO is likely to have a strong organizational presence in districts with a large unionized workforce, and representatives from those districts are likely to share many of the same concerns as does the union. In

---

[56]The vast majority of individual contributions to PACS are less than $250. Typically individual contributions to PACs are $75 for associations, $100 for corporations, and $20 for unions. These figures are taken from a national survey of PAC officials. See footnote 61 for details.

[57]See Table 2 in Janet Grenzke, "Comparing Contributions to U.S. House Members from Outside Their Districts," *Legislative Studies Quarterly* 13 (1988): 83–103. Grenzke's analysis is based only on individual contributions to PACs of $500 or more (except for 1977–1978, which is based on contributions of $100 or more). However, the vast majority of individual contributions to PACs are less than $100. Grenzke assumes that all PACs treat large and small contributions equally.

[58]Ibid., p. 95.

general, the greater the organizational presence of the group in the legislator's district, the more likely it is that the legislator's political and policy interests will coincide with those of the group. Consequently, even if PACs redistribute money across district lines, if they do so in such a way that they concentrate money in districts where their economic or occupational interests are already well established, they may enhance the representation of *local* interests. In such instances, PAC money would enhance extradistrict, not extradistrict, ties with the representative, even when the money comes from outside the district.

As mentioned earlier, an information-based theory of campaign contributions and access does not specify to what extent PACs draw together lobbyists and legislators with fundamentally dissimilar interests. The theory suggests only that this is a possibility, and in light of concerns about the representative process, one that must be considered seriously. Although extant theory is silent on the question of whether PACs reinforce or undermine the connections that legislators have with their local constituents, empirical analysis is not. The available empirical evidence indicates that PACs generally *reinforce* existing constituency ties rather than create new ones. Eismeier and Pollock, after comparing the contribution patterns of PACs with headquarters in Washington to those with headquarters outside of Washington, observed that PACs often contribute to candidates in the same state or region in which the PACs are headquartered. They conclude that "there appears to be a good deal more localism in the behavior of political action committees than the prevailing wisdom would suggest," and that "the nationalization of campaign finance may not undermine, and in fact may reflect, the local representation of functional interests."[59]

After studying the extent to which PACs contribute to legislators from districts in which they have little or no organizational

[59]P. 16 in Eismeier, Theodore J. and Philip H. Pollock, III, "The Political Geography of Political Action Committees: National Cash and the Local Connection in Congressional Elections." Paper presented at the annual meeting of the American Political Science Association, Washington, DC, 1988, and p. 15 in Eismeier, Theodore J. and Philip H. Pollock, III. "The Geopolitics of PACs." Paper presented at the annual meeting of the Midwest Political Science Association, Chicago, IL, 1985.

membership base, I reached a similar conclusion.[60] The contribution patterns of 30 corporate and trade association PACs with interests before the House Agriculture and Ways and Means Committees provided virtually no support for the hypothesis that PACs contribute disproportionately to districts where they are organizationally weak. To the contrary, these PACs concentrated their contributions in districts where they already had a clear organizational presence.

Additional evidence consistent with this general result is provided by responses of PAC directors in a national survey. During the summer and fall of 1988, I mailed questionnaires to all labor and trade association PACs as well as to a randomly selected sample of roughly 40 percent of all corporate PACs registered with the FEC. The final tally of responses included information from 364 PACs on how fundraising was conducted within each PAC, who within each organization was most responsible for contribution decisions, and various other organizational characteristics and practices. Overrepresented in the final sample were large PACs and association PACs, but otherwise the sample was quite representative in terms of the percentage of money that all PACs contributed to Democrats and to incumbents.[61]

To gain some insight into the extent to which PACs reinforce existing organizational connections to representatives or introduce new ones, PAC officials were asked, "About how often does your PAC contribute to a U.S. House candidate from a district where your PAC,

---

[60]John R. Wright, "PAC Contributions, Lobbying, and Representation," *Journal of Politics* 51 (1989): 713–729.

[61]The total number of questionnaires mailed was 1953, making for an overall response rate of 18.6 percent. Although disappointing, this rate is comparable to that achieved by Diana Owen in a similar survey. See "Information Resources for PAC Decision-Making." Of the final sample of 364 PACs, 19 removed the number identifying the name and type of organization. The proportions of each type of PAC in the sample and all PACs registered with the FEC in 1988 are as follows:

	Percent of All PACs	Percent in Sample
Corporate	41.5 (2008)	37.6 (137)
Trade/Health/Membership	17.6 (848)	45.9 (166)
Labor	8.3 (401)	11.3 (41)
Nonconnected	27.8 (1341)	———
Other	4.8 (230)	———

The contribution patterns of PACs in the sample mirror closely the patterns of all PACs registered with the FEC in 1988. Comparisons of the percentage of total contributions given to incumbents and to Democrats are as follows:

or the parent organization, has little or no membership base?" Four response categories were offered: "never," "once in a great while," "occasionally," and "frequently." As it turned out, only 25 percent of the 350 officials who responded to this question claimed that their PACs made such contributions "frequently." A larger share—34 percent—claimed that their PACs "never" made such contributions or else did so only "once in a great while." The remaining 41 percent noted that contributions of this sort were made only "occasionally." While we do not know precisely what "frequently" or "occasionally" means in this context, the clear perception among these PAC officials was that contributions from their organizations tended to coincide with their organizational concentrations of members.

These same PAC officials were also asked to evaluate the influence that professional lobbyists, national PAC officials, local PAC officials, rank-and-file members, and candidates themselves had over contribution decisions.[62] Table 5.10 summarizes the results. Officials from the vast majority of all PACs rated the importance of recommendations from rank-and-file members as equal to or greater than the importance of recommendations from any other source.

(continued)	Percent to Democrats	Percent to Incumbents
Corporate		
Sample of PACs	44.2	82.3
All PACs	44.6	79.5
Labor		
Sample of PACs	90.7	76.6
All PACs	94.4	70.3
Trade/Health/Membership		
Sample of PACs	54.1	82.8
All PACs	55.1	82.4

Finally, the sample slightly overrepresents large PACs. Of all PACs registered with the FEC in 1988, 75.2 percent made total contributions of less than $50,000. The comparable percentage in the sample is 68 percent. Ten percent of the sample PACs made total contributions in excess of $250,000 compared with only 5.5 percent of all PACs.

[62]The exact question asked was "How much weight do recommendations and requests from each of the following sources—professional lobbyists, national officers of the PAC, state and local PAC officers, and rank-and-file members—carry in the final contribution decisions?" Respondents rated each source as carrying "a great deal," "some," or "little or no" weight.

Table 5.10 Relative Importance of Rank-and-File Membership in PAC Decision Making

Rank and File Rated as Important or More Important Than	Percent of PACs	Number of PACs Making Comparison
Lobbyists	70.0	317
National PAC officials	78.2	270
Local PAC officials	81.0	265
Candidates	81.4	308

Only 30 percent of officials ranked lobbyists as more important than rank-and-file members, and less than 22 parent ranked national PAC officials as more important. Despite popular concerns, contribution decisions are made far more often by the local rank and file (not in Washington, D.C.), by the organization's professional lobbyists, or by national PAC officials.

Also of interest in Table 5.10 is the relative influence that candidates themselves have in the decision process. As discussed earlier in this chapter, Frank Sorauf has described the relationship between PACs and candidates as bilateral rather than unilateral, in that candidates sometimes aggressively seek money from PACs. He notes that PAC managers sometimes describe solicitations by candidates as "arm-twisting" or "extortion," implying that candidates threaten to withhold support or favors from the group unless a contribution is made.[63] This importuning may be relatively frequent, but the data in Table 5.10 indicate that it seldom takes priority over recommendations or requests from the rank and file. The rank and file were judged by 81.4 percent of the PAC managers to carry at least as much or more weight than candidates in the decision process. Although the importance of candidates' requests should not be overlooked, it appears that importuning by candidates does little to disturb the local orientation of most PACs.

[63] Sorauf, *Inside Campaign Finance* p. 68.

All of these findings paint a consistent picture of local influences at work in the decision making of most PACs. This result is understandable when considering the responsibility that rank-and-file members of PACs assume for raising money. Like any other political group, PACs are plagued by collective-action problems, and this ultimately shifts the responsibility for fund-raising to the rank and file. PACs provide collective benefits in the sense that their contributions increase or decrease the chances that various congressional candidates will be elected or, alternatively, the chances that various pieces of legislation will be enacted. The primary way that PACs overcome the free rider problem is to appeal to prospective donors' feelings of organizational loyalty and to their beliefs about the importance of participating in the political process. These appeals are typically made either through direct mail or through personal, one-on-one contacting; but it is one-on-one contacting that is most effective, as it is so much easier for individuals to ignore an impersonal letter than a personal contact. The only catch is that raising money through one-on-one contacting requires a large cadre of rank-and-file activists at the grassroots level who can knock on doors and make telephone calls. Since these individuals exercise considerable control over the supply of money to PACs, they also exercise considerable control over how money is spent.

Some evidence of the connection between responsibility for fund-raising and control over allocation decisions is provided by responses of PAC officials to the survey question: "What proportion of the actual fund-raising work of your PAC is conducted by active rank-and-file members?" In those PACs where the rank and file or local officials were deemed to be more influential in final allocation decisions, the rank and file was reported to be responsible for 86 percent of the fund-raising work; but in those PACs where lobbyists and national officials were seen to be most influential in the allocation process, only 55 percent of the fund-raising work was attributed to rank-and-file activists.

The unmistakable influence of local activists in PAC decision making suggests that accounts of the demise of geographic representation in the United States are, if not greatly, at least a bit exaggerated. In more than two out of every three PACs, the preferences of local officials and activists are perceived to carry as much or more weight in contribution decisions as the preferences of Washington lobbyists and national PAC officials. Most PACs maintain strong local roots because the challenges of fund-raising give their active rank-and-file members an important voice in the operation of the PAC. To the extent that the main function of PACs is to acquire access, the available evidence indicates that the access they acquire is predominantly from representatives with whom they share similar geographic interests, not from those with fundamentally dissimilar interests.

Even if PACs do not alter the geographic basis of representation, they may still have an important impact on the representative process by redirecting the attention of legislators *within* their districts. Those interests that contribute may simply receive more attention from their elected representatives than those that do not. In this sense, PACs may encourage functional representation—that is, representation based on socioeconomic or occupational interests—but it is functional representation constrained by geography.[64] Thus, in spite all their appearances of impropriety, it cannot be said that PACs are exclusively, or even chiefly, the tools of Washington elites.

[64]Robert Weissberg makes much the same point in describing "collective representation." See Robert Weissberg, "Collective vs. Dyadic Representation in Congress," *American Political Science Review* 72 (1978): 535–547.

CONSEQUENCES OF INTEREST GROUP POLITICS

Fairly or unfairly, interest groups are often blamed for many of the problems of modern society. Policy gridlock, unchecked governmental growth, economic inefficiency, and political equality are some of the negative economic and political consequences that interest groups allegedly create, encourage, and sustain. Special interests contribute to governmental growth, it is argued, by lobbying for policies that benefit them narrowly, and they create gridlock by vigorously defending those policies, making it virtually impossible for politicians to reduce the size of government or impose costs on specific groups for the sake of the larger public interest.[1] Interest groups are also thought to reinforce and further political inequalities. Many reformers charge that the economically privileged have an organizational advantage that exaggerates representational differences between economic classes. These political inequalities lead to economic inequalities, which then lead to further political inequalities.

In this chapter I examine the basic assumptions of and the evidence for arguments relating interest groups to policy gridlock, governmental growth and inefficiency, and political inequality. I then consider the extent to which each of these problems is consistent with or implied by an informational theory of interest group influence. Application of the theoretical perspective yields additional

---

[1]See Lester C. Thurow, *The Zero-Sum Society: Distribution and the Possibilities for Economic Change* (New York: Basic Books, 1980).

insight into the nature of these problems and the extent to which interest groups should be held responsible. I conclude the chapter by discussing one positive consequence of interest group politics.

Policy Gridlock

President Clinton, in his first address to a joint session of Congress, attacked interest groups for paralyzing the policy process. He characterized special interests as "defenders of decline," and he remarked that "our political system so often has seemed paralyzed by special interest groups."[2] Such assertions are commonplace and often politically convenient, but whether they are true and who suffers as a result are not entirely clear. While it is true that defenders of the status quo have a great strategic advantage in American politics, not all organized interests are defenders of the status quo; many pursue progressive, change-oriented political agendas.

The concept of policy gridlock as applied to interest groups, though seldom defined precisely by those who use it, seems generally to suggest a process in which some set of organized interests manages successfully to block any proposal put on the table, with the result that no new legislation is produced. Since some form of legislation is usually assumed to be in the larger public interest, the absence of legislation is viewed as a suboptimal situation in which special interests have obstructed the realization of the public interest. Classic policy gridlock is broken only when conditions reach crisis proportions, when groups tire of battling one another and cooperate to develop and propose "predigested" policies, or when the president steps in and provides political leadership.[3]

---

[2]Presidential Address, "Clinton Outlines His Plan to Spur the Economy," *Congressional Quarterly Weekly Report* (February 20, 1993), pp. 399 and 403.

[3]"Predigested" policies are policy solutions that groups themselves have attempted to work out on their own outside the formal legislative process. For discussion, see Douglas W. Costain and Anne N. Costain, "Interest Groups as Policy Aggregators in the Legislative Process," *Polity* 14 (1981): 249–272. For examples of presidential initiative, see Christopher J. Bosso, *Pesticides and Politics: The Life Cycle of a Public Issue*, (Pittsburgh: University of Pittsburgh Press, 1987), pp. 261–262.

Factors other than interest groups also contribute to gridlock. Divided control of government, a political agenda increasingly dominated by emotional and contentious issues, and greater media attention to the political process all make political bargaining and compromise more difficult. Yet one can hardly ignore the contribution of interest groups to policy paralysis. Just the sheer number of interest groups alone is bound to place serious demands and strains on the policy-making process. As E. E. Schattschneider once noted, "if all interests could be mobilized the result would be stalemate."[4]

Interest groups have been active in American politics for a long time, but gridlock has only recently become a salient concern. It takes more than interest group mobilization, therefore, to bring about gridlock. Gridlock requires not only the mobilization of interests but also *conflict* among them, with various factions attempting to block or counteract one another rather than cooperating to resolve differences and find a common solution. Importantly, along with the mobilization of groups in recent years has been an increase in the conflict among groups. Various investigations into the amount of conflict or cooperation among groups in particular policy areas have indicated change in the direction of more gridlock, not less.

The Changing Nature of Interest Group Politics

The growth over the past several decades in the number of interest groups is well documented.[5] Less dramatic, but equally important, however, has been a corresponding change in relationships among interest groups. Political scientists often describe the relationships among groups and their connections to the policy process in terms of geometric figures, and the complexity of these figures has greatly increased over the years.[6] Originally, a simple triangle was used to

[4] E. E. Schattschneider, *The Semisovereign People: A Realist's View of Democracy in America* (New York: Holt, Rinehart, and Winston, 1960), pp. 34–35.

[5] For an excellent review in relation to congressional politics, see Barbara Sinclair, *Transformation of the U.S. Senate* (Baltimore: The Johns Hopkins University Press, 1989), pp. 57–64.

[6] For an excellent review and synthesis of various conceptions of interest groups and policy making, see Andrew S. McFarland, "Interest Groups and Theories of Power in America," *British Journal of Political Science* 17 (1987): 129–147.

describe a relatively cooperative relationship among interest groups, legislators, and bureaucrats. However, as the number of organized interests multiplied, as conflict increased, and as the process became more complicated and prone to stasis, more elaborate geometric structures have been employed. The most recent, a "hollow sphere," describes a policy process characterized by a large number of conflicting interests with no central mediators. A brief review of these geometric descriptions of interest groups and policy making is useful for understanding the increasing scope and intensity of interest group conflict.

Triangles

Interest group politics of the 1940s and 1950s were much less contentious than, or at least not as visibly contentious as, today. Cooperation among interest groups and policy makers in the formulation and implementation of public policy was typical of political decision making within special areas of public policy known as *subsystems*. A subsystem, according to J. Leiper Freeman, is "formed by an executive bureau and congressional committees, with special interest groups intimately attached."[7] Also called "subgovernments," "cozy little triangles," or "iron triangles," these alliances of legislators, bureaucrats, and lobbyists dominated policy making in limited, low-visibility policy areas through mutual accommodation of one another's interests.[8] A classic subsystem, and one that is still largely intact today, is that of veterans' affairs, where the House and Senate

---

[7]J. Leiper Freeman, *The Political Process: Bureau—Legislative Committee Relations*, Revised Edition (New York: Random House, 1965), p. 11.

[8]Journalist Douglass Cater introduced the term *subgovernment* to describe the military-industrial complex in *Power in Washington* (New York: Random House, 1964); and Dorothy James introduced the term *cozy little triangle* to explain how bureaus deal with the struggle over their control, or supervision. She argues that because the bureaucracy is too large and complex for the president to supervise closely, agencies become controlled by alliances of interest groups and members of Congress. She argues that the "most successful way for a bureau to deal with the struggle for supervision is to form a 'cozy little triangle' through established accommodations between the bureau, its organized interest groups, and the chairmen of the relevant subcommittees." See Dorothy B. James, *The Contemporary Presidency* (Indianapolis: Bobbs-Merrill, 1969), p. 126.

Veterans' Affairs Committees in Congress, the Veterans Administration, and organizations such as the American Legion and the Veterans of Foreign Wars (VFW) work together in developing policies on education, health care, and housing for veterans. However, even this subsystem has experienced conflict in recent years as the interests and needs of Vietnam veterans are often distinct from those of World War II and Korean War veterans.

Interest groups are pivotal in triangular subsystems. They help bureaucrats build coalitional support for programs in Congress, and they provide information and electoral support for legislators. Legislators, in turn, create programs for the bureaucrats, and bureaucrats administer benefits to the groups. Since interest groups are sources of political support for bureaucrats within Congress and for legislators within constituencies, all of the actors within a subsystem share the same basic policy goals. Policy making within subsystems entails little conflict, and the policies that result are generally distributive, or pork barrel in nature, having concentrated benefits and dispersed costs.[9] Educational benefits for veterans, for example, are concentrated narrowly on the veteran population, but the costs of these programs are shared by all taxpayers, veterans or not.

Although policy making within subsystems tends to be relatively harmonious, conflict and competition among subsystems is often intense. This is particularly true when federal budgets are shrinking, for it is then that senior citizens, farmers, veterans, and various other occupational and demographic groups fight to maintain their favorite programs. The competition that results from subsystem politics, therefore, is generally competition over how to slice the pie, not competition over the details of specific policies.

Hexagons and Issue Networks
In its classic form, a subsystem or cozy triangle is a relatively closed system, with participation limited to just a few groups, agencies, and committees. This model seemed to characterize policy making of the 1940s and 1950s quite well, but as the interest group system expanded in the 1960s and 1970s, the triangular analogy began to

[9]See James Q. Wilson, *Political Organizations* (New York: Basic Books, 1973), pp. 327–337.

break down. Charles Jones, for example, observed that participation in energy policy making in the 1970s did not conform very well to the model of cozy triangles. As a result of the Arab oil embargo in 1973 and several nuclear power plant accidents, a whole new set of participants—public interest groups, environmental groups, congressional party leaders, presidents of companies and foreign governments—became involved in energy issues. Jones notes that "the cozy little triangles which had come to characterize the development of energy policies had become *sloppy large hexagons.*"[10]

A similar transformation has occurred in the environmental policy area. Christopher Bosso describes how participation in decisions governing the regulation and use of pesticides has expanded dramatically since the 1960s. Whereas the key players in the pesticides policy area once included only the producers of agricultural chemicals, the House Committee on Agriculture, and midlevel personnel within the U.S. Department of Agriculture (a classic triangular subsystem), key participants now include environmental groups, the Environmental Protection Agency, and the Senate Agriculture and Commerce Committees. Bosso explained that what was once a cooperative or "self-regulatory" policy area "dominated by a limited and relatively exclusive set of actors" is now one involving "broad issue conflict among multiple competitors."[11]

One of the first to recognize that triangles did not adequately describe many contemporary policy areas was Hugh Heclo, who argued that the notion of an iron triangle was not so much wrong as it was "disastrously incomplete."[12] He suggested that the notion of an "issue network" better described the constellation of actors participating in policy areas with large numbers of participants. Issue networks, according to Heclo, have less well-defined boundaries than iron triangles, and they allow for greater diversity among groups' policy positions. He notes that "participants move in and out of the networks constantly," and that "rather than groups united in

---

[10]Charles O. Jones, "American Politics and the Organization of Energy Decision Making," *Annual Review of Energy* 4 (1979): 105.

[11]Bosso, *Pesticides and Politics*, p. 13.

[12]Hugh Heclo, "Issue Networks and the Executive Establishment," in Anthony King (ed.), *The New American Political System* (Washington, DC: American Enterprise Institute, 1979), p. 102.

dominance over a program, no one, as far as one can tell, is in control of the policies and issues."[13]

Interest group politics characterized by hexagons or issue networks are inherently more contentious than the politics of triangles simply because there are more groups and hence potentially more divergent points of view represented. Unlike triangles, issue networks are not dominated by one powerful set of interests, and hence bargaining, negotiation, and compromise are much more important to the resolution of conflict. The costs of arriving at a final decision are also higher in issue networks, and as a result the overall decision process is generally slower.

Hollow Spheres

The number of interests and the conflict among them has increased in virtually all policy areas; yet, policy making in some areas is more contentious and hence more prone to gridlock than in others. In an effort to explain variations in conflict across policy areas, Robert Salisbury and several colleagues investigated patterns of alliance and opposition among interest groups in four policy domains—health, energy, agriculture, and labor.[14] They discovered that the energy and labor policy areas were much more controversial than agriculture or health and that this difference was related to differences in the presence or absence of "peak associations" in each of the policy areas. Peak associations, which typically have as members specialized groups or trade associations, seek to represent an entire economic sector, not simply the interests of one specialized producer. The quintessential examples of peak associations are the AFL-CIO and the U.S. Chamber of Commerce, but organizations such as the American Farm Bureau Federation and even the American Medical Association are also sometimes considered peaks.

What Salisbury and his colleagues discovered was that strong peak associations *increase* the conflict and competition among groups within a policy area. They concluded that the "more prominent and

[13]Ibid., p. 102.
[14]Robert H. Salisbury, John P. Heinz, Edward O. Laumann, and Robert L. Nelson, "Who Works with Whom? Group Alliances and Opposition," *American Political Science Review* 81 (1987): 1217–1234.

unified the peak associations in a policy domain, the more polarized its group structure and policy struggles become."[15] In the case of labor, they found that the peak associations of business and labor tend to "pull the specialized groups into one orbit or another," but in the case of agriculture, where peak associations are divided and weak, policy making was dominated by "narrower and often shifting coalitions and...articulated with less partisan or doctrinal flavor..."[16]

Having determined that each of the four policy domains they investigated involved substantial conflict or opposition among groups, albeit in varying degrees, this team of investigators next inquired into the extent to which political elites—the most "notable" interest group leaders, Washington lawyers, and government officials within a given policy domain—serve to ameliorate conflict.[17] Noting that elites have a particular interest in maintaining the system that made them elites, they hypothesized that elites might manage conflict by integrating political demands and harmonizing divergent views, thereby furthering societal cohesion and permitting the polity to function. Heinz, Laumann, Salisbury, and Nelson tested this proposition by asking each of 72 Washington elites to note which of the other 71 elites he or she knew well enough "to be confident that they would take the trouble to assist you briefly (and without a fee) if you requested."[18] By examining the correlation patterns in the responses of all 72 elites, they were able to identify communication networks among elites.

Contrary to their expectations, Heinz and his colleagues discovered that the overall rate of interaction among elites was surprisingly low. They found that when elites communicated with other elites,

---

[15]Ibid., p. 1229.

[16]Ibid., p. 1229.

[17]See John P. Heinz, Edward O. Laumann, Robert H. Salisbury, and Robert L. Nelson, "Inner Circles or Hollow Cores? Elite Networks in National Policy Systems," *Journal of Politics*, 52 (1990):356–390; and John P. Heinz, Edward O. Laumann, and Robert L. Nelson, and Robert H. Salisbury, *The Hollow Core: Private Interests in National Policy Making*(Cambridge, MA: Harvard University Press, 1993), Chapter 10.

[18]Heinz et al., "Inner Circles or Hollow Cores? Elite Networks in National Policy Systems," p. 359.

they typically did so only with their allies, not with their adversaries. They found little evidence that elites function as "mediators" or "deal-makers" who facilitate the resolution of conflict and thus found little support for the notion that elites bridge the policy differences among competing interests. Given evidence that elites generally do not play the role of mediators, the investigators concluded that the structure of each of their four policy networks resembles a sphere with a "hollow core."[19]

The absence of mediators or deal makers among the elite representatives of private interests implies very clearly that conflicts among organized interests are almost always handled *within* the institutions of national government—the Congress, bureaucratic agencies, and the courts—not by interest group leaders themselves. Thus, the interactions between organized interests and governmental institutions, not the interactions among interests themselves, are the important connections for understanding and explaining policy outcomes. Although organized interests sometimes hammer out agreements among themselves before appealing to government officials, cooperation and deliberation among organized interests appear to be the exception, and competition seems to be the norm. In such a world, the prospects of gridlock are nontrivial.

Gridlock and Information

The politics that transpires in the situation of hollow spheres and issue networks is what Christopher Bosso has termed "presence politics." Presence politics describes the "activities of a rather stable,

---

[19]Heinz et al. found it puzzling that the core is empty. They contended that the core is the position that should maximize elites' influence, because it is from the core that they can coordinate and control the flow of information. They suggested, however, that the core is empty simply because it *is* such an attractive, powerful position. Elites, they argued, will not allow any individual to occupy the core position because that individual would be too powerful relative to the others. They suggested (p. 306) that "there will be a strong tendency to push actors out of the core, or not allow them to occupy such a position for very long, so as to avoid dependency." Any elites who attempt to occupy the central position would be so influential that "the market would bid up the price of their services until they were converted from mediators to advocates." See *The Hollow Core*, p. 307.

if somewhat inchoate, set of lobbyists and other policy activists."[20]
The fundamental resources needed to compete effectively in the
world of presence politics are information and expertise. Compared
with the politics of subgovernments, presence politics involves a
much broader range and diversity of actors, and thus influence
depends on expertise and information rather than exclusivity of
jurisdiction. It is information, argued Bosso, especially information
about policy problems and conditions, that threatens the cozy
dynamics of subgovernments, drawing the public and other actors
into the fray. As more and more people become informed about how
conditions affect them personally, subgovernment politics, argued
Bosso, "explodes into pluralistic policymaking."[21]

Bosso's view of the policy-making process as presence politics
fits comfortably with an informational theory of interest group
influence. Access, multiple actors, competition, a focus on institutions, and especially expertise—about both policy and politics—are
central components of the informational perspective. In the informational model, groups have conflicting policy preferences, and
they use information strategically to cancel out or correct misleading information they expect to be provided by their opponents.
Moreover, groups do not resolve conflicts or disagreements on
their own; instead, all information is transmitted to legislators, and
any conflicting information is checked and resolved by legislators
themselves. The basic assumptions of an informational theory of
interest group influence, therefore, are entirely consistent with the
prevailing perspectives of interest groups and the policy-making
process, whether characterized as presence politics or hollow
spheres. Gridlock is a distinct possibility in Bosso's conception of
presence politics and in images of interest groups and policy making characterized by issue networks, hollow spheres, and information transmission.

The informational theory of group influence suggests that if
gridlock occurs, it is a consequence of the way that policy proposals
are framed and the agenda is set, not simply a consequence of multiple groups with conflicting objectives. Recall that one of the impor-

[20]Bosso, *Pesticides and Politics*, p. 257.
[21]Ibid., p. 256.

tant consequences of competitive lobbying in the informational model is that all relevant information about policy outcomes and political outcomes will be accurately and fully revealed to decision makers. Thus, if one side or the other has a true political advantage, or truly advocates a superior policy position, then legislators will almost surely discover this and behave accordingly. Clearly, then, one group can successfully block a policy proposal of a competing group by introducing information that successfully counters the information provided by that group. One instance of this does not constitute gridlock, however. For gridlock to result, blocking must occur repeatedly, which implies that the blocking group or coalition of groups always have superior information to the proposing group or coalition of groups. However, this kind of asymmetry is unlikely to occur regularly unless the blocking coalition group controls the political agenda, in which case the source of gridlock lies in the way that proposals are formulated and introduced, not in the lobbying process per se.

Although policy gridlock is almost always used pejoratively, it is important to recognize that all stalemate is not invariably bad. Although interest groups will occasionally succeed in misleading legislators, an informational theory predicts that this will only occur when legislators are lobbied by groups on just one side of the issue. When groups from both sides of the issue lobby, as would be expected in policy areas where multiple groups have access to legislators, then all relevant information is revealed to legislators and no group can successfully mislead. A successful blocking action, therefore, implies that legislators have made the right political or policy choices—that is, they have not adopted a policy that will not work as advertised or that is not what a majority of the attentive voters wanted. Blocking actions of this sort, which may appear as stalemate, are not always inimical to the public interest.

Governmental Growth and Inefficiency

In contrast to claims that interest groups lead to policy gridlock are claims that interest groups create an almost opposite problem: unbridled governmental growth. That interest groups should at once be blamed for both gridlock and growth may seem ironic, but both outcomes are possible. Which occurs depends largely on the types of issues on the political agenda. When the agenda is dominated by policies that *concentrate benefits* and *disperse costs*, government will tend to grow; but when the agenda is dominated by policies that *disperse benefits* while either *concentrating* or *dispersing costs*, stalemate is the more likely outcome.[22] Veterans' benefits, agricultural subsidies, and tariffs—what are sometimes referred to as policies with "particularistic" benefits—concentrate benefits on particular segments of the population but disperse costs across the entire population of taxpayers. National defense and public transportation, policies with "universalistic" benefits, disperse both benefits and costs widely. Regulatory policies, such as restrictions on smokestack emissions, disperse benefits—clean air in this case—broadly, but concentrate costs narrowly on particular industries.

Interest groups are much more likely to lobby for policies with particularistic rather than universalistic benefits. In fact, groups will generally *not* lobby for policies with universalistic benefits unless those policies are modified to provide particular benefits as well. Consider an urban transportation system, for example.[23] An urban transportation system offers universalistic benefits such as a reduction in automobile traffic congestion, a reduction in air pollution, reduced transportation costs brought about by economies of scale, and so forth. Any specific interest group, however, cannot be expected to lobby for such benefits, because the benefits are dispersed across so many different interests that each particular group would

[22]For an analysis of the effects of different types of issues on governmental growth, see Peter J. Coughlin, Dennis C. Mueller, and Peter Murrell, "Electoral Politics, Interest Groups, and the Size of Government," *Economic Inquiry* (1990): 682–705. They concluded: "It is the existence of goods whose benefits are concentrated on a particular group that can explain why an increase in the number of organized interest groups might lead to an increase in government size." The classification of policies by the concentration of costs and benefits was originally offered by Wilson, *Political Organizations*, pp. 327–337.
[23]This example is taken from Peter H. Aranson and Peter C. Ordeshook, "A Prolegomenon to a Theory of the Failure of Representative Democracy," in Richard Auster and Barbara Sears (eds.), *American Re-Evolution* (Tucson: University of Arizona Press, 1977), pp. 23–46.

find it in its interest to free ride on the lobbying efforts of other groups. Only if groups received particularistic benefits—perhaps an expectation of profits and higher wages for contractors and their employees, or improved access to central city businesses—would they be expected to lobby on behalf of the transportation system.

There will be little or no interest group opposition to policies that disperse the costs of particularistic benefits across the entire population without regard to group membership. Any group that opposes another group's particularistic benefit can at best hope only to reduce the tax bill for all individuals in the population. However, since a lower tax bill for the population as a whole is itself a collective, or universalistic good, no group will be expected to lobby for such an outcome, or equivalently, against another group's particularistic benefit. Since legislators profit politically from such policies, it follows that when there are many groups seeking many particularistic benefits, there will be a large number of governmental programs benefitting those groups. In fact, since groups will not oppose the particularistic demands of other groups, governmental programs will grow unchecked.

Robert Dahl explains that the tendency for interest groups to lobby for policies that convey particularistic benefits is a consequence of the *centralization* and *inclusiveness* of interest groups within the political system.[24] *Inclusiveness* refers to the proportion of the population included in organizations, and *centralization* the extent to which organizations are concentrated in peak associations whose leaders are able to negotiate and enter into decisions on behalf of the members of the entire coalition. Dahl argues that decentralized bargaining by exclusive associations generally results in the costs of bargains to be passed on to others not involved in the bargaining process, with little incentive or opportunity to consider general and long-run consequences. Since interest groups in the United States are largely decentralized organizations with weakly inclusive or exclusive memberships, organizational leaders, according to Dahl, "have strong incentives to foster the particularistic interests and demands of their own members and little incentive—indeed a strong

---

[24]Robert A. Dahl, *Dilemmas of Pluralist Democracy: Autonomy vs. Control* (New Haven: Yale University Press, 1982), pp 68–80, 192–194.

disincentive—to exercise their influence on behalf of the interests and demands of nonmembers."[25]

Interest group lobbying for particularistic benefits not only leads to big government but, according to economists, is also economically inefficient. If the government is to award a defense contract to build submarines, for example, then whichever manufacturing interest is awarded the contract essentially acquires a monopoly on the building of submarines, and various producers will compete for this governmentally created monopoly by lobbying the Congress and the Department of Defense. However, because lobbying efforts are costly, firms that commit scarce resources to lobbying cannot apply those resources to economically productive activities such as investment in new equipment, research and development, and so forth. Economists refer to lobbying efforts of this sort as "rent seeking." As Tollison explained,

> To the extent that real resources are spent to capture monopoly rents in such ways as lobbying, these expenditures create no value from a social point of view. It is this activity of wasting resources in competing for artificially contrived transfers that is called rent seeking.[26]

"Artificially contrived transfers," or particularistic benefits, are themselves economically inefficient in that they are not goods that groups could acquire or would attempt to acquire on their own in the private marketplace. It is only because they expect to be able to pass the costs along to the unorganized, thereby making their benefits greater than their share of the costs, that groups lobby for them in the first place. Moreover, once policies that benefit particular groups are put into place, there will be incentives for additional investment, which will in turn lead to further inefficiency, because the economic returns from these investment will be artificially high as a result of special interest legislation rather than market forces.

Inefficiency also takes the form of slow economic growth and arrested technological development. Political interest groups contribute to these problems when, for example, corporations lobby for

[25]Ibid., p. 74.
[26]Robert D. Tollison, "Rent Seeking: A Survey," *Kyklos* 35 (1982): 577.

bailouts of failing firms or when labor unions repress labor-saving innovations to protect jobs.[27] These sorts of problems result not from clashes between opposing and well-organized factions but rather from "distributional coalitions" of groups—what Mancur Olson defined as organizations "overwhelmingly oriented to struggles over the distribution of income and wealth rather than to the production of additional output."[28] He claimed that distributional coalitions "slow down a society's capacity to adopt new technologies and to reallocate resources in response to changing conditions, and thereby reduce the rate of economic growth."[29] The overall effect, Olson argued, is that special interest groups "reduce efficiency and aggregate income in the societies in which they operate."[30] Even worse, when special interest groups and distributional issues become significant, political life becomes divisive because people come to resent the favorable treatment given to the interest groups, which in turn can make governing difficult.

Information and Governmental Growth

Although the governmental growth argument depends critically on the existence of policies that convey particularistic benefits, the precise extent to which the political agenda is dominated by these issues and exactly how they get there is unknown. Much more study is needed of the types of issues that dominate the national political agenda, how the mix of issues has changed over the years, and exactly what the role of interest groups is in setting the agenda. As the number of interest groups continues to grow and as the politics of cozy triangles gives way to broader, more inclusive decision processes, it seems likely that more and more issues will involve organized conflict of some sort. Whether and to what extent these issues are likely to crowd distributive issues from the political agenda is much less clear.

[27]Mancur Olson, *The Rise and Decline of Nations: Economic Growth, Stagflation, and Social Rigidities* (New Haven: Yale University Press, 1982), pp. 61–65.
[28]Ibid., p. 44.
[29]Ibid., p. 65.
[30]Ibid., p. 47.

The key characteristic of policies that involve concentrated benefits and dispersed costs is that they are seldom controversial. As explained earlier, interest groups will generally not lobby against distributive policies, for when the costs are distributed widely, then any gains from reducing costs are also distributed widely. Thus, organized opposition to distributive policies involves a classic collective-action problem. Even though many groups may prefer smaller government or lower taxes, the expected gain to any single group from lobbying against another group's particularistic benefit is sufficiently small relative to the costs of lobbying that it is not rational in cost-benefit terms to lobby. Consequently, when the agenda is dominated by policies that convey particularistic benefits, there will be no competitive lobbying.

In the absence of competitive lobbying, the informational theory of group influence predicts that legislators will not always be fully informed and that groups will be able to mislead them about the true policy consequences or true preferences of constituents. Indeed, this is precisely what occurs when legislators are lobbied to vote for policies that convey particularistic benefits. A majority of constituents may oppose such policies because of their adverse consequences for the size of the bureaucracy and the federal deficit; yet, this information is usually not communicated to legislators because it is not cost-effective for opposition groups to lobby. Legislators in this situation behave exactly as an informational theory predicts they should: they act on incomplete information provided by those groups that lobby them.

Why, when it seems so plainly obvious that continued congressional support for particularistic policies is not good public policy, does Congress persist in supporting them? The answer, in short, is that politics, not public policy, dominates legislative decision making on these sorts of issues. Even though it may not be in the long-term public interest for legislators to vote repeatedly for pork barrel projects, there are sufficiently few organizations lobbying on behalf of the broader public interest to convince legislators that it is in their political interests or in the interests of good public policy to vote them down. As demonstrated again and again, unless there is a groundswell of public opposition to higher taxes and larger government, members of Congress will not act on their own accord to eliminate particularistic policy benefits and reduce the growth in government programs and spending. The greater problem, then, is not that the public interest could not be accommodated through interest group activity but rather that public interest groups have difficulty organizing and lobbying at all. Whatever bias exists in favor of special interests over the public interest problem is due to problems of organization and collective action, not in the lobbying or legislative process itself.

Political Equality: The Representation of Unorganized Interests

The individuals most likely to participate politically in the United States or in other democracies are those with relatively high levels of education, income, and professional status. These resources enable individuals to find the time and information necessary to volunteer for political candidates, contact their representatives, or engage in assorted other political activities. Political inequality, therefore, is to some extent a natural consequence of economic and social inequalities. Political inequality is more severe in some countries than others, however, and depends in part on the structure of the interest group and political party systems in those countries. In some countries, affiliation with political parties or interest groups actually *lessens* the political inequalities naturally associated with social and economic inequality. The United States, unfortunately, is not one of these.

In cross-national comparisons of political participation in seven democracies, Nie, Verba, and Kim discovered that organizational involvement has the greatest effect on political participation when divisions among social groups coincide with divisions among political groups. When religious or occupational groups, for example, have strong ties to political parties and organizations closely aligned with those social groups, then individuals are more likely to join political organizations and participate at levels above and beyond that expected on the basis of their socioeconomic resources alone. Presumably, organizational membership provides political exposure that can either create or substitute for participatory attitudes such as efficacy and citizen duty that typically are associated with high social or economic status. As Nie, Verba, and Kim explained,

> Where there are clearly defined competing groups and the groups are well organized, one is more likely to have political activists recruited on other bases than their socioeconomic resource level. Where such competition is blurred or absent, the individual forces associated with socio-economic resource level take over, resulting in a greater disparity between the haves and the have-nots.[31]

The United States, unlike some European democracies, has a distinct social and political structure in which cleavages are *cross-cutting*. Social divisions in the United States do not generally coincide with political divisions, as some Catholics, for example, identify with the Republican Party and others with the Democratic Party, and some farmers belong to the relatively conservative American Farm Bureau Federation and others to the more liberal National Farmers Union. Cross-cutting cleavages generally *exaggerate* political inequalities, because socioeconomic factors, not social group identifications, are often the primary determinants of organizational membership. Catholics, for example, are attracted to the Republican Party not because of their Catholicism, but because of other economic or social interests; farmers who join either the Farm Bureau or the Farmers Union do so not because of their identify as farmers, but because of their economic philosophies about agricultural policy. When group identity is not the principal motivation for joining an interest group or political party, social and economic factors dominate the decision to join political interest groups. The consequence is an upper-class bias in the American interest group system.[32]

One exception in the United States involves African-Americans, who because of a group-consciousness that evolved during the 1950s

---

[31]Sidney Verba, Norman Nie, and Jae-on Kim, *Political Participation and Political Equality: A Seven-Nation Study* (New York: Cambridge University Press, 1978), pp. 198–199.
[32]See E. E. Schattschneider, *The Semisovereign People: A Realist's View of Democracy in America* (New York: Holt, Rhinehart, and Winston, 1960), pp. 32–37; and Kay Lehman Schlozman, "What Accent the Heavenly Chorus? Political Equality and the American Pressure System," *Journal of Politics* 46 (1984): 1006–1032.

and 1960s are as likely or more likely to join political organizations as a result of their group identification than as a result of their socioeconomic resources. Consequently, they participate at higher rates than would be expected given their socioeconomic characteristics alone.[33] There is also some evidence that unskilled workers who belong to unions are more likely to participate politically than unskilled workers who do not belong to unions.[34] Still, it is primarily the middle- and upper-class citizen, not the lower-class citizen, that is drawn to political organizations in the United States, and thus interest groups are a double-edged sword when it comes to participation and representation.[35] On the one hand, they exaggerate differences in participation rates between high- and low-status citizens, and on the other, they amplify the concerns of those who do participate. The net effect is to increase political and economic inequality, as the unorganized generally have fewer economic resources.

Under what conditions, if any, will the unorganized be represented in American politics? Arthur Denzau and Michael Munger have shown that legislators will take into account the policy preferences of unorganized citizens when three conditions are met: (1) unorganized citizens are informed about legislators' efforts to enact policies they care about, (2) they vote accordingly, and (3) legislators know precisely the number of votes they stand to gain or lose among unorganized voters as a result of their policy efforts.[36] In the event that the unorganized voters are uninformed, legislators may exchange policy favors directly for campaign money or other

---

[33]Sidney Verba and Norman H. Nie, *Participation in America: Political Democracy and Social Equality* (New York: Harper and Row, 1972), pp. 252–259.

[34]See V. O. Key, *Public Opinion and American Democracy* (New York: Knopf, 1967), p. 506.

[35]Even though high-status individuals are much more likely than low-status individuals to join interest groups in the United States, once individuals become members and gain political exposure within groups, some of the differences in participation among members with different socioeconomic characteristics are reduced. See Philip H. Pollock, III, "Organizations as Agents of Mobilization: How Does Group Activity Affect Political Participation?" *American Journal of Political Science* 26 (1982): 485–503.

[36]Arthur T. Denzau and Michael C. Munger, "Legislators and Interest Groups: How Unorganized Interests Get Represented," *American Political Science Review* 80 (1986): 89–106.

resources from interest groups, and then use those resources to persuade the unorganized citizens to vote for them on nonpolicy grounds. However, when unorganized citizens are sufficiently informed to hold their legislators accountable for their policy actions at election time, legislators will provide policy favors only to interest groups with policy goals similar to those of the unorganized voters in their constituencies.

If the interests of each citizen were represented by at least one organized group and if unorganized citizens were sufficiently informed to hold their representatives accountable for their policy actions, then there would be no serious representational disparities resulting from interest group politics. These are two big ifs, however. The interests of poor people, for example, are not very well represented within the interest group system at large because very few groups have been organized to work on behalf of poor people. Also, most of the empirical research on congressional elections demonstrates conclusively that citizens make their congressional voting decisions far more frequently on the basis of partisan identification and familiarity with the candidates than on the basis of legislators' policy decisions. Half the electorate cannot even recall the name of its representative in Congress, let alone how he or she voted on various bills. Interest groups, therefore, almost certainly introduce and sustain some degree of bias in the representational process. This bias may be of relatively little consequence if excluded citizens do not have intense interests at stake; however, when interests or opinions are intensely held and the possibilities for participation are limited, the consequences can be severe. As V. O. Key once observed:

> The combination of intense opinion and low sense of efficacy with alienation from participation in the political system may not be the most healthy condition for a democratic order. Such population blocs may be of serious consequence only when they are of considerable magnitude. Such blocs may, if sufficiently agitated, seek to work out their concerns through mob action or by other more direct routes to their ends than the tortuous process of popular politics; nonparticipators may yearn for short-cuts.[37]

[37]Key, *Public Opinion and American Democracy*, p. 232.

Information and Inequality

What, if anything, can be done to reduce political inequality? One option is to restrict the political activities of the economically advantaged; another is to encourage the participation of the economically disadvantaged. Only this second option is viable, however, because First Amendment guarantees effectively preclude restricting political activities, even those of economically advantaged citizens. One means of stimulating participation among the disadvantaged is to subsidize their participation through direct cash transfers or through special tax benefits. Although this is possible in principle, in practice it is unclear that such efforts would do much to enhance the influence of previously unorganized interests.

One implication of an informational theory of organized influence is that any information a group provides is credible only when it is clear to lawmakers that groups have expended costly resources to acquire expertise about policy or electoral outcomes. If it were easy for any organization to become an expert about policy matters or electoral mobilization, then information would no longer be scarce, and information would not be a source of influence for groups. Subsidized groups might achieve some credibility on policy matters (for example, they might convince lawmakers by hiring well-known policy experts to present their case), but it is much harder to imagine subsidized groups carrying much credibility about electoral mobilization. While any organization can hire pollsters, slick advertisers, or direct mail specialists to give the appearance of a strong grassroots organization, and even though organizations sometimes clearly attempt to exaggerate or distort perceptions of their grassroots capability, such efforts by subsidized groups would be totally transparent. There would be common knowledge about which groups were subsidized and which were not, and thus one would expect legislators simply to discount the electoral implications of grassroots efforts from the subsidized groups.

To be sure, many organizations are subsidized in some sense by an outside patron and yet compete very successfully in the American political arena. Citizen groups in particular receive substantial support from individual gifts and foundation grants, and many nonprofit organizations are the beneficiaries of governmental grants and contracts from federal agencies seeking to coordinate policy and collect data. The American Public Transit Association, for example, has received federal research contracts to apply new technology to bus and rail systems; the American Council on Education receives federal funds from the Department of Defense to evaluate military courses for academic credit; and The Planned Parenthood Federation of America receives federal grants to set up family planning programs both internationally and domestically.[38] In general, however, the amount of federal support that groups receive is typically quite small. According to the Walker survey, only nonprofit groups receive on average more than 10 percent of their revenue from governmental sources, and according to a *National Journal* survey, the nonprofits receiving the greatest support are state and local governmental organizations.[39]

That efforts to subsidize collective political action are likely to fail reveals an important irony about collective action. The factors that make organized political action difficult are the very same factors that make it effective. If there were no costs to becoming organized, then the very fact of being organized would mean very little. While it is certainly true that impediments to collective action produce negative multiplier effects in terms of participation and representation, it is by no means clear that artificially removing the impediments through governmental regulation or subsidization would reduce inequalities.

Interest Groups, Representation, and Legislating

One of the fundamental dilemmas of republican government, at least in the contemporary United States, is that elected representatives often find it difficult to meet the demands of policy making in Washington while at the same time stay attuned to the demands and concerns of their constituents at home. As Richard Fenno has noted, there is a considerable tension in pursuing both Washington and constituency careers simultaneously, as the "twin requirements that

[38]See Rochelle L. Stanfield, "'Defunding the Left' May Remain Just Another Fond Dream of Conservatives," *National Journal* August 1, 1981, pp. 1374–1378.
[39]See Jack L. Walker, "The Origins and Maintenance of Interest Groups in America," *American Political Science Review* 77 (1983): 400; and Stanfield, "'Defunding the Left'."

Congress be a representative and a legislative institution" pose a dilemma for many House members.[40] To be effective legislators, members of Congress must be in Washington, but to be effective representatives and continue to be reelected, they must spend a great deal of time in their districts. As Fenno put it:

> Under the best of circumstances, the tension involved in maintaining constituency contact and achieving legislative competence is considerable. Members cannot be in two places at once, and the growth of a Washington career exacerbates the problem. But, more than that, the demands in both places have grown recently. The legislative workload and the demand for legislative expertise are steadily increasing. So is the problem of maintaining meaningful contact with their several constituencies. Years ago, House members returned home for months at a time to live among their supportive constituencies, soak up the home atmosphere, absorb local problems at first hand. Today, they race home for a day, a weekend, a week at a time.[41]

One apparent manifestation of this fundamental dilemma is the relatively large number of congressional retirements in recent elections. Frequently, members explain their retirement decisions in terms of the basic tension between electioneering and legislating: the strain of raising money and waging continuous campaigns detracts from the loftier goal of making good public policy. Yet, the legislative process goes on, and despite the disillusionment that obviously exists, many members of Congress do succeed in managing both electoral and legislative careers.

One of the reasons—but surely not the only reason—that legislators are able to achieve legislative competence and also stay attuned to their constituents' concerns is because of the informational role that interest groups play in the legislative process. While it is sometimes possible for interest groups to manipulate legislators' perceptions of the political or policy consequences of a bill, there is one important situation in which all relevant information is revealed accurately to legislators through the lobbying process. As explained earlier, when legislators are lobbied by groups on both sides of the issue, all groups have strong incentives to present information fully

---

[40]Richard F. Fenno, Jr., *Home Style: House Members in Their Districts* (Boston: Little, Brown, 1978), p. 216.
[41]Ibid., p. 222.

and accurately, for conflicting information implies that one side or the other has been less than entirely forthcoming. In order to avoid damaging their reputations for credibility, or perhaps even losing access, groups will not take a chance on misleading legislators when they are likely to be discovered, and the chances of discovery are almost certain when there is lobbying by groups on both sides of an issue.

Whether legislators will be lobbied by groups on both sides of an issue depends in part on their position in the legislature. Some legislators, given their committee assignments or their leadership positions are more important legislatively than others, and it is these representatives that groups are most likely to lobby. Thus, one natural consequence of legislators' gaining seniority and moving up in the legislative hierarchy is that they are more likely to be lobbied in general and, therefore, more likely to be lobbied by groups from opposing sides of the issue. When these groups engage in grassroots lobbying campaigns, legislators can become informed about the direction and intensity of their constituents' policy preferences without having to spend inordinate amounts of time in their districts acquiring information firsthand.

Unfortunately, because senior legislators generally receive the best information through the lobbying process, interest groups are not an effective bridge between the Washington and local environments for all legislators. However, for those legislators who manage to stay in office long enough to acquire legislative seniority, interest group lobbying can play an important role in bridging their Washington and local environments, and this redounds to the benefit of constituents as well as the legislative process more broadly.

Clearly, all of the consequences of interest group politics are not nearly so positive. The problems of political inequality, excessive governmental growth and spending, economic inefficiency, and policy gridlock are associated in varying degrees with interest group politics. The source of most of these problems, however, lies in the organization of interests in the first place, not in the transmission or processing of interests once they are organized. In other words, the system works for those who are organized, and sometimes even for those who are unorganized. For the unorganized, however, there are no guarantees, and, unfortunately, there appear to be no shortcuts or quick fixes to remedy organizational deficiencies.

C H A P T E R 7

CONCLUSION

The central argument of this book has been that special interests can hold great sway over the American policy process through their control over and strategic use of information. One telling example of interest group influence over the years has been that of the National Rifle Association (NRA) and its opposition to gun control measures. Despite several recent setbacks to its agenda, most notably the passage of the Brady bill in 1993, the success of the NRA and its allies in fending off gun control legislation for so many years demonstrates clearly how a passionate and well-organized minority interest can prevail over an unorganized and dispassionate majority interest.

The NRA's success over the years has stemmed primarily from its large and active membership, which, when fully mobilized, presents compelling information to members of Congress about the electoral consequences of their stands on gun control. Legislators who ever witnessed the exceptional grassroots opposition to gun control proposals that the NRA was able to generate made the obvious connection: if the NRA could mobilize so many constituents over one roll call vote or procedural decision in Congress, it surely could do the same thing at election time. Whether the NRA could or, in fact, did unilaterally bring about the defeat of incumbent members of Congress is questionable.[1] Nevertheless, many incum-

---

[1]Some political observers have concluded that the electoral defeats of Maryland's Senator Joseph Tydings in 1970 and Vermont's Representative Peter Smith in 1990 were due in no small part to the NRA's efforts. See Josh Sugarman, *National Rifle Association: Money, Firepower, and Fear* (Washington, DC: National Press Books, 1992), pp. 173–176.

189

bents in Congress *believed* that the NRA could impose serious electoral consequences and, in the absence of credible information to
the contrary, had little choice but to support the NRA.

The NRA's long battle against gun control legislation illustrates
not only the strength of special interests in American politics but also
their vulnerability. The NRA's recent failure to defeat the Brady bill's
requirements of a waiting period and background check shows that
even the most powerful organized interests lose occasionally. Two
basic forces brought about the NRA's defeat on the Brady bill: (1) a
mass public that held its opinions on gun control more intensely than
in the past because of heightened concerns about violent crime and
(2) the organized opposition of Handgun Control, Inc., which,
because of more intense public opinion, was able to counter the NRA's
claims about the electoral consequences to members of Congress of
opposing gun control.[2] The forces of intense public opinion and organized opposition are forces to which all special interests are vulnerable.

The vulnerability of the NRA on the Brady bill illustrates clearly
that there are *natural* limits to the power of special interests in American politics. Organized opposition, together with an aroused public,
can constrain and check the power of special interests. That the power
of special interests often goes unchecked and unconstrained, therefore,
is partly a consequence of the fact that no one cares. In such cases, it
can hardly be claimed that special interests distort or obscure public
opinion, for there is not much opinion to distort or obscure. This may
be small comfort, however, to those who are concerned about other
ostensibly pernicious consequences of interest group politics, such as
the underrepresentation of the economically disadvantaged.

Not only does mass public opinion sometimes check and limit
the power of special interests in American politics, but interest
groups themselves also check and constrain one another. Counteractive lobbying prevents organizations from exploiting the informational advantages they often have over legislators. When confronted
with organized lobbying by groups with opposite policy preferences,

---

[2]For evidence of the effectiveness of grassroots lobbying by gun control advocates on
earlier legislative issues, see Laura I. Langbein and Mark A. Lotwis, "The Political
Efficacy of Lobbying and Money: Gun Control in the U.S. House, 1986." *Legislative
Studies Quarterly*, 14 (1990): 414–440.

groups can ill-afford to exaggerate the facts or otherwise present misleading information. Discovery is likely to be swift and the punishment sure.

The mobilization of many new interests over the past several decades, especially the mobilization of many public interest groups, is a highly significant development in terms of the legitimacy and integrity it lends to the interest group process. Counteractive lobbying by these organizations provides a very real and substantial constraint on the ability of special interests to distort the public interest and manipulate the political process to their advantage. Given the active participation of organizations on each side of most political issues, the lobbying process is to a large degree self-regulating. Ultimately, the checks that groups provide on one another naturally are far stronger and more effective than any that might be imposed artificially through the legislative process.

Despite the natural constraints on interest group influence, many individuals still believe that additional limitations are necessary. During the 103rd Congress (1993–1994), both the House and the Senate renewed their efforts to reform the laws governing lobbying and campaign contributions. The reforms of the 103rd Congress closely resembled reforms proposed, but never enacted into law, during the 102nd Congress. The lobbying reforms of the 102nd Congress languished at the committee level in 1992, and the campaign finance reform bill was vetoed by President Bush. In the 103rd Congress, continued public disgust over the relationship between special interests and Congress, together with strong support from the Clinton administration, inspired new action, but again to no avail. Both the campaign finance and lobbying reform bills met their ends in the Senate in 1994 under Republican-led filibusters. Still, a brief review of these legislative efforts is instructive for what it reveals about the political and constitutional difficulties associated with the governmental regulation of organized interests.

Campaign Finance Reform

There are many dimensions to recent campaign finance reform efforts, some of which have more to do with electoral margins and partisan control than with the relationship between interest groups and members of Congress. Rather than provide a comprehensive review of the many provisions of campaign finance, I will focus only on those that bear directly or indirectly on interest group activities.

The primary goal of all reform efforts with respect to interest groups is to reduce the dependence of members of Congress on PAC money. Three aspects of campaign finance reform are particularly relevant to this goal: overall spending limits in congressional campaigns, individual contribution limits for PACs, and aggregate contribution limits for PACs. The relevance of contribution limits on PACs is fairly obvious; such limits ostensibly reduce their influence in the process. The relevance of overall spending limits is less obvious, however. These limits are important only in conjunction with limits on the total PAC money that candidates can receive. Clearly, the higher the overall spending limits relative to aggregate PAC limits, the lower the dependence of candidates on PAC money.

The House and Senate have historically taken very different positions on regulating PAC contributions. The Senate has demonstrated its willingness either to ban PAC contributions altogether, as it did in 1993, or else to place much greater restrictions on PAC contributions than those proposed by the House. The more restrictive position of the Senate is due to the fact that senators are generally less dependent on PAC money than House members. Recall from Table 5.4 that House incumbents in 1992 received 52.6 percent of all PAC contributions, whereas Senate incumbents received only 19.4 percent. The preference that PACs have for House members, combined with the lower cost of House campaigns, means that House members receive on average a much larger share of their total contributions from PACs than do senators. For the 1991–1992 election cycle, the average House candidate received 32.8 percent of total campaign receipts from political action committees, whereas the average senator received only 19.8 percent of total receipts from PACs; and the average House *incumbent* received 47 percent of total receipts from PACs, whereas the average Senate *incumbent* received only 32.8 percent.[3] The lower dependence of Senate candidates on PAC money is largely a consequence of their larger electoral districts. Senate candidates can more easily raise large amounts of

[3]Data are from FEC (Federal Election Commission) press release, March 4, 1993, p. 6.

money in small individual contributions from their constituents than can House candidates.

In 1993 the Senate banned PAC contributions entirely in its bill (S 3), whereas the House left standing the PAC contribution limit of $5000 per election (HR 3). Instead of reducing the individual PAC contribution limit, the House imposed a $200,000 aggregate cap on the amount of PAC money that any congressional candidate could receive during a given election cycle. In combination with this aggregate limit, the House bill also called for an overall voluntary spending limit of $600,000 per campaign, thus limiting PAC contributions as a share of total expenditures to one-third. Ultimately, this discrepancy between the House and Senate positions on PACs is what killed the legislation.

Given that House incumbents in 1991–1992 received on average 47 percent and Senate incumbents roughly 33 percent of total receipts from PACs, the limitation of PAC contributions to only one-third of expenditures in the 1993 reform bill would appear to yield a significant reduction in candidates' dependence on PAC contributions.[4] Closer analysis, however, reveals that legislators would be only slightly less dependent on PAC money under the reform proposal. For the 1991–1992 election cycle, House Democratic incumbents received an average of $283,887 in PAC contributions and Republican House incumbents an average of $211,597.[5] In practice, then, even though the $200,000 aggregate cap does limit PAC contributions somewhat, incumbents will continue to receive nearly as much money from PACs as they have in the past. Moreover, since the growth in PACs and PAC contributions has leveled off in recent years, the $200,000 aggregate cap is not much different from the cap on PAC contributions that has evolved naturally.

The net effect of the House reform proposal is to decrease incumbents' dependence on PAC money in relative terms—that is, relative to other sources—but not in absolute terms. The flow of PAC contributions to legislators will be affected very little; instead of spending less time raising money from PACs, legislators will simply spend more time raising money in small individual contributions. These changes should have very little effect on the role of PACs in the

[4]Data are from FEC press release, March 4, 1993, p. 6.
[5]Ibid., p. 4

legislative process. The argument of Chapter 5 is that campaign contributions are simply a way for groups to convince legislators that they share a common policy perspective and, therefore, that any information provided by the organization's lobbyist is worth listening to. It is in this sense that contributions purchase access, and thus as long as there is no significant reduction in the absolute dollars that PACs are allowed to contribute, their ability to gain access through contributions will be disturbed hardly at all by the new regulations.

The difficulty of imposing artificial, that is, statutory, constraints on the activities of interest groups is illustrated clearly by the campaign finance reform bill that emerged from the Senate in 1993. Constitutional questions were raised by several important provisions in the bill. The ban on PAC contributions raised the question of whether individuals would lose their rights of association guaranteed under the First Amendment. Similarly, a prohibition on contacts between lobbyists and representatives to whom they had made campaign contributions raised the question of whether lobbyists would be forced to choose between their right of free speech and their right to petition the government for redress of grievances, both of which are also guaranteed under the First Amendment. The Senate was so uncertain about the constitutionality of these and other provisions that it included a special provision in the bill that made the entire act invalid if any portion of it were struck down by the Supreme Court.

In addition to the constitutional impediments to reform, political considerations also played a significant role in campaign finance reform during the 103rd Congress. The larger political issues of reform, whether during the 103rd or any other Congress, are electoral security for incumbents and partisan control of Congress. These concerns, far more than dependence on PACs or even the apparent corruption of the electoral process, are ultimately the concerns that determine the outcomes of the reform process.

Lobbying Reform

The main thrust of the lobbying reforms of the 103rd Congress was to tighten registration procedures and to provide for greater financial disclosure of lobbying activities. The Lobbying Disclosure Act of 1993 (LDA), introduced originally in the Senate by Senator Carl Levin (D, MI), required registration on a semiannual basis by anyone who is paid to make lobbying contacts with either the legislative or the executive branch of the federal government. As defined in the act:

> The term "lobbyist" means any individual who is employed by or retained by another for financial or other compensation to perform services that include lobbying contacts, other than an individual whose lobbying activities are only incidental to, and are not a significant part of, the services provided by such individual to the client.[6]

Under the bill, an individual's lobbying contacts are deemed significant enough to require registration when lobbying expenses or income from one's efforts exceed $1000 on behalf of a single client or $5000 on behalf of multiple clients in a semiannual period.[7] Thus, once these thresholds are exceeded, the act covers representatives of national organizations, even if lobbying accounts for only a small percentage of their professional activities, and Washington lawyers who regularly contact officials on behalf of a client or clients, even if almost all of their work is litigation or counseling.

The act defined *lobbying activities* very specifically:

> The term "lobbying activities" means lobbying contacts and efforts in support of such contacts, including preparation and planning activities, research and other background work that is intended for use in contacts, and coordination with the lobbing activities of others. Lobbying activities include grass roots lobbying communications and communications with members...[8]

The term *lobbying contacts* was further defined to include communications with members of Congress and their staff, officers and employees in the executive office of the president, and ranking officials in other federal agencies. *Not* included as lobbying contacts in the act are communications that involve requests for appointments

---

[6]*Congressional Record*, 103rd Congress, 1st session (May 6, 1993): S5580.

[7]In the legal definition of *client*, an organization whose employees act as lobbyists on its behalf is a client. Importantly, organizations that contribute more than $5000 to a coalitional lobbying effort would be considered "clients" under the act and would be identified as such.

[8]*Congressional Record*, 103rd Congress, 1st session (May 6, 1993): S5580.

or status of an action, testimony before congressional committees, participation in agency adjudicatory proceedings, the filing of written comments in rule-making proceedings, and routine negotiations of contracts, grants, loans, and other federal assistance.

The disclosure requirements of the 1993 bill went well beyond those specified in the 1946 statute. Under the new bill, individuals would have had to disclose the name of the individual or organization on whose behalf they lobbied; a list of the specific issues on which they lobbied, including a list of bill numbers and references to specific regulatory actions; the committees of Congress and the federal agencies contacted; and a "good faith estimate" of the total income or expenses connected with the lobbying activities, including those connected with grassroots communications.

The media in 1993 and 1994 reported relatively little about the substance of the LDA itself and instead focused most of its attention on various amendments to restrict the gifts that lobbyists traditionally have given to members of Congress. Following the Ethics Reform Act of 1989 and amendments to it in 1991, members were allowed to accept an unlimited number of gifts worth $100 or less from any source. They could accept no more than a total of $250 worth of gifts over $100 from any single source in a given year, however. Not counted as gifts were meals, drinks, transportation to speaking engagements, retreats, and so forth. Public interest groups such as Common Cause and Public Citizen lobbied extensively to tighten the restrictions on lobbyists' gifts in the LDA of 1993.

The Senate eventually passed an amendment to the LDA that banned all gifts from lobbyists worth more than $20, and limited the total value of all gifts that a member of Congress could accept from a single lobbyist to $50 per year. Counted as gifts in the Senate's amendment were meals, drinks, transportation to speaking engagements, retreats, and the like. The House passed a much weaker version of this amendment. Under the House bill, lobbyists were banned from giving members gifts, including meals and entertainment; however, groups were allowed to pay for members' travel, meals, and entertainment associated with political events, retreats, conventions, and so forth.

The Lobbying Disclosure Act of 1993 narrowly missed being enacted into law during the 103rd Congress. Both the House and

Senate approved virtually identical versions of the bill, and a conference report was issued in September 1994. Ultimately, however, the Senate refused to approve the conference report because of concerns that the bill would have required information to be disclosed about individuals who contributed money to groups' grassroots lobbying campaigns. Although the bill's sponsors adamantly denied that this would be the case, opponents—particularly conservatives—became convinced that the bill would discourage grassroots campaigning.

The LDA would have accomplished much of what previous legislation dating back to the Hoar Resolution of 1876 failed to accomplish—patching up many of the loopholes and exceptions in lobby disclosure laws. Neither the LDA nor the prohibition on gifts, however, would have seriously curtailed the influence of special interests in Congress. Interest groups are influential with members of Congress because of the information they provide, not because of the gifts and favors they bestow, and disclosure provisions alone, despite their symbolic importance, will not interfere with the acquisition and transmission of information from groups to legislators.

However, lest one becomes cynical of the reform process, it is important to recognize that the original intent of the LDA of 1993 was not to curtail the influence of special interests. Senator Levin's remarks on the floor of the Senate when he introduced his bill in the 103rd Congress made clear his support for the lobbying process.

> Lobbying—that is, seeking to influence legislation and government policy—is not bad. Far from it. It is a vital part of our participatory democracy. We deal every day with lobbyists for cities, counties, and States; lobbyists for public hospitals and and private relief groups; lobbyists for police organizations and lobbyists for the Girl Scouts. Some lobbyists try to protect the jobs and benefits of our workers; others seek to improve the competitiveness of our industry. Some lobbyists work to keep our streets safe; some want to keep our air and water clean; other seek to reduce taxes.[9]

The purpose of the LDA was not to check lobbying influence but rather to provide information about and to create public awareness of lobbying activities. According to Senator Levin, one reason the

---

[9]*Congressional Record,* 103rd Congress, 1st session (February 4, 1993): S1466.

public is suspicious and distrustful of the relationship between lobbyists and government officials is the "cloak of secrecy that currently covers too many lobbyists and their activities."[10] Thus, the presumption underlying full public disclosure of lobbying activities is not that that lobbying is inherently corrupt; to the contrary, the presumption is that lobbying is, if anything, inherently good, and that disclosure will reveal this fact to the American public.

Had the LDA been enacted, its main impact on the operation of lobbying itself would have been through the ban on lobbyists' gifts. Although gifts do not secure influence per se, they are useful to lobbyists for keeping communication channels open to legislators, allowing them to monitor legislators' thoughts and actions, and thereby provide them with important information about the legislative process that could be converted to influence. Thus, a ban on gifts would force lobbyists to find other ways to maintain access to members of Congress and to do favors for them. Organizational prestige and reputation, for example, might become even more important, so that representatives of established and well-known groups would have an even greater advantage with members of Congress. Under the current law, even small or nascent organizations can afford to take a member to lunch occasionally or to deliver a basket of fruit at Christmas time; consequently, a ban on all gifts might very well impose greater hardships for these organizations than for the larger and wealthier organizations. There are other important reasons, however, for banning gifts from lobbyists to members of Congress. A prohibition on gifts would be an important symbolic step, if nothing else, in restoring the public's esteem in Congress and its trust in the legislative process.

Taken as a whole, this latest wave of reforms would have infringed hardly at all on the basic processes by which interest groups seek and achieve influence over the legislative process. The essential components of successful lobbying—access and the strategic acquisition and use of information—would have been the same in the post-reform era period as in the prereform period. Thus, in terms of their scope, the reform efforts of the 103rd Congress were not much different from reform efforts of earlier periods. With the

[10]Ibid.

exception of the FECA of 1971 and the amendments of 1974, congressional reforms of lobbying and campaign finance historically have been mostly superficial rather than fundamental. This should not be cause for disillusionment with the integrity of the political process, however. The interest group system, in spite of some of the problems it raises, is largely a self-regulating one that is not prone to significant misrepresentation and abuse.

That the latest reform efforts were no more profound than they were should not be construed as evidence that the forces of reform are inherently weak or that Congress is hopelessly dominated by special interests. Historically, it has been very difficult for Congress to regulate groups and at the same time ensure that their political rights under the First Amendment are not jeopardized. Perhaps of equal importance, however, in understanding the reluctance of Congress to enact far-reaching reforms is the fact that Congress *needs* interest groups. Interest groups are an important source of information to legislators, not only about policy consequences but also about the direction and intensity of their constituents' policy preferences. Some mechanism for aggregating and revealing citizens' preferences is indispensable in a republican form of government, especially one as large as that of the United States. Without interest groups, legislators would be even less proficient than they currently are at legislating, and they would be seem even more distant from their constituents.

Summary

Elected representatives must pay constant attention to their electoral and legislative environments. Other politicians are constantly trying to take their jobs, and other legislators or interest groups are usually trying to upset their policy plans. To stay apprised of the political situations at home and in Washington, they must frequently turn to others for information and advice. Among those they turn to are organized interests.

Interest groups are valuable sources of information to legislators because they typically have intimate connections to legislators' districts *and* to the Washington policy-making environment. They influence constituency opinion on important policy questions, they organize and mobilize voters, they provide campaign money, they help shape the legislator's reputation at home, they conduct research and disseminate policy information in Washington, and they make it their business to know what other legislators and groups are doing and planning.

Legislators can learn a great deal by observing groups' activities and by talking with their lobbyists and policy experts. Legislators learn about the direction and intensity of their constituents' policy concerns by observing groups' grassroots mobilization efforts. They learn about how policies work, whether there are legal and constitutional issues that must be addressed, and what the administrative difficulties are and how agencies are likely to handle them by talking to groups' policy experts. In addition, they learn about the policy stands of their fellow legislators and strategies for handling bills by talking with Washington lobbyists.

Interest groups are much more than "service bureaus" for legislators, however. They have clear-cut policy agendas, and they pursue them vigorously. Their legislative successes and failures often have significant economic, social, or political implications for their members as well as for citizens at large. Since the stakes are high, groups are understandably selective about the content of the information they provide, and they are strategic about when and how they make it available. Naturally, they like to present only information that is favorable to their interests, and, occasionally, they may even exaggerate their claims or create a distorted impression of their true organizational strength and support among constituents. In short, there is always a possibility that interest groups will try to manipulate the beliefs and behavior of legislators with the information they present.

Even with the possibility of misrepresentation, interest groups are still important informational assets to members of Congress. In fact, legislators are generally better informed about politics and policy with interest groups than without them. Unfortunately, it cannot be claimed that groups never misrepresent the facts, but there are strong incentives for them not to do so. Members of Congress have considerable resources at their disposal to acquire much of the same information that groups provide, and although it is often more costly for legislators to acquire information through their own resources than to rely on interest groups, they do have the ability to verify lobbying information. Groups recognize and respect this ability and generally reveal truthfully what they know, for nothing can be more debilitating for lobbyists in the long run than for legislators to lose confidence in them. Providing an even more effective check on interest groups, however, are other interest groups. Any group that exaggerates, distorts, or does not fully reveal what it truthfully knows risks exposure by a competing group that presents the facts accurately. Competition among interest groups, therefore, is crucial for keeping groups honest. In the final analysis, unrestricted competition among groups is likely to be the most effective means of regulating interest group behavior.

Ultimately, interest groups help legislators bridge the gap between what they do in Washington and what they do at home in their districts. Through contact with groups, they stay in contact with their constituents, and through interest groups they have access to the legislative and policy expertise necessary to enact their own and their constituents' political agendas. Thus, the bridge that interest groups provide between Washington and the district runs both ways. Interest groups not only improve the job security and policy performance of legislators, but they also serve as a mechanism by which citizens can bring their concerns to the attention of their representatives. Of course, a political system in which legislators rely heavily on interest groups to formulate policy and stay attuned to their constituencies is not, and never will be, perfect. Inefficiency, policy paralysis, and political inequality are all dangers associated with a political system in which interest groups play a dominant role in the governing process. Yet, in a system in which the political parties lack the ideological cohesiveness, discipline, and responsibility to govern effectively, there is really no alternative, short of constitutional reform, to interest group politics.

INDEX